Merry christmas to
the best teacher
in the world!!!!!

From Dominic
Stauffer

To: Ms. Pfeil

WOOF!

WOOF!

Writers on Dogs

EDITED BY

LEE MONTGOMERY

VIKING

VIKING
Published by the Penguin Group
Penguin Group (USA) Inc., 375 Hudson Street, New York, New York 10014, U.S.A.
Penguin Group (Canada), 90 Eglinton Avenue East, Suite 700, Toronto, Ontario,
Canada M4P 2Y3 (a division of Pearson Penguin Canada Inc.)
Penguin Books Ltd, 80 Strand, London WC2R 0RL, England
Penguin Ireland, 25 St. Stephen's Green, Dublin 2, Ireland
(a division of Penguin Books Ltd)
Penguin Books Australia Ltd, 250 Camberwell Road, Camberwell, Victoria 3124, Australia
(a division of Pearson Australia Group Pty Ltd)
Penguin Books India Pvt Ltd, 11 Community Centre, Panchsheel Park,
New Delhi – 110 017, India
Penguin Group (NZ), 67 Apollo Drive, Rosedale, North Shore 0632, New Zealand
(a division of Pearson New Zealand Ltd)
Penguin Books (South Africa) (Pty) Ltd, 24 Sturdee Avenue, Rosebank,
Johannesburg 2196, South Africa

Penguin Books Ltd, Registered Offices: 80 Strand, London WC2R 0RL, England

First published in 2008 by Viking Penguin, a member of Penguin Group (USA) Inc.

1 3 5 7 9 10 8 6 4 2

The essays in this book are the copyrighted property of the respective authors.

"Sleeping with Dogs in a King-Size Bed" by Abigail Thomas and "At Least You Have Your Legs" by Jim Shepard (in slightly different form as "You're Not Going Anywhere Without Me") first appeared in *O, The Oprah Magazine*; "A Good Creature" by Chris Adrian in *TinHouse*; "Dog Lives" by Antonya Nelson in *Texas Monthly*; "My Commodore" by Denis Johnson in *Epoch*; "The Leash" by Tom Grimes in *Narrative Magazine*; and "Schnauzer, Talking" by Lee Montgomery (in slightly different form) in *Bark*.

Images from two letters written by William James reproduced by permission of Bay James.

LIBRARY OF CONGRESS CATALOGING IN PUBLICATION DATA
Woof! : writers on dogs / edited by Lee Montgomery.
p.   cm.
ISBN 978-0-670-02029-4
1. Dogs—Anecdotes.   I. Montgomery, Lee B. (Lee Begole), date.
SF426.2.W67   2008
636.7—dc22   2008003941

Printed in the United States of America
Designed by Nancy Resnick

For the Stinkies

My little dog, a heartbeat at my feet.

—Edith Wharton

Contents

WOOF!

Introduction

ELIZABETH MARSHALL THOMAS

Not another book about dogs! With seemingly over a million books about dogs available, why in the world would we need another? The truth is, while many people love dogs, few can write well about them and even fewer can capture the soul essence of dog as accurately and beautifully as the authors of the stories featured within these pages.

Books by animal behaviorists, pop specialists, psychics, and dog whisperers abound, stacking the shelves of pet and book stores. But how many offer thoughtful observation and insights into the world of dogs? Not those books, supposedly narrated by a dog, recounting events of interest to the author. These include "faux" nonfiction such as in *Millie's Book* by Barbara Bush, a coy memoir allegedly dictated by a springer spaniel to the then first lady. Not only did a dog not write this book, but Barbara probably didn't write it either. More likely it was the work of a ghostwriter with more interest in celebrities than in animals. We don't learn much about Millie except her coat color, which was black and white. Instead we find the names of numerous celebrities and learn what they wore to dinner—details that surely didn't concern the dog. Millie would be far more interested in the alarming number of strangers, the buzz of noisy talk that blossomed as the drinks were served, and the odors in and on the strangers' shoes and clothing. *Where had they walked? Were they menstruating? What had they been eating?* Or more important still, *did they have dogs and, if so, who were these dogs?* Needless to say these probabilities escaped the ghostwriter.

Then there is the Albert Payson Terhune element of the genre— *Lad: A Dog, Lad of Sunnybank,* and the rest. I adored these books as a child but revisit them today with much pain. What was I thinking? Terhune fancied racial "purity" in people and in dogs, so "half-breeds" of both species are his villains, while purebred Anglos and collies are the stars. Sir Percy Fitzpatrick's *Jock of the Bushveld* also belongs in this company. Amid Africans called by racist terms too embarrassing to mention, amid starving village mongrels who were kicked aside by all whom they approached, Jock was a heroic Staffordshire bull terrier whom, evidently, Fitzpatrick didn't bother to take home to England with him when he concluded his hunting safari, although Jock had proved his merit over and over again, bravely attacking everything from kudus to crocodiles in service of his master. There was a time when I couldn't get enough of *Jock of the Bushveld.* Today this book breaks my heart, but at least Jock was presented as a very real, interesting dog who had fascinating if gruesome adventures.

How-to books occupy much of the genre. *How to choose a dog. How to train a dog. How to feed and care for a puppy.* These books reflect an underlying assumption—that a dog must be purebred, must be spayed or castrated, must never know freedom but must be crated or kept on a leash, and must undergo obedience training. Thus these books reflect much of current thinking about dogs—dogs are property, to be chosen like clothing or furniture. Fertility is only for dogs kept for breeding, and these dogs get little joy out of it. Their mates may be total strangers, as they are chosen by their owners, and the father dogs may never see their children, who after a few weeks with their mother are parted from her forever. The dogs-as-property aspect of the genre blossoms into books about how to use dogs, whether to cheer the elderly in nursing homes or to retrieve game birds for a hunter.

In the best part of the genre are stories of individual dogs, some as dog biographies, others as accounts of the relationship between certain dogs and their owners, such as readers will find in this anthology. To produce such stories isn't easy. Most dog stories, as J. C. Hallman points out herein, "even as they seem to capture something about the spirit of the animal, are actually pretty interchangeable. We think dogs are expressing their personality exactly at those moments when they're doing what all dogs do." Thus, as an extension of the problem, not many dog stories have depth and subtlety. But some do, including J. C. Hallman's and the others found in these pages. Such writings result from deep interest and insightful observation. They are evidence that a dog "doing what all dogs do" may nevertheless be doing something exceptionally meaningful.

In this anthology the reader will find observations made by the authors of their own dogs—personal, private observations the rest of us may also have experienced, perhaps in the distant past, but still in our hearts.

When encountering some of the essays here, stories with material that is fresh and unexpected, I was reminded of the famous haiku by the great Japanese poet Bashō:

> *The sudden chill I feel*
> *My dead wife's comb*
> *In our bedroom*
> *Under my heel.*

While reading Abigail Thomas's story, "Sleeping with Dogs in a King-Size Bed," I felt just such a chill. Thomas slept side by side with her dogs on the bed, as did I with my Australian shepherd, Pearl. Over time I gained thirty pounds (as did Thomas!) and Pearl gained ten, and we didn't fit on the bed as comfortably as before. I published a poem called "Pearl and I Are Far Too Fat" that mentions how, after we both became too wide, we began to push each other in our sleep. Even so, we never slept apart. Each of us liked to feel the warmth of the other's body throughout the night, no matter how near the edge of the bed the other might have maneuvered us. To my infinite sorrow, Pearl died of cancer, but reading the story, I felt her presence once again, her back against mine. I also had to admire Thomas, because while Pearl and I continued to struggle over meager territory, Thomas wisely bought a bigger bed.

I experienced the chill again when I read Yannick Murphy's "The Big Kahuna." In it, Murphy tells us that Tom, her Newfoundland, didn't like to be groomed. But sometimes she groomed him anyway. When the fur pulling got too strong, Tom would first warn Murphy with a single bark and then would take her wrist in his mouth and apply a little pressure with his teeth. *Stop now,* the dog was saying. When I read that, my mind flew back to the entry hall of my childhood home. I was sitting on the floor, grooming the tail of my beloved Newfoundland, Brigantine. I was pulling at the tangles. Brig barked once, rather desperately, but I kept pulling. Then, like Tom, she applied her teeth, not to my wrist but to the back of my neck, a firm but well-controlled scare to remind me that she was bigger than I was and that I should respect her feelings. So I stopped brushing, just as Murphy did with Tom. In the fifty intervening years since that episode, I have been reading and writing about dogs but never thought to tell of my experience with Brig, nor have I ever seen her act described by anyone else. Reading Murphy's piece, I actually relived the moment. I saw Brig's tail, the fur black and tangled. I saw the brush, with a brown handle and strong black bristles. I once again smelled Brig's damp fur and saw the pinewood floor in the entry hall, with our muddy boots in the corner. And I remembered looking up into Brig's eyes, knowing that she wasn't happy with me. For weeks after reading Yannick Murphy's story, I thought of Brig, my darling Brig, and longed to put my arms around her.

There are other wonderful stories in this volume that will undoubtedly evoke countless memories of our past loves, our lives and times with dogs we have known. Mary Otis writes about falling in love with and trying to woo her neighbor's dog, Odin. Ron Carlson's "A Hundred-Dog Life" recounts all the dogs the author has encountered and who have touched him in some way. Paul Winner, an author and minister, interweaves the heartbreaking stories of the failing of his beloved dog Bill and the death of his father with his decision to move to New York to go to seminary. In Chris Adrian's "A Good Creature," Adrian, a writer, physician, and student in divinity school, writes about his earnest desire to be a dog. And in Denis Johnson's "My Commodore," his mastiff, The Colonel, narrates a story about Johnson.

It's the freshness of the essays in this collection that awakes memory. A small detail may be common to us all and may seem undramatic, unworthy of mention, but like the tea-soaked crumb of madeleine on the tongue of Marcel Proust, the crumb that evoked a seven-volume work, *À la Recherche du Temps Perdu* (*Remembrance of Things Past*), it is these details that awaken memories of important moments in our own lives. In Antonya Nelson's "Dog Lives," Nelson remembers how her daughter slept on the floor beside their golden retriever, Odette, who was dying, just as I slept on the kitchen floor beside our beloved Sundog, also a retriever, or part retriever, during the last weeks of his life. By day I spent hours at the vet with him, as Nelson did with Odette, and because he suffered as Odette suffered, I sat on the floor beside him, stroking his face, sometimes squirting water into his mouth to relieve his thirst, as Nelson did for Odette. Undoubtedly, other readers of this book will have had the same experience but may never have had the comfort of living it again through someone else's words.

Dogs can teach us about life and death, as in Rick Bass's "Sick Dog," where Bass writes about his struggle to deal with the severe illness of his hunting dog, longing for one last hunt. In "At Least You Have Your Legs," Jim Shepard revisits his guilt over the loss of dogs he loved and for whose accidental deaths he always felt responsible.

Victoria Redel's essay chronicles her struggle with the decision to give up a dog she loves but who bites. Southern author Barry Hannah relives the horror of losing two beloved dogs, run over by the cars of mindless people in his booming hometown of Oxford, Mississippi.

Other stories here recount how dogs become part of the emotional landscape as in Tom Grimes's "Charlie," or step in as child substitutes, as in Lee Montgomery's "Schnauzer, Talking." In still other stories, authors write about how a dog's companionship saved their sanity. Both Robin Romm and Michelle Latiolais write about the dogs who stayed by them after the loss of their beloveds. For Romm it was her mother who died of cancer. For Latiolais it was her husband, whose suicide left her suddenly alone, with only their unruly bull terrier, Damned Spot, for comfort.

Then, too, there is much in these pages that is funny, heroic, and informative. Readers will applaud an author who keeps a dog close even though the dog dislikes the mailman and attacks the mail as it comes through the slot, or who destroys the owner's rugs and shoes and flower beds. Readers will applaud an author who ignores complaints about her dog from passersby, an author who retaliates against offensive passersby, and an author who moves away from a neighborhood where her dog is mistreated. These authors are the good people of the world. They have fathomed the dog-human relationship and are as deeply involved with their dogs as their dogs are with them. As Lydia Millet writes, "we tend to identify so strongly with our dogs, and our dogs . . . come in their own enigmatic way also to identify with us." Dog lovers around the world will read this book, see themselves, their lives, and their dogs, and rejoice in all things human and all things dog.

Sleeping with Dogs on a King-Size Bed

ABIGAIL THOMAS

H ere is some of what I have found in my bed: mulch, grass, leaves, tiny little black things that seem (*thank God*) inanimate, brownish streaks I don't want to examine, feathers, twigs, gravel, muddy paw prints, and plain dirt. I never look closely anymore; I assume the worst. I change the white (hence the information) sheets all the time, but since the mattress on my new bed is waist-high, there is no bending involved and what was once an onerous chore is now almost a pleasure. The only hard part is getting between the radiator and the right side of the bed, where there are only six inches of wiggle room. *Thank God* I have only myself and the dogs to please.

I used to feel about king size beds the way I do about Hummers and private jets and granite countertops, but over the past seven years I gained three dogs and thirty pounds, and my old bed, a humble queen, just didn't cut it anymore. It was either lose the weight, lose the dogs, or buy something bigger. King-size is what I needed, and king-size is what I got.

I fell in love with this particular bed because it was hand-made. The headboard is fashioned of a single piece of wood, more than an inch thick, like a really good steak. It was designed originally as a rope bed, and my son spent a day outfitting it with wooden slats because I had researched rope beds and didn't want to sleep on anything I needed to tighten regularly with a special tool. The mattress I picked out is as high as a wedding cake. When I'm up there, I am thirty-eight inches off the floor. I feel like the ruler of a small, rumpled country.

It is an exaggeration to say my nose grazes the ceiling.

My two dogs, Rosie and Carolina, jump up with ease, but my old beagle, Harry, can't make it. He was able to manage the other bed, but he had to back up to the wall to get a running start. Now there is no space left for a running start. This bed takes up the whole room, so I heave him up every night. I hope never to need a heave up myself. So far I am troubled only by arthritis, and if it gets worse, I can always ask my son to make me some stairs. I imagine covering them with red velvet.

My whole perspective has changed. When I lie in bed, I am at eye level with the top of my bureau. I can see the photograph of a horse chestnut tree and a white chair beneath it, almost hidden by leaves, where my father liked to sit. I can see, I think, the charger for my cell phone, lost these many months. I am closer to the ceiling fan, which came with the house and resembles something trying to resemble something out of an old saloon. It doesn't move the air around much but makes a pleasant sound.

I love it up here.

I bought these new white king-size sheets for thirty-nine dollars. They have a one-thousand thread count (although my daughter tells me that anything over six hundred is a waste). They are heavy and soft; it's like sleeping inside a loaf of bread. There are some mornings when I can't think of a good enough reason to get out of bed, but this is where the dogs come in handy. Even if I put my head under all four pillows, Rosie seeks me out. She is relentless. Whichever way I turn, her cold nose is poking in my face. So this is what it's like to be hunted down.

The four of us sleep in a huddle. Harry dives under the covers toward my feet on the left, Rosie on the right, and Carolina on my (our) pillow. During the night Harry gets out from under and arranges himself on top of the blanket; Rosie inches up to lay her head on my shoulder; and Carolina, who tends to start compact and neat, softens and unwinds during the night, extended by morning to her full length. When I open my eyes, there is Rosie, her eyes already open, watching my face.

Dogs make good company. Dogs don't question the fact that you are going to take a nap twenty minutes after getting up from the last one. They are happy to accommodate you. Sometimes Rosie hops off the bed the minute I hop on, but she has her own dog reasons, and it is never because of something I said at breakfast or because she had an unhappy adolescence.

I have slept with dogs for seven years. Every now and then, I remember sleeping with a man, but if I hold still, the memory fades. Strange, when I consider how much of my life was spent in pursuit of being pursued for the purpose of going to bed. I'm just not interested anymore.

But wait.

There is Marky Mark. I tell my friend Claudette. She absorbs this, and I can feel she does not understand completely. Perhaps Marky Mark is not on her A-list.

"Who would you rather sleep with," she asks, "Marky Mark or Johnny Depp?"

"Marky Mark," I say. "Johnny Depp is too beautiful."

"Johnny Depp is too *thin,*" says Claudette.

Anyway, no matter how irresistible a man might find this sixty-five-year-old grandmother of twelve, or I him, there are the dogs, and the bed is big, but not that big. Rosie's breath smells like fish, Carolina sheds, Harry growls if you touch him when he's sleeping—or even when he's not if he thinks you want to push him around. He has his quirks. He'll bite if you move him aside with your hands, but he takes no umbrage at being shoved by a hip. He will not go near a bowl if you forget to take the spoon out. No matter what's in it, no matter how badly he wants to lick it, he stays at a safe distance and barks until the spoon is removed.

Sometimes I wonder if I might be missing something with only dogs for companionship, but then I think about mornings. First there would be the discovery that there is no milk for someone who takes it in his coffee. Then the likelihood of conversation. I need to be quiet with my (black) coffee. I want to listen to the mourning doves. I like to sit on the sofa with the dogs, stroking Carolina's silky chest and Rosie's satin flank. Harry sits on my feet, standing guard. Suppose another person were here? What if he had opinions? What if he used the word "postmodern" with a straight face? What if he wanted to explain how many feet from a dwelling a cesspool needed to be? What if he wanted to talk about the pros and cons of raising the prime mortgage rate? What if he wanted to talk about his *childhood*? Or worse, mine? I can put up with Carolina's barking because she'll stop for a treat (and because I love her so much), but people are different. You can't shut them up with the offer of a dog biscuit or a little piece of broccoli.

Lots of people in my somewhat leaky boat are on the lookout for a human companion. Not me. I have learned to love the inside of my own head. There isn't much I'd rather say than think. Of course there is the rare bird with whom I am in sync, the odd person who can make me laugh my head off and with whom conversation is not an imposition or a chore, but these people are few and far between. I can talk to them on the phone. I can invite them for coffee.

So where am I going with this? Probably back upstairs with the dogs. It is starting to rain. I have made my bed, and I want to lie in it.

Let's Go, My Love

ANNA KEESEY

Once, in a parking lot, in the rain, I saw a weary-looking woman in overalls and a fleece jacket open the rear door of a beater Subaru and a brindled monster of a dog heave himself into the backseat. I didn't pay close attention but kept on loading the groceries into my own beater Subaru. It was Oregon, after all, and fleece, Subarus, overalls, dogs, and weariness were all in healthy supply. But something had gotten into me, some spore. The woman was driving away, thinking her thoughts, and behind her the dog was riding and looking out the window, thinking his thoughts, so *together* that their togetherness was unremarkable to either of them. The sight vegetated in me, and grew. The dog does not have to be coached or invited to jump into the Subaru. The dog is *with* you. The dog *knows the drill*.

I was thirty-nine (*cliché*), unmarried (*yawn*) and childless (*duh*). The outlook on that front was not good. For ten years, weddings among my friends and the births of their children had occurred with what I thought was inconsiderate frequency. I'd tried to *figure it out*, working an everlasting Rubik's Cube of self-appraisal: I was too much— tall, talkative, impatient, with hairs on my chin—or not enough—not kind, not mild, not satisfied. I had read too much, I had learned too

little. I was too self-sufficient or too love-hungry; I was not configured for partnership; I was a mess. Clickety-click, working the cube
in front of my friends, in therapy, in the garden, in bed in the morning before I could bring myself to move. My heart, I was sure, was
atrophying and flaking, returning to dust. No wonder weariness
prevailed.

Occasional boyfriends, whom despite their niceness I couldn't be
sure about, moved on. Without fail—apparently having been prepared by the magic blossom of my ambivalent company—each fell
hard and permanently for the next creature that crossed his path.
"Yeah," said my mother. "I have that effect on men, too."

Seeking power over my own destiny, I considered having a baby
on my own, but every time I began preparations, I became demoral-
ized. I sniffled as I perused the online gamete catalogs. In down-
loaded donor profiles, I heard the voices of potential daddies, men I
would never meet, and I ached at having come to such a pass. I closed
the files, silenced the cautious, friendly, gentle voices. What a lousy
universe. I was furious.

But while we're waiting, we indulge in stopgap loves. One (rainy)
November day, I found myself moving from enclosure to enclosure
in the rather spiffy facilities of the Portland Humane Society, daz-
zled by dogs. There were so many dogs doing dog things: running to
the fronts of their cages, barking, standing on their hind legs, or lying
on rucked-up blankets looking back at me blankly, afflicted with a
Newgate jaundice of the soul. Smaller bins held puppies in rolling,
schnarfling heaps: huskies like puffs of gray marshmallow; blunt-
nosed, soulful pit bulls; taut and deranged little terriers. I snuck my
hand into their midst, feeling their selves, the sweet plump energy of
them: delicious.

But in another cage, alone, stood a puppy who had recently been
neutered and, in an unrelated misfortune, had an angry staph infection on his tender belly. He was a little bigger, a little older than

the other puppies, and had a history. I read his paperwork. As a grapefruit-size, scrabbling grub he had been taken from his litter in some small town to a pet store and thence to a home where he was fed My-Te-Fine dog food and encouraged to rassle and fight.

The sign on his cage said that he was a mix of rottweiler, golden retriever, and St. Bernard: THIS WILL BE A VERY LARGE DOG. But come on—how big could he really get? I'd grown up with what I'd thought was a large dog. It was Oregon! Who wanted a little dog? *I can handle a large dog,* I thought, feeling momentarily competent.

I summoned an attendant.

In the concrete room where one test-drove the dogs, the puppy hustled along the perimeter. He sniffed and urinated, sniffed and urinated. Then he approached me, took my pant leg in his mouth, and looked up at me with the shrewd brown eyes of a chimpanzee. His needly white teeth made a small tear in the corduroy. But who cared? Not me. His face was pure red velvet with a pale gold mask, his muzzle was short and soft, his gargantuan paws benign, unconscious of their absurdity.

The My-Te-Fine household had surrendered the puppy because he had come up lame once or twice after playing, a bad omen for the future. But the X-rays of his hips were inconclusive. He *might* need an operation, someday, and such operations could be expensive. I seized on the ambiguities. *Might* need an operation that *might* be expensive. Besides: lame after playing? The poor puppy. The poor, poor little puppy.

Thanksgiving. I had a puppy, a crate, books, chew toys, and a handsome collar with an address tag. I meant to raise my dog properly. In my mother's living room, I released him so that my mother, a sucker for cute, could feast on his babyness. He barreled out of the crate, bucking and twisting like a devil on methamphetamine. His chimp eyes were empty. He was consumed. He went to my mother, who stood there in slippers and a robe, ready to love, and flashed and sharked his bitter teeth all over her bare ankles. Like a Cossack, he drove her up onto an armchair, and when she pulled down her robe to protect her feet, he went after her hands. When I seized his collar, he twisted and deformed and got his needles onto me. It wasn't a bite. It was a pricking, a multiplicitous, simultaneous threat of puncture. I dragged him, as I remember, back to his crate and shoveled him in. My dismay was indescribably complex. I suddenly felt very weary.

A few days later, observing a similar toothy performance, my sister, who knew dogs, patted her infant daughter on the bottom and said, "That dog isn't normal."

I knew he wasn't. I knew he was a hurting unit. But so was I. And the first words into my mind were retaliatory, ones I muted with difficulty. *You know what?* I wanted to say. *Your BABY'S not normal.*

I was thirty-nine: no lover, no children, and saddled with a maniac.

I thought at first I'd keep him for a week. I did. Another week. All right. Another week. He was still hell, a whirling djinn of anxiety and white needles. I brought him into the natural-pet-food store, where the owner took pity on me and gave me a card for a trainer. The trainer came to the house, accompanied by her feathery, gnomish dog, a papillon. The papillon was perfect. It lay calm and alert, its inordinately large ears perked, watching as the trainer encouraged my puppy to lie down. He would not. He rolled his watery eyes, he worked his needles. She turned him on his back. He would not submit. He struggled, he struggled, he would not be held down. It wasn't fear or anger in him. He was like a mosquito larva in stagnant water, primitive and jerking. There was a mindless defiance in him that didn't even rise to the level of protest.

The trainer was dubious.

Was there love in there somewhere? Where was that dog thing that made them come to the old fires and lie down, even after the food was eaten?

———

He crapped five times a day on the rugs. I organized a basket of tools: plastic bags, paper towels, a spray bottle of water, a spray bottle of coprophagic enzymes, but I was dog-naïve—it took me weeks to understand that when the puppy began to wander away with his head down and swinging, he was looking for a place to unburden himself. He chewed the fringe off my Oriental rug, he knocked down his dog gate, he whined when separated from me and sharked me when we were together. He looked for anything chewable, un-tethered, and expensive and, when I was distracted, snaked it off the shelf or table and destroyed it. You could see him patrolling the house looking for objects to mouth, shred, disassemble: he shopped until he dropped. Happening upon him as he mauled an antique book, a friend shook her head. "He's a mastermind," she said.

In order that I could have a respite from repeating "Leave it!" ad nauseam, I sent him to dog day care a couple of times a week. There he was socially awkward and bit other dogs and was bitten. His day-care provider suggested I follow her lead: every morning she split her Prozac tablet in half and shared it with her pit bull.

I couldn't get him to walk on a leash. "Let's go, my love," I said, jerking on his collar. He just sat down on the sidewalk and flashed me a chimpish look—with one eye, not both, because both would have been too agreeable, too intimate. No, he deployed one eye only, which rolled darkly in its yellow-white, full of sullen resistance: the stink-eye. He lay thick and inert on the concrete. He would not move.

A man who passed through my bedroom now and then stretched his silky brown body in the light from the window, put on his glasses, and said, "Why didn't you get a *good* dog?"

"He bites," I mourned. "He destroys everything. He won't walk on a leash."

"I'll show you," the silky man said. He put on his pants, descended the stairs, took the puppy outside on a leash, and dragged him by his neck along the sidewalk. The puppy writhed and strangled for two feet, four feet, seven feet. At ten feet, to avoid death, he got up and trotted, expressionless.

Force. Huh. I'd been unclear on the concept.

The silky man returned the puppy to me and started up his Subaru. Through the window he gave me some advice: "Kick the shit out of him."

But he was so beautiful. As he grew, his gold mask faded and the soft brown of his puppy fur gave way to a glorious red copper, as luxurious as money. He developed a speckled harness of black hairs over his strong shoulders. He had a broad, classic brow on his hefty Teutonic head, which was surmounted by an odd lump of bone. "What a pronounced sagittal crest!" said an anthropologist friend admiringly. The whole facial business was covered with a layer of rich industrial velvet. His ears hung like short brown pennants, as if from a rod on either side of his face, and they were thick and soft. His eyes were almost pupil-less in their darkness, shaped like teardrops, and rimmed in alluring black; his nose was a chunk of rough charcoal rubber, his muzzle pleated and furred and whiskered and frosted with his breath like an otter's.

And what a big, strong, goofy body—the burly chest, the sharp prow of a sternum with ribs sailing backward, the weird taut arrangement of the planes of belly, ghosted with those vestigial nipples. His poor penis, essential little structure, clad in winter white like a rabbit's-foot charm. Under the alert long tail—held up authoritatively for any curiosity, any inspection—were the pink keyhole of his busy pooper and two incongruous puffs of sunshine-colored fur, like pantalets on a shepherdess. When he shook water off his coat, the shaking proceeded from his flappy front lips backward, like the Wave, to these puffs, so there was a millisecond when the body was still except for their glittering shimmy. If Cleopatra and a chimpanzee had had a child, it would have looked like this dog, I thought.

But his bigness—he was nearly eighty pounds. Cleopatra, a chimpanzee, and a bison, then. No: Cleopatra, a chimp, a bison, a cyclone,
a barracuda, and the Marx Brothers.

"He's so cute," said the unenlightened.

He was, and it was a good thing. Because every day I still wanted
to kill him.

One rainy evening, when I'd had him for several months, I was
walking him in Laurelhurst Park. It was getting dark. The puppy
was muddy from some playing he'd done in a hole a little earlier, and
he was actively sniffing every last vertical surface, every blade of
grass, stone, and tree, in an effort to obliterate with his urine all evidence of the existence of other male dogs. In order that he might do
this without yanking me to and fro, I had let him off his leash. I was
spacing out a little, watching the rain fall on the Olmstedishly lovely
duck lagoon, fantasizing, perhaps, that I was a normal person with a
normal dog, a loyal and loving one, who looked over his shoulder
regularly to make sure I was still— But no. I was a fool, and the
puppy—now a sturdy specimen, springy and muscled—was nipping
up the hill with a bone-chilling air of delight and planned mayhem.
I broke into action and called him, but he was soon out of sight in the
dusky trees. I called and called, and looked, and walked in large circles. Surely he'd be over there by the horseshoe pit, or the picnic area,
or, if not there, then surely he had gone back to the meadow to revisit
the muddy hole. Was he somewhere along the rhododendron path?
Near the sculpture, near the stone benches? It was now completely
dark, and the rain was spatting harder, trickling down the backs of
my cold hands. Outside the park cars raced by on Thirty-ninth and
on Stark, and he was senseless when it came to cars. I walked the
perimeter of the park, dreading each time I turned a corner the sight
of a crumpled, muddy heap of suffering animal. I couldn't believe
that this had happened, and I was sick, sick with pain. But as I
trudged up the hill one more time, rain dribbling off my anorak,

some part of my mind thought, *If I don't find him, I won't have to fight him anymore.*

Finally I had to give up and walk home. I would sleep a little and look again in the morning. Drenched, I turned the corner and slogged up to the house. And there on the porch, tied to the door-knob with a length of decrepit speaker wire, sat the puppy. The address tag had done its job. He had been returned to me. He looked over his shoulder, his velvet brow furrowed and his eyes black hiero-glyphs of distress. He saw me. His brow cleared, his eyes lightened. He lowered his head and put out his nose slightly toward me and beat the porch with his tail.

I had had ten minutes of freedom, and now they were over. Before I untied him, I used all my strength to hold him still, and I kissed his face.

I learned to train him. He was, after all, a mastermind, and when he applied his considerable cunning to the project of getting me to dispense treats, he found that it took nothing more than to snap himself into a soldierly sit or to lie down and kill a little time. Treats! I myself discovered that if I packed a rubber toy with cheddar cheese, he would relax and nurse on it for many minutes, minutes in which he was not crunching a burned-out lightbulb down to the metal screw or mincing a twenty-dollar bill I had carelessly left on the coffee table. There were moments of rest and moments when I woke up at night and heard with a sense of comfort the smacking of his lips, his breath, his dreaming paws trembling against the floor.

When he was a year old, his game hips fulfilled the promise of their youth and required bilateral, experimental surgery. His pelvic bones were buzz-sawed and bolted and grafted, and my bank account underwent a similarly aggressive cashectomy. He was unable for some time to stand, much less crouch, and with misery in his eyes had to poop where he lay. I cleaned him up and administered Demerol with anxious exactitude. As I sat, and sometimes lay beside him,

I realized that I loved his body as I had never loved any other body, as I had never been philosophically free to love one. The self-consciousness of the human being is a sovereignty over that realm. A human's repeated and sometimes urgent attempts to see a reflection in mirrors and windows, to present, perform, alter, and improve the self, all mean that in the country of the body he or she is king. One can't abjectly love a body that can evaluate itself, or you. But the dog didn't think about himself. He couldn't see himself in mirrors. He was only feeling and action, and I was free to adore him.

On the day that he could once again jump in and out of the Subaru, I, too, felt recalled to life.

Suddenly, it seemed—as it probably seems for everyone—I was forty. For those who aren't yet forty, let me tell you that forty is galvaniz-ing. Forty is a motivational speaker, but not the kind you click past on TV. Forty is the speaker you go to because your shiftless friend told you it would change your life, and you know that it won't, but you go to a hotel ballroom anyway, just to be nice and because you think it will be weird and fun to talk about later, and the motiva-tional speaker turns out to be this fucker who *has your number.* Forty was like that. I sucked in my breath and blew the dust off my life. I applied for jobs. A very good job was offered, a job in the Midwest. Oh, no, I mewed. My house! My friends! My garden! My weak-ass routine! Then I shut up and accepted. I drove dog, stuff, and Subaru cross-country through a summer of forest fires, set up house a couple of blocks from Lake Michigan, and began to work like mad.

The dogs in this new neighborhood were smaller than in Oregon. There were toy dogs of various kinds, fluffy little pooches. They and their owners were scared of my dog, who now topped a hundred pounds. My dog was unmoved by their vulnerability. He bit them anyway, which was extremely demoralizing for everyone except him.

But I found, in this new place, that while I'd been distracted by

jobs and moving, my psyche had sloughed off the dream of traditional baby making. It was now an easy decision to begin a series of
efforts familiar to many twenty-first-century single ladies. These involved donors denoted by four-digit codes, slim plastic tubing, jovial
monsieur le docteur pronouncements on the "dogleg" in my cervix
that had to be negotiated with the tube. Drugs, blood draws. A chilly
encondomed probe that imaged my ovaries, which, urged on by
hormones, began racking up eggs like pool balls. More drugs, in
hypodermics this time, which—alone in my apartment—I myself
introduced into the innocent upper outside corner of the innocent
upper outside quadrant of my butt. Sometimes the puncture seeped
a little, and several of my skirts became marked, there, with tiny dots
of brown blood. A twilight sleep, a "harvest," a sore belly. A gelatin
print of four embryos, like silver brooches studded with gleaming
cells. It was strange. It was magical. A tube again. And a bizarre
time known as the two-week wait.

It was November again, the day before Thanksgiving. In my office I waited and shuffled papers. Woolly galaxies of snow blew sideways past the tall window. The lab results were delayed by the weather.
Everyone else was leaving the building for the holiday. Doors shut.
My heart swooped to and fro, on a skateboard of anxiety.

At last the phone rang, the shocking raw ring of an old campus
phone, and the nurse was speaking. Before that moment, I believe, I
had not been pregnant. But afterward I was.

That evening, wearing a princess dress of interior joy, I went
home and lay on the sofa. I contemplated the magic. I had never been
pregnant before and had imagined that in the same way my heart
fled partnership, my body, slim, strong, even boyish, would wiggle
out of conception. But now the citadel had been taken. I had no doubt
that the hard part was over, that now I was in the clear, because nur-
turing something smaller than myself was something I was practiced at. Witness the badness in fur, who got up that evening onto the
sofa with me and did something he'd never done before: curled up

like a dog Danish in the space between my bowed legs. He put his head on my thigh and gazed up at me. Inside me a tiny thing was doubling, tripling, octupling. There we all were, together. I touched the crunchy velvet of the dog's furrowed brow. "You're my first baby," I told him.

At six weeks an ultrasound showed the heartbeat, a flickering dot, a Seussian Who keeping time on a micro-bongo. The chance of miscarriage went down to one in twenty. I wasn't just pregnant, I was expecting. Sometime around August 1, I would become a mother. The pleasure and peace that suffused me were unprecedented. For the first time in my life, rather than regarding myself with a feeling limited to the continuum between disgust and rueful tolerance, I began actively to love myself. I cherished and reveled in my body, I was tender and protective toward it, as if I were my own doting husband. I ate kale and drank carrot juice, I did yoga. I brushed my hair a lot, slowly.

And the relief, the change in the way I thought about romance! It became clear to me that for years, probably, I had put aside looking for a partner for myself and looked, more crudely, for a child's biological father. My eggs had nagged me into foolishness with men whose faces flew the flags of Prague, Cairo, Minsk; my German-Irish DNA had been seeking hybrid vigor, knowing that at conception's buffet table I could supply the potatoes but someone else would be the spice. Now that helpless confusion was over. I would have a child with a key assist from a smart, brown-eyed, myopic, bookish, and apparently generous sperm donor, and afterward my relationships would be different, undisrupted by the tantrums of the egg.

Since I would be a mother by midsummer, I reasoned, my free time for finishing my languishing novel was limited, and I would forgo Christmas with my family in Oregon to work on it. I would nip up to Wisconsin for a couple of days and visit some friends and their baby. Hence, two days before Christmas, I took the dog to be boarded, did a few errands, and went to the OB for a checkup. The baby would be bigger now, and I'd be able to see more of that peculiar cellular sculpture, so tiny and so huge.

"Huh," said the doctor.

How I admire the clarity and assertion of what she said next. She was like a prince facing a dragon. "I'm very sorry to say this, but I don't see what I should be seeing."

There was no heartbeat any longer. The little life was over. Tests showed, later, an unusual chromosomal anomaly. I was, after all, forty-one. Tests showed, later, a boy.

It was December 23, in the late afternoon, almost dusk. It was eight degrees above zero. The sky over the houses across the street was that brilliant, waning, Maxfield Parrish blue. As I trudged through the parking lot, squeaking over the snow, I seemed to myself a great system of error, my body not precious but merely an incompetent twin of my mind. The future had collapsed, as a telescope collapses. There was no such thing as August anymore. I had only myself and this bleak instant I was living inside, and both were inadequate to support life.

I didn't want to call anyone. Not my mother or father or sister, not a friend. I wanted no one to hold my hand. I couldn't be bothered to tell them how I felt. I couldn't teach other people how to help me. I was too wounded to pretend to be a person. I just wanted my dog. I wanted my dog, my darling dog, my companion, my constant love. I just wanted my fucking dog.

Once, out on the neighborhood Lake Michigan beach, I let the dog off his leash. It was very early in the morning, and there was only one fellow jogging, way down at the other end near the breakwater. The dog, aroused and delighted by the pink morning, pounced on the small surf with both front paws. His exuberance was undimmed by this gesture, and he turned and trotted down to the man coming up the beach, who halted and stood stock-still. *Uh-oh,* I thought. I ran to the dog and began to clip him onto the leash.

"Madam," said the man, "why do you have your dog on the beach? This is not a dog beach. There is a sign just there. Madam!"

"We're leaving," I said. To the dog I said, "Let's go, my love!"

He pursued me. "Madam—"

I said, "Buddy—"

"Madam! It is not a question of 'Buddy'—"

"Fuck you," I said, quite reasonably.

"It is not a question of 'Fuck you,'—it is a question—"

Give me a break, I thought. *It is a question of this is the creature who helps me bear my life.*

I think in grief we need to do two things: to feel our feelings and to be protected from the world. When you are trying to feel your feelings, the world abrades with its noises, its gravity, its temperatures and atmospheres. In the world, even having a self is a burden. For better or worse, the self has relationships, and then, in service of the relationship, the self must be performed, using that agreeable puppet the body. It's too much to ask sometimes. One needs to retreat into nowhere, be nothing, be relieved of existing. And with the dog there is no performance. One can be just feelings and instruments of perception. One cannot see oneself in mirrors; one cannot see mirrors at all. When the self is forgotten, all mirrors turn to glass.

One can, in fact, become a dog.

After some time, when I was reunited with my self, I—as they say— assessed my options. Options were pursued. And after some more time—now, that is—the dog and I are expecting again. This time our baby is coming from another country. A friend who has both children and dog said to me, "Get ready for the dog to become just the dog." But how can it happen? He has been at my feet through every doubt, frustration, and fear, head on his paws, trusting two things: the present moment and me. I trust his trust now. I believe in myself. I was tenacious with him, and he has repaid my tenacity. He fostered love in me and fathered faith. I don't know the name of what he has been to me. Sweetheart? Friend? Comrade? Brother? He is surly, innocent, eager, fretful, and flawed. So am I. And probably this child, too. If the dog becomes the afterthought, if I'm throwing him a handful of food on the way out the door, let me now remind my future self: the child in my arms has a father in the dog.

Sick Dog

RICK BASS

His belly remained swollen like a watermelon. The tests at the veterinary hospital in Pullman, Washington, continued to show nothing. I had to make the choice whether to put all our cards on the table and just walk away or keep playing. I feared I was going to lose him—no dog lives forever, I told myself—and after ten hunting seasons what I desperately wanted—if he would not live forever—was just one more hunt.

In the old days, Elizabeth and I had always joked about the proverbial hundred-dollar pheasant, or the three-hundred-dollar pheasant, or whatever: the crude math that totaled gas and hotel and food expenses accrued on a journey to Montana's east side and then divided that sum by the number of pheasants procured. We had always laughed about it, with the unspoken punch line being the realization that the journeys were about passion and need, not money or meat—about feeling alive, and about the deepest possible engagement with the senses. But it was profoundly sobering to realize that what I was now pursuing, with all the tests and surgeries, could easily be a five-thousand-dollar pheasant.

Live long enough and all weaknesses will be illuminated. But again, perhaps that is not all bad, for cannot they then begin to become strengths?

And even if they remain a weakness, is not a weakness, deeply felt, better than a numbness or nothingness—an unfeeling, if safe, neutrality?

There was one more little piss-ant test—something under a hundred dollars, as I remember it—that they wanted to run, to see if Point was even a candidate for surviving exploratory surgery, should I choose to pursue that option. My choice was to keep playing—to try to make him completely better—or go home and hope he lasted the nine weeks till pheasant-hunting season. I chose to keep playing.

We had a little bit of time before the test—it would not be until the next morning—and so I was able to spring him from the hospital late that afternoon.

I thought about making the long drive back to Montana, to be home for just one more night—with the long summer twilight I might be able to arrive just before dark, between nine and ten, and then set the alarm to get up early—4:00 A.M.—and be back in Pullman when the sun was coming up over the hills and the sleeping summer college town was just beginning to stir.

It was tempting. But I was so tired from having gotten up to make that morning's drive, and from the sleepless night before, that I decided to just stay.

I cried when they brought him out to me, because it seemed already that he had been resurrected, brought back from the dead, and because I was simply so happy to see him, and most of all, I think, because he was simply so happy to see me and to be sprung from the hospital: straining against his leash to gallop, claw-scratching across the tile floors of that sunlit atrium, ignoring all the other people and all the other dogs and cats, intent only upon closing that distance between him and me, and with his little stub-tail rotoring with excitement, and grinning with happiness: so utterly, wonderfully unaware of the discussion we were having in the world above him.

As unaware of that world, I imagined, as I was of the lower or other world of bird scent, and all other scent, that he inhabited—a world in which invisible things manifested themselves to him with the density and clarity of color, texture, substance, and meaning, while I, unseeing and unknowing, blundered happily along behind him, hoping for a bird.

He collided against my leg with the density of reality, not memory—not yet—and I crouched down and thump-petted him, grabbed his ears and scratched behind them in his bliss spot, the dog ecstasy trigger—and thought not for the first time what guardians dogs are, like shields or protectors against the distant and pervasive complexities of the world that saturate our news and dim consciousness these days—increasingly insoluble complexities of our own making.

Dr. Mordecai and Laura handed the leash to me, smiling a little and, I could tell, hoping for the best.

"See you tomorrow," they said.

It was uncomfortable, feeling like I was keeping a secret from him— he was so in-the-moment, happy and alive, while I was carrying the burden, the mantle of dread—but his pleasure, even joy, in the world was infectious, and I quickly readjusted, shifted my sorrow and grief to gratitude. It was a joy and pleasure to lift him out of the kennel and take him on a lunging walk down the dusty, gravelly hill behind the worn-out old hotel, to walk along the railroad tracks in the afternoon heat, grasshoppers springing from out of the thistles, and take in that peculiar and beguiling scent of small towns in the West in the summer, as the edge of the great heat finally first begins to fade and the sprinklers, the miners of underground aquifers, come on, watering the parched lawns that have been waiting all day, dying all day.

You can smell the pulse of moisture, in those small towns, when the sprinklers come on and the first shadows begin to widen beyond the carefully nurtured and utterly illogical shade trees—cool, leafy green maples, oaks, box elders, ginkgos, Lombardy poplars, where by all rights there should be nothing, only heat and wind—and you can smell the fresh scent of the grass growing and a loosening of the day's previous tautness, like an exhalation of relief.

It is a wild bartering of the future for the present, this business of watering lawns and cool green parks, in the small towns and communities of the West—a cultural, multigenerational mainstay— but it struck me that just because it had been this way for as long as I could remember, this fact in no way guaranteed that it would be that way forever: and that indeed, for anyone who cared to look even just a little bit beneath the surface—to ascertain the facts and extrap- olate from the given and quantifiable resources below—there could be no conclusion other than that someday very soon such bounty— such extravagance—would have to come to an end. You could not quite put a date on it, but you could know irrefutably, that which you probably had never bothered to consider before, the fact that something precious and wonderful and somewhat taken for granted was not just draining away but was being spent in wild, profli- gate excess. And that there was beauty, if not prudence, in such spending.

I was no longer trying to save Point's life, for I did not think his life could be saved, any more than any of ours can be saved. I was trying to keep him hanging on until September, at which time we would joyously, grievously, intensely, wantonly, spend the remaining hours, minutes, seconds doing what Point loved best. Pheasant sea- son, in October, seemed as distant as the gilded gates and streets of heaven. But the approach of dove season, and grouse and Hungarian partridge—that was close enough to hope for. With Point's belly swelling the way it was, it was the longest of shots, a big dream, but maybe not impossible. Time would not stand still, but maybe we could somehow slow it down a bit, could even fool or deceive it somehow—like the rooster pheasants that sought to skulk and scurry and twist along beneath the hiding cover of the tall grass waving just overhead, while the sound of the hunter's footfalls, and the hot breath of the hound, approach.

In the meantime there was the now, and despite my knowledge of that leaking-away, we were square in the middle of the now, going for an afternoon walk in terrain that was new and yet familiar. And was it my imagination or did time seem to be slowing, and maybe even willing to suspend for a moment or two, as Point stopped to sniff at the base of a shady willow tree or as he scent-marked the sun-heated rails of the train tracks, with mirage shimmers rising from the gravel and the heat-hazy cloudless blue sky above?

It is an ancient lesson, one we must learn and then forget and then relearn, every time someone gets sick and then travels on: that perhaps the seams, the laminae, between the various worlds—the past, present, and future, as well as the living and the nonliving—may not be as distinct and clear-cut as we have been taught, or as our somewhat arbitrary clocks and calendars have led us to believe.

We walked around a little more, down through an industrial section at the edge of town, where the wheat fields began—strolling, wandering, investigating, as if we had all the time in the world—and then went back up to the old hotel room, so nearly identical to the ones in which we stayed in eastern Montana that it was almost possible to believe that it had been translocated, picked up and tornado-whirled to this location, two states away, and to this point which for a long time had been the future but was no longer the future; that we had finally gotten here.

I left him sleeping in the room—ever the Spartan, he would not get up on the bed the way his brother Superman loved to do but instead groaned and curled up on the carpet, Antaeus-like, a ground nester, as afraid of heights as he was of water—only with the scent of birds, and the pursuit of them, was he ferocious—and I walked downtown to get a little exercise and to eat dinner.

It's corny, as well as extravagant and wasteful, but I ordered a full entrée instead of an appetizer, knowing I probably wouldn't be able to finish it and knowing what I would do with the leftovers.

The meal was good, and it was nice to step away for a moment from the unchecked drain of emotion involved with ceaseless caregiving. I read from a book as I waited for my meal and enjoyed again the space and leisure of a college town in summer—remembering, from time to time, parts of my youth, and my past, that I had long ago forgotten, from my distant days in just such a town, while in college myself—but then midway through the meal, I started to feel anxious and could not wait to get back to the room to check on him. Even if only to watch him sleep.

So it goes, in the caregiving mode. You have to get away; you have to get right back. For a long while, your time and even your emotions are not really your own; for a long time, it is you, at least as much as the patient, who is entrapped, held hostage.

He was asleep when I got back to the room, but he awakened stiffly, slowly—like an old man, like an old dog—when I held the leftovers, the chef's finest offerings, beneath his nose; and as Point rose gradually from one land or layer and ascended through the strata of dreams, it was like watching a birth or resurrection: a recovery.

Disbelieving at first—was he still dreaming?—he nudged the food tentatively, as if unsure of which land he was inhabiting, before evidently deciding that, dream or not, he might as well eat it and then find out whether it was real.

I could almost see the invisible layers of infirmity, the invisible residues of his long life and his illness, falling away as he roused more fully from sleep and began to wolf at the dinner offering with gulping inhalations, his front legs braced as if to defend a carcass over which he stood guard, but with his little rotor-stub of a tail spinning happily. I remembered the old adage about being able to tell whether a dog was healthy or not based upon its appetite—and while I knew that Point wasn't healthy, it was almost possible to pretend that he was. Regardless of what was the matter with him, there could be no denying that he was taking pleasure in the moment, and in the world. And though I could never know the answer for sure— I would have to make it up myself—I found myself wondering, as I would often through the course of this journey, whether Point's buoyant optimism, his ceaseless and habitual relish for life, was simply that—the good fortune, the random cant of relentless habit—or was instead something somehow more noble: a considered response, a choice made despite the long-term evidence presented to the traveler upon awakening each morning.

He was just a dog. I knew that. But he was probably dying, maybe dying fast—surely, with the millennia-honed integrity of his animal body, he understood that things were not right—and yet he persisted in sucking the marrow-pleasure from every turn of the clock and every turn of the world, whether majestic or mundane.

In this, as when out in the fields in autumn, I felt that I was trailing him, following his every lead, or trying to.

Homesick with maybe the worst kind of homesickness, end-of-summer homesick, I called home and gave Elizabeth the specific update and Lowry the general one. (Mary Katherine was still at summer camp.) Lowry of course wanted to know if Point was going to be all right, and when I told her that I couldn't honestly tell her that he was, that we just didn't know, she wanted to know the next-best thing, asking when he would be coming home.

"Soon," I said. "Real soon. Tomorrow, I hope."

"Can I talk to him?" she asked.

These ridiculous, wonderful moments of childhood, of family: how many more years, months, weeks would she be asking such things? "Of course," I said. And, like a sap, I didn't just pretend to put the phone down by Point's ear but really did it. How to guard the heart? Shouldn't one be a bit more restrained, a bit more cautious—a bit more protective?

I could hear the bell of Lowry's voice, tiny and indistinct to my ears but surely clear to Point's, and I laughed as he furrowed his brow and tried to look under the rug, just beneath where I was holding the phone. I let her talk on, and then after a short while I took the phone from Point and told her of his initial reaction—she was pleased—and then told her good night and hung up.

What an utter homebody I have become in these last years. As a freelance journalist, I could choose to travel anywhere in the world, could pitch any story—and certainly, there are stories that captivate me and places I would love to visit—but what I want and choose and crave most of all now is the day-to-day and day-after-day sweet pre-dictability of domestic routine: knowing somehow that beneath that veneer of sameness there is not really sameness, only the illusion of it, that things are changing, always in motion.

This illusion of secure routine is particularly keen in summer, with the early sunrises, and the high-hanging middays—a walk down to the lake, a swim, a nap—and the long twilights: venison burgers on the grill, bats in the dusk, nighttime, sleep, and then time to start all over again. Given the choice, I would choose this over any-thing or anyplace else in the world. I am hostage to my contentment. And without question, the speckled old hound that was now gulping water from his bowl, his surprise dinner consumed, is a part of that regular domestic structure.

He was sleepy from the long journey and from all the tests; after satisfying himself that there were no more treats, he curled up on the thin carpet—the poured concrete dense just beneath him—heaved a groan of . . . what? accomplishment? satisfaction that all was right in the world?—and soon drifted back down into sleep, occasionally opening one eye as he descended, as if to check on me, to see that I was still there.

I was tired, too. If I couldn't be home, at least I could take my plea-sure in where I was. It was a comfort to hear the steady old-hound sounds of my dog snoring, the same as he always has.

I lay on the bed reading, and he lay at the foot of the bed asleep and content, unconcerned by what I knew or sensed, and we were close, so close, to September. Perhaps that knowledge alone was the source and fuel of his contentment, his happiness.

And lying there just before sleep myself, I felt it, too: despite my affinity for home, I was ready and yearning for the time of my seasonal leave-taking, which becomes more bittersweet each year, as I love home more and more each year—pulling me with twin affections, stretching and attenuating and expanding the tendency I have otherwise to contract and hunker down.

There in the little Palouse prairie room, I was hungry for, craving, Montana's east-side prairie. The little dim-lightbulb hotel rooms over there, the diners, the candy bar and Cracker Jack and Coke for lunch, out in the field—why bother going back into town?—in Indian summer—the space, the emptiness, but not a hollowness—and best of all the distance from the relentless responsibility and ceaseless failures and occasional frustrations of a regular life, a life one has renegotiated to largely avoid dreaming and to instead merely accept—and relish—in the moment, even as tides and pressures of responsibility and obligation continue to buffet the traveler and the aging negotiator. . . . On the east side, with a dog, or dogs, that renegotiated life—for all its sweetness and for all your desire for that, and only that—draws back just a bit, and in its place there emerges a briefly mythic life, over on the other side of the Great Divide: a life where you can stride all day from horizon to horizon and not once be reminded of that other, and in some ways smaller, life behind you.

In the east, on the prairie, you have not yet renegotiated your dreams and probably never will. At any second, a bird could get up. At any second, your amazing dog could catch the scent trail of one that is in hiding, and one you would otherwise have passed right by.

Both you and the dog are young and strong—tireless, limitless—and you possess the key to the gates of the world. Even the most robust imagination cannot envision reduction, much less infirmity.

I listened to him breathing steadily, heavily, as he slept—knowing that in the morning, if he had what his vet, Doug, feared he had, Point very well might not awaken—and finally I fell asleep.

Hammered from the long night drive and the sleepless night after that one, I awoke feeling finally rested when the first light flowed in over the fields and came through the eastern window. I awoke feeling rested and positive. It would have been a perfect day, were Point not sick. How many other days had passed by in which I had possessed those three elements and yet had been less than exuberant? Here I had two of them, and were I to be granted the third one, Point's health, all would be clean and well, I would be exuberant; so why, on all those previous days when I had indeed awakened possessing those three things, had I been anything less than euphoric? *Waste, utter waste.* In this learning, too—or this remembering of what I already knew—Point was leading me again, I was following him again, as if across a field we had both hunted many times before but with a different breeze blowing this time and a different quarry, a different prize, hidden in the field this time.

One last little test this morning and we would be good to go: it was Friday, and even if he was able to withstand the exploratory surgery, they wouldn't perform it until next week. One last little test and we could go home for the weekend.

I was lying in bed thinking these things, listening to his old-dog Aqua Lung breathing and watching that sunrise, feeling good about arising so early—when I heard him stir.

I laughed at the familiar ear-flapping body rattle of his rising and shaking, and the long slow groan-and-yawn as he stretched, just the same as he had always done, back when he was young and fit.

On sleep-stiff legs and still groaning, he walked over to the side of the bed and nudged my hand toward his top-of-skull petting spot, and shook again as if in galvanic ecstasy, and then urged me up and out and into the day.

We made a walk around town, maybe his last. Everything in the town was new to me, and I had the thought that no one who saw him would be thinking what I was thinking—that this could be this dog's last walk through the town—but that instead they would have glanced at him and imagined they were seeing a dog normal and average and healthy in every way.

For a long time I thought my heart had been closed to him because of the previous dog I'd had—his older brother, Colter. But how can your heart still be open to the brilliant white collars of the rooster pheasants, and the blue sky of the winter days, and the endless gold of the wheat stubble and winter grass, and not be open to the dog?

We stopped to rest. We sat on a curb beside a small city park. He was as strong as ever but tired easily. I watched him closely, and whether he was pretending not to notice that he was tired, and that that was why he'd had to stop, or whether he truly wasn't paying this diminishment any mind, I couldn't tell. I tried to study his eyes surreptitiously. I thought I knew this dog—I *did* know this dog—but I just couldn't tell.

The sun was up over the trees, and the town was beginning to stir with car and pedestrian activity. The downtown coffee shops were abuzz, freight-delivery trucks were a-rumble on the little highway that passed right through the downtown—and the heat and glare of the day was already beginning to build, though it was barely eight o'clock. I watched it all from the time-out, single-purpose vantage that Point and I now occupied—our one goal of making only one more hunt—and it seemed to me that I was now watching the other travelers in some kind of fast-forward, speeded-up motion: that they were each and all humming and bustling like ants, or even faster—moving here and there at a pace that seemed barely possible. I had been a part of that pace and buzz, before Point got sick, and I sat there in the bright morning light and watched them, every one of them, hurrying on, buzzing on, heads down—even as I also knew that someday, long after this was all over and we had either gotten, or not just gotten, that one last pheasant, I would rejoin them all in that frenetic if not ceaseless flow.

It was time to go. Point's short coat was warm with the sun. We stood up and went to the car—I was glad I had left the windows down—got in, and drove up the hill, toward the glinting sun, and the university.

Dr. Mordecai and Laura were back in the sunlit atrium, ready and waiting, dressed in their white smocks like church choristers, like angels. By now they had the routine down, and the three of us hefted him, still in his crate, and carried him as if he were a sultan and we his porters.

Even for the relatively mild test that day, they had to tranquilize him, send him under; such was his terror and strength within the castle walls of any vet's office that he had to be restrained chemically, his one-track mind altered in such a way as to tell his muscles to relax. I sat in the waiting room while they readied him in the back, and I could hear a brief gurgling fit, a hoarse barking. Up and down they would send him, up and down, over the course of their explorations and his treatments, like a flag at sunrise and sunset, descending quickly and then rising more slowly through those various laminae of consciousness. Perhaps for him it was only as if he was still running, but was also as when the winds and breezes shifted, or the bird turned, taking him out of its scent cone; or even as when the bird flew out ahead of him, unseen by him, so that the invisible thing he had been following, though still as real as it had ever been, was now made to seem even more vaporous, as the last discernible wind-washed molecules of scent slid off the bird's wings as it lifted into flight.

Sometimes—not always, and I think I could even say rarely—but still, sometimes, I perceive that there is a stillness and a wholeness in the world, or in some portion or corner or fragment of the world, for some little place in time, where things just feel so right and huge and powerful and easy that I will have the perhaps blasphemous thought that maybe there are layers of heaven, and that, with our species' dependence upon visual acuity, we might fixate too much on notions of streets-lined-with-gold as indicator or marker of when a traveler arrives in that place.

For once perhaps we are guilty of looking ahead too much, and too far. Maybe such gilded environs and such a place of peace—or the capability of reaching such a place—does lie ahead for each and all, at some further and farther point. What if the further and denser reality of heaven—and whether such heaven is "just" a mental or spiritual state, like the dream or thought of a journey, or like the journey itself, or is in fact an object, as real as a mountain range or a deer, an elk, a wild duck—is composed of strata and laminae, like that of an intensely folded mountain range?

For once perhaps we look too far ahead, particularly with regard to the prophecies of old. Perhaps the gilded cities and streets lined with gold are before us now; perhaps we have even already passed through and by them.

What if right from the very start we are somehow already in on the ground floor of such a heaven and possess, on the remainder of our journey, the capability of being incorporated deeper and further into those strata, those laminae—rising and ascending into the body of that other and farther place?

There are definitely moments in time and places in the world where we have each felt the peace and wholeness, the stillness, spoken of in such prophecies and promises. For me it is experienced most often when I am deep in the wilderness, or up on the ridges of mountains, or in the fields and prairies with nothing but field and prairie to the horizon, or when I am simply in the presence of family. In such moments I think very much that the case could be made that we are already ankle-deep in heaven.

There in the waiting room, I heard his howls and bayings grow gradually more subdued and spaced wider apart. There was one last howl, which then faded into a kind of strangled gargling, and I imagined that finally he was going under, descending, or ascending, again. The only patient in the entire hospital making such protestations: a rank, unruly outsider, completely unfit for civilization in any way.

Hang in there, bud, I think. *I'm here with you.* But am I? I think I am and imagine that I can feel him looking for me, then making his way down into darkness, which I imagine for him might be like the cool ponds into which he would sink gingerly on a hot day—and only on the hottest of days, nervous as he was around water.

There's no certain way to reconstruct the parts of the journey we did not experience or witness firsthand, but it occurs to me only now, with so much of this receding—hurrying—into the past, that one of the reasons Point might have been so frightened of water—deep water, that is, in which the bottom could not be seen or felt—could have had something to do with the time when, so long ago, he was shot by the neighbor lady when he was out on the ice, barking at a deer. For all I know, maybe he went through the ice or was tossed into the river but somehow escaped; and somehow, three days later, straggled back home, hole-ridden, with his naughty brother, Superman, who was also bullet-pierced. I had never really given it, the fear of water, much thought: it was just a Point thing that he did, another Antaeus thing, where he felt more comfortable when his feet were on the ground from which he drew his strength. We accepted it, rather than laboring to change it.

Just this last season, however, Lowry and I were delighted when he finally made his first official water retrieve on a hen mallard that went down on the other side of an irrigation ditch, in early October. How we cheered him when he made the three strokes across the little ditch (before he even knew what he had done) to reach the duck, and then, best of all, after much consideration and summoning more courage than any of us would likely have possessed or knew he possessed—a lifetime's worth—he finally plunged back across, crossing his great fear in three strong strokes again, the duck gripped firmly in his jaws and the two of us cheering like crazy, like a whole stadium full of cheerers, rather than two tiny figures standing there isolated on the prairie and beneath that great sky, while a tiny dog paddled earnestly—the blink of an eye would miss it—across the even tinier thread of the irrigation ditch.

It seemed no time at all—less than an hour—before Dr. Mordecai and Laura emerged back into the spacious atrium. He had passed the test and could take the surgery. There was always the chance, they warned, that he might shut down midsurgery anyway, and they asked me to be thinking about what kind (if any) of life-support or resurrection measures I would want them to perform, were such a thing to happen. There was also the possibility that when they opened him up they would find him so riddled with the illness— eaten up from head to toe, with the invisible now made visible—that there would be no sense in trying to put him back together—*system collapse*—and the best thing that could be done for him would be to let him keep on sleeping, to let him remain down in the cool pond of his dreams, if that was where he was: the cool pond of Indian summer that was absorbing his panting body heat, in the shade of the cottonwoods—not quitting or ending anything but just resting up, cooling off for just a moment before going back up the bank and out onto the yellow stubble of the prairie, the gray-black sod and soil warm on the pads of his feet and the yellow sun warm again, already, on his damp back: with years and years ahead of him still. The leaves of the cottonwoods by that pond would still be green that early in the year, with only the first few of them beginning to turn yellow.

All that stuff—the resuscitation attempts, the possible decision to administer euthanasia midsurgery, depending upon the various findings—didn't have to be made right away, Dr. Mordecai explained; all I had to decide now was a surgery date. I could wait until Monday or I could wait as long as I wished—two, even three weeks, if I wanted; except for the swelling, things seemed relatively stable, if one were willing to reduce one's perspective, one's scale and sense of time, from months or years at a time down instead to hours or, if one were feeling really profligate, days.

I felt like a coach or quarterback, faced with making a profound call, a decision that would have as its rootstock more of a fundamental philosophy than any analysis of facts, circumstances, existing conditions. The odds no longer seemed a consideration, only a larger, underlying question: was I—were we—playing to keep from losing any more ground—to delay the rate of losing—or were we playing to win, win in one bold stroke and go home?

I chose the latter and scheduled the surgery for the following Monday morning. The best thing I could hope for, it seemed, was some large honking tumor, utterly benign, that could be easily excised, at which point they would stitch him back up and we would go home and, in a few weeks, back out into the fields for another autumn, at least one more autumn.

No, I thought then, remembering: it couldn't be a big tumor, because all the various other tests, including the MRI I'd already run on him (hoping to spare him the indignity of surgery—of being gutted stem to stern and then having to emerge back into the physical world he once commanded and limp around, shorn and stitched)— all those previous tests would easily have detected a big tumor. I had to hope for a little one, something invisible—pea-size, or seed-size— even an unruly fragment of old porcupine quill, having journeyed far over the years before lodging in some obstructing place: something the surgeons could see, which the machines and robots could not. Something the human eye could see but which was undetectable by the blood profiles, the chemical assays, which continued to indicate that all was fine, all was well, as the red blood continued to fill his heart and then squeeze back out, carrying him along, miraculous vessel that he was, with me following him.

———

I had been like a boxer caught in the ring with a much larger opponent; I had been trying to focus on the possibility of one short-term goal, pheasants, rather than the larger reality, death; and under such battering circumstances, I had even been balling up, protecting myself against joy, cautious against and, as a defensive mechanism, even disbelieving of every counsel directed toward the thing I most wanted to hear: that he was going to be all right, that the tests could find nothing, that it was simply an infection causing a temporary blockage, treatable with antibiotics, that it was simply an old dog's leaking heart valve, treatable with medication.

But now, having been up and down so much, having run through so many tests, and, like a gambler who had encountered a bad run of luck, having quickly run through about five thousand quick dollars—for nothing, really, not even the rarest of things, knowledge, but instead more absence of knowledge—now, having him released back to me for the weekend, when I had been prepared for the possibility of not having him at all this weekend, or ever again, I allowed myself the largest spike of joy I had been able to experience during this new stage of the journey: and even for joy it was surprisingly delicious, pure, and transcendent, like the joy of childhood.

It was like the joy that comes from an unawareness of any other larger factors or connections beyond the moment—an unawareness that can help deliver that purity of focus. What was so strange about it, of course, was the fact that unlike a child I was acutely aware of those other larger and not-so-distant further factors and connections; but the joy came flooding in nonetheless, totally displacing those fears and worries and that pain. It was almost a biological response— again, pure and elemental—that was delivered to me, not because I had earned or deserved it, and certainly not because greater external circumstances dictated it—he was likely dying—but instead was delivered to me, flooded into me, simply because I needed it.

I had been trying to hold out the world's pleasures for too long, and at some stage, I had not been able to continue that resistance— one puny human—against so great a force in the world, and finding the weak chink in my armor—my love for Point—that force, that joy, came flooding in, and suddenly I was simply happy to be driving back to Montana with him, and no matter that he was uncured or that it was only for the weekend: there was only joy, delight, and this time, rather than trying to guard against it, I reveled in it.

This was not any wise or noble or otherwise conscious decision on my part: it was instead that the joy was just too complete and powerful to resist or withstand.

He hopped up into the front seat, grinning—as if we were escaping something and were complicit in our getaway—and we headed home, with no tubes or wires or pills or needles, no pain of mortal flesh or, that afternoon at least, foreknowledge of pain and loss to come. It was just a summer afternoon in the American West, and I drove and petted his head and later, as he slept, admired the sun through the windshield or on his dappled, ticked coat.

I listened to the news of the world the same way I used to listen to it, as if it mattered—as if I were not in the throes of a more immediate personal crisis, so tiny to the world yet so large within the confines of my heart—and I admired the passing landscape—the summer sky, the tall fields of wheat not yet cut, soft wheat appearing to blanket the rolling hills—and in so doing I was even able to think about the upcoming hunting season without bottomless despair.

Homeward! One more day at least, and even if he died in his sleep, it would now be in his home, with the all and only ones who loved him around him and every object familiar to him—sacred in that familiarity—and with every scent, every sound, every rhythm, every sight, terrain, over which he had dominance in his life, through virtue of his love of life. One more day *at least*! I had prepared for the possibility of not having even this one.

It was midafternoon, easing to late afternoon, but the days were still long. There was a fair chance I would get in before dark. I drove on, and he continued to sleep, exhausted not just from the tests but also from the stress of being away from home. As well as (even in my afternoon's joy, I could not sugarcoat this) from the illness, or the problem, or whatever it was, itself.

We were nearing the farthest northern edge of wheat country: about to leave the still-bucolic (and yet here in summer, heat-stricken) farm country, which in August seemed to just be waiting, hanging on, poised suffering and paused, waiting for September's rains—and soon we would be at the edge of the mountain-and-lake country, which was to say also the land of clustered strip malls and the ever-expanding continuum of commerce and truck-roar that was Coeur d'Alene and, farther north, Sandpoint—and so I stopped, there on a hill not too far from the place where the wheat country finally ran out and where the pace of the world would quicken and the density of mankind, the blur of our coming and going, would become magnified a hundredfold. I gently awakened Point, lifted him from the front seat, and set him down on a dirt road so that he could walk around and stretch a bit, pee, do his business.

He was a little wobbly at first. The sun was lower in the west now—not setting, but low enough to announce that part of the day that really has no name in summer up here—somewhere around five o'clock, in which a description of neither "late afternoon" nor "early evening" is quite accurate—and after Point had peed, he did an odd and unsettling thing. Never before in the least bit contemplative, he turned so that he was facing that five o'clock sun, and the rolling hills between it and us, and stood there and stared out at the horizon. There was a hot dry wind pouring toward us from the west, and I tried to tell myself he was just standing there like that as he tried to parse out some scent.

But I had seen him take the scent of a hundred thousand or maybe a million things over the years, and as the wind stirred his eyes and his nose twitched only once or twice, I could see that though he was scenting something, the primary senses going on for him that moment were his eyesight and something else: something going on in his mind.

He stood there, for once almost seeming to ignore his ability to scent things, and instead stared out at the horizon. There was a tentativeness and a vague curiosity both in that stare—I would like to say it was free of concern, but I cannot—and one of the impressions I got, with that dry, warm wind pressing against us, was that he was almost bracing himself, though the wind was not really quite that strong.

The malls and commercial frenzy—the dissipation of the earth's vitality, and of life, is what it felt like to me—passed, with the unpleasantness of this leg of the journey forcing me to detach, relegating those external surroundings to the emotionless blur that they were—hunger is not an emotion—and then, later, we were on the other side of it and back into western Montana, and then, a bit later still, we were beginning the journey up into our wild little valley, with the afternoon's, or evening's, first cool breath coinciding with the moment we turned up the small road that led far back into our valley.

The road followed the winding, rushing river as it flowed down from out of the mountains. The river was bony at that time of year, at its shallowest points, with boulders and even cobbles exposed in places that were usually never showing; and in many ways it was the time of year when the river was, to my eyes, most beautiful. We were almost home now, were assured of being home before dark, and once more I felt a wave of great joy, as unreasonable as it was elemental, though this time there were finally, and once more, the first threads of the other things starting to form within that joy, the impurities of bittersweetness. Still, it had been a good afternoon, taking a long drive with my dog, and I petted him as he continued to sleep, and drove with the windows down, taking in the rich, lush odors of the green valley as it finally cooled against the day.

———

I thought I had been doing a pretty good job of protecting myself—of preparing for the worst—but maybe I had done too good a job, for as I pulled onto the long gravel road that led to my house and then up the long gravel drive through the woods—driving with the windows rolled down now, and breathing the cool air of high mountain summer, delicious in any age but all the more rare and refreshing in this era of global warming—I realized that despite playing to win, running the tests necessary to have a chance at cleanly saving his life (as opposed to messily prolonging it), there was a huge part of me that had not expected that the two of us would ever come driving back down this light-dappled little lane in the summer, would never stop once more and take a long, satisfying piss in that wonderful long light of late summer ending-of-day. The scent of decaying logs, ancient forest mulch, drying, as the remnants of the day's heat, which had percolated down beneath the carpet of old pine needles and kinnikinnick and Oregon grape, continued to tick silently, the olfactory equivalent of a heated engine that continues to expand and then contract, ticking, even after the engine has been shut off.

The lovely, nostalgic scent of a distant forest fire somewhere far away—maybe an entire state, maybe two states distant. Maybe up in Canada.

Traveling farther down the gravel drive, slowly, to the point where we were close enough for Superman, alone in his kennel, to pop out and begin barking, protesting the scratch of gravel. Barking at any vehicle, whether known to him or not. Barking as he always had, as if everything were still always the same, and with the house coming into sight now, and Elizabeth and the girls sitting out on the steps waiting, and with the marsh down below the house still green, even in August, and with the mountains beyond greener.

Point leaning his head out the open window, whining, eager to rejoin Superman—in ten years they had probably not spent more than two or three days and nights apart—and it was that simple: he was in no pain, he was glad to be home, and I had given him one more summer day, had given us all one more summer day; we were home.

You know the end to this story. It's the end to all dog stories. But before it came, we still had more time, and good time. And were home again, once more.

A Good Creature

CHRIS ADRIAN

My ex-boyfriend tells me he's thinking of getting a dog. This is significant to me for a few reasons. We have only been broken up for about a month, and in that time I've managed to put off absolutely none of the habits of mind I developed when we were together, so it still feels like we are together, and so in some pathetic way I consider him to be thinking of getting a dog for *us*. And it seems to me that the lonely woundedness he is feeling now must be considerable if it requires so soft and formidable a patch as a puppy, and that is a perverse comfort somehow, since he dumped me. And he left me in large part because I have developed a Problem in the past few years that gives me in general a horror of the ground and anything that's touched it, along with peculiar notions of uncleanliness that led to frequent hand washing (and boyfriend washing), making everyday expressions of intimacy harder and harder and harder. He left me in particular because I could not sit on a park bench with him and stare at the river (people put their feet on park benches, after all), or sit on the floor of his apartment, or hug him spontaneously without having to assure myself he hadn't been too close to something unclean, and more importantly because my failure to overcome my unreasonable fears in the specific context of *him* denoted for him a weakness of affection and suggested an absence of love. He left me, it occurs to me, because I could not be more like a dog.

My family had a St. Bernard named Moose who died just after I was born. I have no memory of him, but he was made familiar to me by my mother, who was close with all her ghosts and liked to talk about them with us incessantly, telling the same old stories about the same dead people over and over and over in any night of drinking. Moose was a person to her, and something of a hero to her in the way that all her dead were heroes to her (except for evil old Aunt Mary), mostly just on account of their being dead. Moose was probably a better hero than the tragical Irishmen that constituted the rest of her ghost posse. He saved my oldest sister from suffocating in a toy chest and stopped her one night when she was a toddler as she tried to wander out onto a Southern California mountainside to be stung by snakes and eaten by coyotes. He caught her as she was climbing out a first-floor window and kept his teeth in her panties until our parents came, summoned by his bottom-muffled barking. He died of heatstroke after pulling my sisters in a summer parade, in a little cart my father built for him. I think he was supposed to pull only one of them at a time, and never either of them in July, but my father got overly excited at the prospect of being the only dog-pulled cart in the parade, and his judgment lapsed. My mother liked to describe a tender dog-deathbed scene at the vet's in which she or my father fed Popsicles to Moose as he expired, giving him a taste of cold St. Bernard heaven before he got there.

When I was very young, I had a great affection for all my mother's ghosts (except, of course, evil old Aunt Mary), because she described herself as happy back in the days when they were around, and she made them sound so much better than us, the living family she was most unsatisfactorily stuck with. But I had a particular affection for Moose, and even outside of my intoxications-by-association with my mother, I imagined him still with us, massive yet insubstantial, concerned now with protecting us from spiritual rather than physical dangers, ready to sink his teeth into my metaphysical panties if I ever strayed from the path of good. It seems strange to say it, since I never really met him, but he was the first dog I ever loved.

It will be some sort of retriever, a Labrador or a golden, with exquisite young fur. It will follow him everywhere and sit on the floor and on the ground outside and lie down on its belly without a care in the world for what's beneath it. It will put its paws—its terribly filthy paws—all over his apartment and even on his pillow. It will never be moody or depressed or feel guilty when something good happens to it. It will love him unconditionally.

Moose had a retarded younger brother named Shefton, who outlived him by seven years. I say brother, though Shefton was an English sheepdog, because they were puppies together and grew up together in the house. Shefton had spastic limbs and made processing errors and was very fearful. He was my first living dog. I was the youngest in the family and took no responsibility for him. I don't think I ever walked him once, or even filled up his water bowl, but I loved him very generously, and somewhat enviously. Toward the end of his life, when I was in second grade, I decided that he had the better life of the two of us. This was roughly when I saw *The Shaggy D.A.* and *Freaky Friday* for the first time, and I devoutly wished some random magic would bless me into his body. I wanted to stay at home all day while he went to school and watch him while he did my homework.

He died before I could figure out how to make the switch. I remember very clearly knowing that something was wrong even before I went into the house—he'd been put to sleep while my brother and sisters and I were all at school, and our parents were waiting inside with the bad news and a coffee can full of ashes and remnant bone. I cried so hard I threw up all over myself, but that was the only time I ever cried for a dead dog.

He was buried in a ravine in back of the house, under an arrow-shaped stone, and his grave drew to itself all sorts of illicit activities. I showed my penis to about seven different boys and girls down there before I was eight years old, and my brother and sisters drank or did drugs over his headstone. I faced toward his grave but was too afraid to go down to it the night I tried to talk to him with a Ouija board. I turned on every light in the room I shared with my brother in the hope of scaring away Captain Howdy, since my chief fear aside from my family's being murdered by a burglar was that I would get possessed by the devil like Regan MacNeil, and even I knew it had happened to her because she was messing around alone with a Ouija board.

I asked him if he was happy, if Moose was with him, if he could come back, if he could tell me, now that he was dead, the secret way in which a boy can become a dog. I asked what dog heaven was like, and stared and stared at the board, and finally got an answer to just that one question (I am sure, looking back, that I was pushing the planchette). He said it was blue.

I can imagine a life for them, beyond the heady, frustrating days of puppyhood. Months and then years pass, and they begin to realize that they are more to each other than master and servant, man and man's best friend. They are companions, and each contains everything the other ever wanted. Suddenly the old trick of taking the Pup-peroni from his master's mouth is charged with new significance. Bank accounts are merged. The dog, who has better credit than me, is able to buy a house with my ex-boyfriend, and not very much longer after that they begin to fill it with children adopted out of Africa: Chimwemwe, Chifundo, Mphatso. Of course the children are officially adopted by the retriever, since homosexuals will be granted the right to adopt only many years after it's granted to dogs. I can see them now, the whole family scattered on the floor, and nobody is haunted by anxious associations, or notions of uncleanliness, or concerns for the future, or traumas of the past. Like dogs, they are entirely in the present and entirely happy there.

After Shefton died, we got a miniature schnauzer named Schatzi. Our mother drove us at night through an incredible thunderstorm to pick him up. I don't know why we all risked our lives to go get him. I remember the sound his claws made in his cardboard box on the way home every time the thunder broke. He was terrified, but the trip didn't scare me until years later. When we got him home, we nearly killed him overfeeding him. His belly swelled up so much it dragged on the floor, and he could only walk a few steps before he tripped over it.

I am embarrassed for him that his name made him sound like a fat Potsdam whore, but it certainly didn't bother him. He was psychotic around vacuum cleaners, but otherwise he was a serene personality, and he was a good creature. He taught me that dogs are good in the way that Shefton taught me they were lucky, and I wanted to be him, not out of envy but out of agony. I was eight when we got him, and he lived through my adolescence, when I was learning that I was bad and accumulating and suppressing the memories and miseries that would turn me into a cringing, hand-washing mess fifteen years later, and I was terribly concerned with the state of my soul. In Adam's fall we sinned all, but schnauzers were not involved. They were not culpable; they were excused. And I only had to look at my dog, at any dog, to see why. He was never spiteful. He did not lie. He did not want to kill his parents. He never had sex with a man. He was at peace with himself and with the world. I wanted to be like that, a creature at home in creation.

He died after a long dog life. I would discover later that he died a lot like people die. He moaned in his sleep just like my father did as he was dying, and twitched his paws in a way analogous to the way my father made swatting motions at nothing with his hands, and they both got great comfort from benzodiazepines in their final hours. My mother called me at school, weeping, to say the dog was finally dead. I was surprised to find that I wasn't very sad, and this seemed further proof that I was no good, and that of the two of us the dog was the better man.

When I was a kid, my second-favorite cartoon was a piece about a man who gets run over walking his dog. An ambulance comes to resuscitate them both, and a confused (or maybe just mischievous or crazy) paramedic mixes up the dog plasma and the people plasma, and after their transfusions the man and the dog switch personalities. This aired after I stopped wanting to physically become my dog, so I never tried transfusing myself, but my brother and I would play out the cartoon over and over again, taking turns being the man, the dog, the paramedics. We both loved to shout "Dog plasma!" and "People plasma!" but never got very far past the accident in our game.

Now I imagine a lawsuit, a scandal, and, eventually, further research. The self-evident is discovered, that people can benefit from a carefully titrated infusion of dog plasma. Centers spring up in the abandoned offices where people once went for high colonics. I am among the first to go in for a visit.

A giant shambling doctor who seems to have a gotten a touch of Newf interviews me and asks me to describe my symptoms. "I am afraid of the ground," I say. He nods and makes a little check on his clipboard. "I am haunted by the past. I always do the wrong thing even though I know what the right thing is. I am afraid to touch my boyfriend. My sense of smell is not acute."

"You've come to the right place," he tells me, shaking my little white hand with his gigantic one. In his big brown eyes, I can find absolutely nothing but kindness and reassurance. A poodle-faced nurse takes me into the treatment room and starts my IV. "Labrador," the doctor says, drawing up the golden fluid. "A fine choice!"

"People plasma!" says the nurse, and they all have a good laugh. Then they drug me up and start the infusion, and for hours I am dreaming, running through tall grass or on the beach. I am just barely aware that my feet are pedaling on the table. In my dream I am carefully placing one bare paw on the ground, and then another, and then I am picking up a ball from the ground *with my mouth,* and there is nothing at all wrong with that.

"Wake up, sir," says the nurse. "You're all done."

My ex-boyfriend wants a dog, and I want to be like a dog. You'd think we could come to some sort of accommodation. I could meet him halfway and sit with him on a clean pillow on the ground. I could fetch a new ball if he threw it in the confines of a clean room. I could get a wig of shining Lab hair.

But of course he left me for deeper and better and worse reasons than my not being a dog, and if he gets a dog, the hole I left in his life will be very partially stoppered. I want to be a good creature for reasons beyond sharing a life with a good man. There's not enough dog plasma in the world to make me new again. In what horrible factory were they going to extract all that dog plasma?

Anyway, I hope he gets the dog and pray I learn to love it.

At Least You Have Your Legs

JIM SHEPARD

My wife Karen found a wolf spider in the shower the other day that was somewhere between two to three inches in diameter. She'd turned on the water before she'd seen it, and now it sat drying out, spread-legged and a little stunned. I was going to kill it but the sheer spectacle of the thing mesmerized us. We put it in a mason jar. When Lucy, our four-year-old daughter, got home from preschool, she put her nose up against the glass, and the thing stood on its hind legs and extended its pedipalps, the way tarantulas do in nature specials. If you touched the jar, it rushed back and forth as much as the space allowed, enraged. It was clear that we had a fairly special spider here.

I figured I'd hang on to it for a couple of days to show various people that I wasn't exaggerating, and then I'd let it go. (After walking a block or two: I didn't need to see *that* son of a bitch again. And if I *did* see him again, his little reprieve was history.)

So a day later, feeling a little like the neighborhood St. Francis, I trooped across the street to a brushy slope, holding the jar out in front of me like someone carrying an isotope of radium, the spider hunching and gathering itself as if grimly trying to figure out what *else* could go wrong, and when I turned the jar over, it spread its legs and caught the lower branches of a young maple, scrambling up and stabilizing itself on a leaf, its weight bending and bobbing the leaf toward the ground. Its fierce little head tracked me while it crouched there swaying, looking more homicidal than grateful.

That week was Wildlife Week, in fact. We live near a protected forest in Massachusetts, which means that deer and turkeys and rabbits and the occasional muskrat periodically scuff through our yard. Even so, not so much in the predator line happens by. Two days before the wolf spider, though, Karen settled into her desk in our study to find herself nose to nose with a huge black bear outside her window. The bear was on his butt and had pulled the bird feeder down with both paws and was snarfing the seeds inside. He was so big that even on his butt he could reach it, and we had it hanging at about shoulder height. He was so strong that he had the thirty-foot pine on which it hung bent toward him as he pulled. (We use wire to hang our bird feeders, the squirrels tear them down so often.)

I was around the other side of the house shooting baskets with the kids. Karen called for us in that voice that unmistakably signals that something's hit the fan. By the time we all arrived at her study window, Dino, our three-year-old beagle, had come out of his customary unconscious sprawl atop the couch, had pieced together what was going on, and was sprinting around in such desperation that he appeared to be levitating by at high speed, ricocheting from window to window and generating enough noise for a one-dog fox hunt.

The bear came off as mostly methodical, and about as dignified as something that obliviously single-minded can look. He was putting both paws into the effort of tilting the feeder enough to empty the last of the seeds into his mouth. Dino bicycled the glass with his front paws, hysterical with outrage, and the bear gazed over at him with some serenity and returned to the mysteries of the feeder. This went on for some time—the humans oohing and aahing, Dino beside himself, the bear unhurriedly bobbing the feeder over his open jaws, like someone shaking sugar into his coffee—until finally *I* started banging on the glass with my palm and shouting (he *was* only four feet away).

You might have thought I was shouting at a movie screen. Not enough noise, eh? I thought, and gathered up some pots and pans from the kitchen and went out into the yard. Dino pinwheeled and gyrated like something on an electrified surface, trying to get to us, but Karen had him hooked by the collar.

I ventured to within ten feet—how fast *could* they run anyway?— and banged my pots and pans together. That he did notice, the way a fat man on a bench notices distant traffic. Poor Dino was now hurling himself at the window, his metal license ringing against the glass. I started bracketing the bear with rocks from the front walkway. One that whizzed by his butt made him drag himself to his feet and then to his hind legs. I was unhappy to discover that he was as tall as I was.

I made cattle-drive sounds. He gave me some thought. I bracketed him with more rocks, and he turned and lurched into motion, at first toward me, and then he changed his mind on the fly and half loped away with that rolling bear gait, looking back once, like an old man put out by hooligans making too much noise to let him watch TV.

Put out or not, he came back a half hour later. Same thing. Same pots and pans, different rocks. This time after he disappeared back into the woods, at Karen's suggestion I took the emptied bird feeder down—it was grooved with claw marks the thickness of pencils raked down both sides of the clear plastic—and she put it in the cellar.

That next Saturday night, Dino went nuts again, and, given the giant, featureless plain that is my thoughtlessness, I let him out the back garage door without fully taking my mind off whatever it was I was doing. When he refused to calm down once outside, I followed him out, mostly for the purpose of yelling at him, and in the darkness I could hear something that sounded like a washing machine being dragged through the woods. I called him, but he just kept barking. Our motion light was out, naturally, so I had to go inside for a flashlight.

When I got back to the driveway, I played its beam around. Dino was invisible at first, his bark noticeably more hoarse. But there was the bear, lugging our full garbage can, its lid still on, up the hillside and through the woods, his arms around the widest part, the frat boy humping a keg. Apparently he hadn't been able to get the bungee cord off the top and had opted for just walking off with the entire thing. I yelled for him to drop the can, and he did. Which disconcerted us both. Later on when I told the story, people said, Wait—the bear understood English? To which I answered, Hey, what can I tell you? I told him to drop it, and he dropped it.

I caught his face with the flashlight beam, and he looked at me like he was suffering from a headache. He gave me his second memorable look: this one more along the lines of, *You are* one *pain in the ass, boy.* Then he left again. I could hear the crashing through the undergrowth for a full few minutes, even over Dino's noise.

It looked as if someone had dragged a boat through the woods. The next morning I was able to follow his trail all the way down to a stream that runs off our property.

Soon after that he came back again and pulled the bag of bird seed out of the garage and tore it open and spread it around. Lucy's babysitter surprised him and apparently lopped a few years off her own life expectancy doing so.

Now we shut our garage doors when not going in or out. And when Dino goes into alarm mode—which is not a very common occurrence, given that he's one of the mellower beagles around—we investigate outside a little bit ourselves before we let him out.

Because in fact it's not true that when Dino was going nuts the night of the garbage can that I let him out without fully taking my mind off whatever I was doing. It was worse than that. I'd been trying to concentrate on something—some reading, or YouTube, or my own vacant look, reflected in the windowpane, who knows?—and I'd lost my patience when his barking had crossed the four-minute threshold, and I'd gotten up and propelled him outside with what they used to call, in the eighteenth century, an angry oath. My family's seen me do it before. Much aggrieved, and never thinking, *Hey, you just* saw *a huge bear out there, and you* know *the bear's been coming around.*

In other words, I could have been throwing him out into one of those monster movies in which the dog, who first sounds the alarm, when he's finally let outside is only heard from again once, with that telltale yelp. Was I sending my dog into harm's way? For that moment when I opened the door, it didn't matter.

That's relevant because I've now had six dogs in my life, and as far as I'm concerned, I killed two of them. I killed them that way, giving in to an irritable self-absorption and taking them for granted in ways that came back, and still come back, to haunt me. As taking things for granted often seems to do.

Karen and I have a lot of childhood photos of each other. One she loves is from around my first Communion, maybe even the day *of* my first Communion; sources disagree. Either on that day or very soon after, as a celebratory gift, my parents gave me my first dog, something for which I'd been pleading since the day I discovered that dogs existed. In the photo I'm probably six. My guess is that it *was* the day of my first Communion, because in the photo I'm posed in front of the white shingles and unpainted cement foundation of our house, decked out in a blindingly new white shirt with my top button buttoned, no tie, and black dress pants so tightly belted that I look like a cartoon. My hair, Brylcreemed, has been sculpted in the fashion of the period into some kind of breaking-wave arrangement. I'm holding Lady, my first puppy, who's on her back and squirming to get loose. My arms are out in front of me, the way someone might carry firewood. You can barely see her face.

What Karen loves about the photo is *my* face, which has clearly just passed some insane outer boundary of happiness, headed for somewhere else equally unprecedented. I remember during the taking of the photo being aware that I was insufficiently able to control my expressions. I remember, in fact, that day as being full of the sort of wild happiness that doesn't allow you to sit still, even when told, repeatedly, by pleased and weary parents, to sit still.

Lady turned out to be a German shepherd–and–something mix, the something being an unspecified hound, probably, given her smaller size. We hit it off, by which I mean I thought about her morning, noon, and night and spoke for her when people asked how she was doing. (As in, "Lady goes, *'I'm* doing fine. How're *you* doing?'")

We sailed through six years like that. She was a supernaturally smart dog, by which I mean that she was certainly the smartest dog *I'd* ever had and that she always seemed to know exactly what was going on with my emotions, which was more than I could say for any of the adults I knew or, more importantly, for myself. If I was sad about something, she'd sit next to me and lean into me. She wasn't impatient with my sadness, as my panicky and overstressed parents tended to be. If I was mad, she'd go sit in her chair with her chin on her paws, keeping a wary watch. She seemed to register that patience was always the best way to deal with anger. And on those occasions when I was exhilarated and ready to head outside, she'd pull her leash down from the hook in the kitchen and circle me with it with her own peculiar and high-energy happy dance, which was a kind of accelerated rocking-horse lilt: dog language for, *It's going to be a great day, isn't it?*

During the night she checked on everyone with the regularity of a night watchman. One early morning when I was sick with the measles, I woke to find her apparently having fallen asleep in the middle of one of her check-ins, sitting next to the bed, her chin on the mattress, snoring.

She was never leashed and roamed the neighborhood judiciously. She never fought with other dogs or took much interest in cats. At least not that we ever heard of. She seemed to handle the unexpected lethality of cars with a kind of casual mastery.

But then when I was eleven or twelve, I was across the street at a friend's house playing with toy soldiers or, as we called them, army men—*why was I playing with army men at the age of twelve? let it go, let it go*—and my friend and I had taken twenty minutes to set up a huge number of guys in some kind of Tarawa beachhead, and here came Lady, jogging by to see how everyone was doing, and she trundled right through the Japanese defenses, churning up ten minutes' worth of work, and I shouted at her and gave her butt a shove, and she spooked and accelerated out into the street and got hit by a car.

I stood over her. My friend did, too, until he got too freaked out and ran into his house. The guy who'd hit her stood over her. He said stuff like it wasn't his fault, that the dog had just run under his wheels. He said he was sorry. Lady was on her side with her mouth open. She had an expression like she had run a mile and was unbelievably hot. Even I could tell she was already dead. The guy said he was sorry again and then pulled her by the paws out of the road and onto the shoulder. I don't remember now whether he went and got the nearest neighbor or the neighbor just came out of the house. I do remember the guy and the car being gone after a while.

The neighbor had his hand on my shoulder. He said I was going to be all right. He said it looked like she hadn't suffered. After a while he gave up and went and got his pickup truck and backed it around next to Lady's body. Then he got out and laid an olive army tarp on the road next to her and pulled her onto it by the skin of her shoulders and butt. I remember feeling piercingly that it was a heartless way to move her. I think he wasn't taking any chances on getting bitten.

He said he was bringing her somewhere, but I didn't register where, or if I did, I don't register it anymore. He drove off, and I stayed there in the street looking down at the spot on the pavement. Then I ran home.

I ran past my mother and into the bathroom and climbed into the tub. I pulled the shower curtain closed behind me. I wasn't ready to see the rest of the human race. I couldn't think of anything in the bathroom that I could use to hurt myself as much as I wanted to hurt myself, but I was also too much of a coward or just too paralyzed to get up and find something in the garage.

My mother located me in there and asked what was wrong. I managed to tell her enough to send her over the neighbor's, where she tried to come up with more information. He didn't have much. When she returned, she tried, alternately, to comfort me and to get me out of the tub. She came from a big Italian family, so this kind of histrionic behavior wasn't new to her experience.

I wasn't comforted, and I wouldn't get out of the tub. I told her by way of explanation that it was my fault. She worked to refute my position. We settled into a stalemate, and I remember she just sat, sad and helpless, on the toilet for while, not knowing what else to do.

My older brother came home from wherever he'd been, got the news, and went to his room. He tended to keep to himself. She'd decided against calling my father, figuring why ruin his day? When he did get home, I heard her tell him out in the driveway, heard him cursing, enraged (at the cosmos, not at me), and heard him go in and make his summer drink—a Tom Collins, with its unmistakable sound of his long metal spoon clinking against the side of his big glass—and then heard him come back out and smash it against the side of the garage.

Eventually he swung open the door of the bathroom and asked me what the Christ I was doing in the tub. He hauled me to my feet and out into my room. He did so principally by showing me how upset *he* was, which had the effect of making my position seem excessive and theatrical. *He* felt the way he did, and *he* wasn't in the tub.

I never fully recovered from that day. Six months or so later, my father mentioned at the dinner table that a friend of his had a puppy that he had to get rid of and that maybe I'd like to go look at it, and I told him, "I'll probably kill it like I killed Lady."

I was reminded that I *hadn't* killed Lady and that I shouldn't think that I had. I understood that, didn't I? Once I made clear that I did, the subject was dropped. A month or so later, he brought home another puppy, this one a male, white, part Dalmatian and part some kind of spaniel. The puppy was white and black with a black patch on his back and black ears. I named him Snoopy.

Snoopy lived to be twelve or so or before he had to be put down. Where was I when that happened? A thousand miles away, teaching in Ann Arbor. My father called after the fact, having employed the same logic my mother had employed about calling him concerning Lady—why ruin his day? So I sat in my attic apartment thinking I'd once again let my dog down: like, where had *I* been at the crucial moment? Where had I been when Snoopy had gotten the injection? Had he been wondering? Had he been thinking, in his foggy dog brain, pretty much what he always did, which was, *It'd be easier, whatever it is, if we were all here?*

When I accepted a teaching job back east, I told myself that my reward for (a) taking a full-time, possibly long-term job and (b) living in the extreme northwest corner of Massachusetts was that I could get another dog. That dog turned out to be Audrey, half Irish setter, half beagle, essentially a slightly larger beagle with that beautiful Irish setter's red coat. Audrey went everywhere, from the Florida Keys to the Italian countryside, always with that endearing and barely controlled beagle's neediness: that skittish, stricken look and little trill that said, *You're not thinking of going somewhere* else *without me, are you?* And after Lady, and after Snoopy, my answer was always, whenever it could be, no. She drank out of scummy fountains in Rome; she sat still for photo shoots over the FDR Drive. (Baffled relatives in Italy remarked, when they first saw her, still petrified and shaking in her little crate in the baggage area, "You know, we have dogs *here*.")

She never needed a leash, and I never needed to call her. If she started to stray, all I had to do was to walk quickly the other way. The instant she caught on, she'd come pounding after me, making little yips, indignant, panicked.

She lived fourteen years. Her muzzle by that time was mostly white—from stress, I told people. Her hearing started to go. It became clear a large part of it was gone. How much? I kept meaning to get that checked out. Then her eyesight started to go. She bonked into things. I meant to get that checked out, too. She got disoriented enough that I started hanging out with her in the yard while she relieved herself.

You can see where this is going. Along came that night when I didn't, when she stood dumbly, her head down, by the door at *the worst possible time,* and I just opened the door and went about what I was doing, and out she went. It wasn't a very busy street. As with Dino, with the bear, nine years later: was I sending my dog into harm's way? For that moment when I opened the door, it didn't matter.

The police called. They said that a woman had reported having hit and killed a dog on the road outside our house a few minutes earlier. They'd found our number on the dog license. Karen took the call and told them that there had to be a mistake, because Audrey was still in the house. It turned out that Audrey was not in the house. Jim had let Audrey out.

———

This time *I* pulled the dog onto the tarp, and *I* loaded the body onto the back of a vehicle. It was my decision what to do with the body. It was shocking to be reenacting that trauma all over again. It was shocking to be standing over my dog's body feeling as though I'd made the same heartless mistake that I'd made before and that I'd never forgotten. She'd probably had no idea where she was when the car hit her. She had relied on me—*You're not thinking of going somewhere* else *without me, are you?*—and that had been a big mistake.

I was raised Catholic, which may or may not be a surprise to hear. Some of my earliest memories of parochial school involve the nuns— Sister Marie Edmund, Sister Justine, Sister Caroline—reminding us insistently of how *lucky* we were, of how many reasons we had to feel fortunate. We had our health, we had mostly intact families, we were never truly hungry or cold. "At least you have your legs," one sister would always say to anyone who whined or complained. And she was right.

W. H. Auden once remarked that there was only one thing that all poetry had to do: "it must praise all it can for being and for happening." One of the great and never-ending blessings of dogs is that they never tire of demonstrating that by example. And one of the great consolations of our relationship with dogs is that we're given the chance, over and over again, to learn that lesson and to behave as though we have, no matter how persistently we seem to refuse to do so.

Dog Lives

ANTONYA NELSON

The first dog I ever outlived was Moe. He came with my family. They were in the process of getting bigger (I was the third child out of what would become five), and they had adopted the dog to appease my brothers in the face of a new sister, me. Moe: a beagle named by boys. The delinquent brother believed he had named the dog after his favorite Stooge; the egghead brother thought "Moe" was short for Geronimo, whose history he was then studying.

Moe was not exactly a member of the family. He lived outside, like the lawn mower, and over the years we spent a lot of time commanding and imploring him to *shut up*. Occasionally my father took him hunting, which left both of them vaguely deaf. It was Moe's baying that prompted my first sentence: "Moe bark."

When the fifth child arrived, my parents moved us from our tiny tract house in Wichita, Kansas, to a giant dilapidated one—we went from a two-bedroom/one-bath to a seven-bedroom/five-bath. Moe and I got lost together our first night in that house, wandering the back staircase that led to the servants' quarters. Everything was different in the new house—we even had a new sister. But Moe was the same. And though he spent the second half of his life in a much larger pen, he still lived outside with the garden tools and bikes, and we rarely visited him. Still, there he sat at the gate, barking, albeit feebly. The big excitement was when he somehow finagled an escape, and we then mobilized—in cars, on foot, on the phone—looking for him, everyone horrified—hearts pounding, eyes leaking—to think he would die or disappear. But who could blame him for trying?

I was twelve when he died, and heartbroken. A piece of my childhood had been irrevocably stolen away—and at the same time I was going through puberty, heading off to junior high, wearing my first bra, sneaking my first sips of liquor, uttering my first curse words. Childhood snuffed, wrapped in a smelly blanket, and buried in the backyard under a brick. For a while there was no replacement for old Moe. My parents made the usual dull excuses: no one ever walked the dog, the dog suffered, sitting outside barking, and they, my mom and dad, would be charged with caring for the dog, no matter the promises we, their hypocritical children, made. Blah, blah, blah.

So it was a stealth operation, acquiring the new dog. It was a forgiveness-rather-than-permission kind of move, very teenage. I located a stray while wandering a neighborhood I shouldn't have been in, smoking cigarettes with people I shouldn't have been with. The dog "followed" me, attached to the end of my white studded belt, all the way home, across town. He became George when he sort of responded to the name. He looked like an English sheepdog cut off at the knees, his tail so long it looked as though he'd tip backward on it, and he acted more like a cat than a dog, aloof and skittish. He rarely barked, and he hid under furniture, refusing to come when called. On walks he picked fights with larger dogs, as if he himself were large. More than once he chased a smaller creature to its death. His one claim to some kind of charm was his right ear, which stood up, while the left lay flat. This made him seem quizzical and sweet instead of malodorous and grumpy, which were his true traits.

As we had with Moe, we took George with us when we went away for the summer. My parents were teachers, and we had a summer cabin in the Colorado Rockies. Across the two states we would drive, all of us in the station wagon, the dog either drooling on my father's shoulder (Moe) or attempting to burrow under the seats or pedals (George).

These two dogs—Moe and George—saw me through my years living at home. When I left for college, George stayed with my parents, just as they'd predicted he would, and when he died and my mother phoned to tell me, I thought for sure the grief in her voice was about my father, or my niece, or any other number of humans we loved. Nope: she was weeping over George, who had finally succumbed.

But I was married by then and had a much more presentable dog to love, a dog who'd fit in at a Pottery Barn photo shoot or running in slow motion on the beach. I had chosen this dog, both her breed and then her herself. Buying a dog is significantly different from inheriting or adopting one. You aren't *saving* a brand-name, bred puppy. There is no *rescue* in that transaction. This dog will have papers— more of them than you yourself have. It's not quite like buying a product, since the dogs aren't assembly-line made, yet it isn't the same as letting fate guide your hand either. Not quite. It's more like dating, I think. You select your type—blond, dumb, sweet—and then watch the litter, looking for the one whose particular blond/dumb/sweet personality best suits your own, knowing in advance that you have some affinity. I wanted a golden retriever. I wanted a girl because I'd had only boys—unneutered ones, at that, my dad of a school of thought that wouldn't think of lopping off a fella's nuts—and had heard the girls didn't stray or fight. I myself have always wanted to be a gentle leggy blonde; why wouldn't I choose her, instead of a fireplug with a Napoleon complex?

And I wanted the most temperate of the girl goldens. Flannery, I named her. (A year later, when I won the Flannery O'Connor Award for Short Fiction, my husband suggested we name our next dog Nobel.)

A golden retriever puppy looks more like a human baby than any other creature. And I loved that dog like a child. She was much more rewarding than my earlier dogs, much more appealing than my cats. Right up until I gave birth to my daughter, the very day, hand on my burbling belly, I can remember thinking, *I will never love anything as much as I love Flannery.*

So Flannery was my biggest dog romance for many years. She was our first project, my husband's and mine. We acquired her in Tucson, which was where I'd gone to graduate school and met my husband, and she grew up there, much photographed and anthropomorphized. She moved with us to Chicago, where she gamely endured living in our tiny one-bedroom apartment, adjusting admirably to a suddenly circumscribed life. Down two flights of metal steps she had to go, several times a day, out beyond the manicured garden and parking lot, us with bags, her with a full bladder. City living in the frozen Midwest. We all suffered.

But soon I had children, and the dog was displaced. Not completely, but profoundly. We returned to the Southwest, to a large house and a big yard, and the dog became like Nana from *Peter Pan,* a patient creature who lay on the floor while they pulled her tail or stood on her head. They learned to walk with her, clinging and tripping and spilling food on her back as she slowly perambulated. They took her existence for granted; they'd been born into a family that included her with the other required members: Mom, Dad, Dog. When she died, at age twelve, my daughter was nine and my son five. I felt her death as the resulting grief passed through them, especially the girl. Those emotions are not diluted by having been refracted through a child; on the contrary, they are enhanced by the frustration of not being able to suffer in the child's place. They are magnified by the ferocity of witnessing not only the death of the animal but the death of the child's innocence. Every coming-of-age story I know has the bittersweet gift of knowledge unwillingly learned. And then never to be unknown.

My family still owns its summer house in the Rockies, and that's where we were when Flannery died. I took her ashes (no backyard burial for this one) up a mountain she particularly enjoyed hiking and scattered them in a waterfall. I had outlived another dog and come some substantial distance since seeing the last one off. All of her predecessors had trekked up this trail. Moe had ridden up it in a Jeep, when it wasn't a trail but a road, when I wasn't a hiker but a passenger as my father four-wheeled. George had skulked along up here with me when I felt a need to escape: leave the house and get high. And now Flannery would always be here. The hikers above me frowned as the gray ash blew about when I dumped the sack and shed a tear.

Three months later I was back at the breeder's.

Sticking with the same breed of dog is sort of like cheating death: having this second golden is a lot like never having lost the first. Same looks, generally, same temperament, same color of fur filling the vacuum bag. The name is different, of course, although Odette seems to understand (and forgive, as is her and her breed's nature) our occasionally calling her Flannery.

My father had a Scottie dog when he was a little boy. In his old age, his children gave him another Scottie (a big step, after the trauma he and my mother had endured over the loss of odious George). He loved the Scottie even though it was an awful dog—self-absorbed, disobedient, flatulent, obese, intolerant, and a biter of small children. It might have seemed to him that we gave him back his childhood, in the form of that rotten little dog. And after having lived with it for twelve years, having watched it die, and then my father die, my mother now imagines that if she ever did get another dog, it would be a Scottie.

My son's idol, when he was young, was his older cousin, Cody. Cody's mother raised West Highland terriers, and so my son grew fixated on owning one. My sister-in-law aided in this fixation by breeding Elmo and Lulu every six months, always offering us a free puppy. Finally my husband succumbed to our combined mewling and whimpering. Oscar the Westie came to live with us.

He imprinted on the golden, so his habits are not as obnoxious as those of most terriers. Still, in the age-old argument concerning

nurture and nature, I think it's safe to say that breed wins out. Oscar
is sneaky the way terriers are sneaky, always hiding small objects
(toys, food, credit cards) and declining to come out of nooks and
crannies. He feels no particular shame in his bad behavior. He ob-
sesses over certain plastic objects, most recently the fly handle of a
pulley on the wire strung in our yard. From the tree house, our children can grab onto the handle and fly across the yard. When they let
loose, the dog runs yapping and leaping at the handle far above his
head. If you send it flying empty along its wire, he chases beneath,
snapping and flipping. If you get in his way, he will bite you.

His life expectancy is well into the double digits.

Eventually disappointed in this creature, my son began lobbying for
a different breed. We had moved to Houston by then; there our family went through a rough patch with our daughter, who finally had
to move away from us in order to survive. She took the golden with
her when she left, and I was glad to think of that dog in her possession, a steady source of unconditional love, radiating like a furnace to
warm our girl, if she would let her.

This left us with one dog, the annoying Westie. Oscar, my son ar-
gued, was lonely. He needed a friend. He even wrote an essay for his
English class on the topic, a persuasive paper that earned him a B
(but when he succeeded in changing his father's mind, I thought he
had a strong case for jacking the grade up to an A).

We scoured the *Houston Chronicle* daily in search of a corgi. We
went on the Internet, we checked out books. The two of us—my son
then thirteen—had a mutual project. And a challenging one at that.
Corgis are popular, it seems. Breeders charge upwards of eight hundred bucks for the little guys. I was interviewed by one breeder, who
lived in Virginia, and apparently did not meet her standards (she *said*
she'd get back to me). Eventually we found what is called a "backyard" breeder, somebody whose credentials (whose *dogs'* credentials,
those crazy important papers) aren't quite top-flight. We met at the

Petco parking lot near George Bush International to make the exchange. The puppy looked flawed, as his ears were lying flat and his markings were subpar. On one ear was a white dot like a thumbprint.

A puppy is a perfect project for a mother and her teenage boy. The two of us treat that dog like our child, commenting fondly on his likes and dislikes, his cleverness and charm, ascribing all manner of intelligence and insight to him. Eventually we were reunited with our daughter, back in New Mexico, and reunited with the big dumb blond dog, too, so, like the Westie, Roscoe the corgi imprinted on the golden retriever. Her lesson of gentle forbearance most definitely took. The corgi's a sociable animal, a little nosy parker. We call him "the therapist," because he genuinely does seem to care about every person in the room, running to greet any newcomer, careful to check up on the others. On walks he takes the lead, weaving back and forth to keep his herd in order. He seems to wish that he could talk; one senses a great many opinions he holds and hopes to express. He spends a lot of time looking us in the eye, tipping his head back and forth as if trying to translate our foreign language into his own. He's like a valet, a very bright valet from some sweet-tempered servile country who has not yet picked up the local idiom. But he will, he will.

Now we have three homes, among which we circulate: fall in New Mexico, winter in Houston, summer in Colorado in that same family cabin. Our dogs travel with us; I hike with the current three up the same trail where I spread the ashes of Flannery. Where I used to hike with George, as a teenager, shrieking at him to stop killing marmots, to stop chasing cats, to come back, come back, come back— to no avail. Last spring Odette, our second golden, began to die. She's been dying for months now, no one thing killing her, but a combination. Seizures, dementia, deteriorating spine, fluid-filled lungs, tremors, dottiness, overlarge heart (and could anything be more metaphorically apt than that, the too-big heart, in a golden retriever?). She wobbles around the yard, she weaves through the house. She tipped over the trash a few weeks ago and consumed everything in it, eggshells, chocolate wrappers, chicken bones. We arrived home to find her in a bloated stupor, a weird panting coma on the kitchen floor.

That night the four of us sat in the kitchen around her, our daughter, now nineteen, at her head, our son, now fifteen, at her haunch. They stroked her, and we talked, for hours. Eventually we moved a pallet in beside the dog so that our daughter could sleep with her. In the morning my daughter and I went to the emergency vet and for the next forty-eight hours occupied, with the dog, a strange little kennel space there.

The dog was X-rayed and evacuated and hooked up to an IV. We took turns squirting water into her mouth, stroking her chin until she swallowed. Around us other emergencies came and went— victims of fights, dogs that had fallen out of truck beds, cats that had been hit by cars—while we sat in our tiny caged room, more like a prison cell than anything else, with its drain in the center. Between forcing fluids and weeping, we ran lines for the play my daughter would star in a few weeks later.

Odette, I think, is my last golden. We bought her from a breeder whose name was Justice, and he was a Texas Ranger. He lived in a trailer and kept his puppies in a kids' play pool in the living room. He had pit bulls in his yard, surrounding the house like a living moat, and the place was so thick with dog odor you almost couldn't breathe. His little daughter was the same age as my son; I wanted to take her, too, when we took the dog. On the way home ten years ago with Odette, I asked the children if they knew what the word "justice" meant. My daughter hesitated, thinking, then said, "Isn't 'justice' just a nice way to say 'revenge'?"

"I didn't like that man," said my son. In that instance it sort of did feel as if I were rescuing a bred dog. I should have bought her siblings, too; the little girl, I couldn't have saved.

I am sitting in my study surrounded by my dogs. There are three, as in a fairy tale: the old golden retriever (dying), the middle-aged

Westie (an asshole), and the young corgi (the apple of my eye). They are easy to please; I enjoy the fact of their kennels, where I can put them when our day is done. It doesn't surprise me that some people prefer their pets to their relatives or friends. There have been dogs present at every stage of my life, silent witnesses, steady companions as I move from house to house and station to station. They've played different roles: irritant, companion, surrogate child. You provide your children with dogs so they have somewhere to pour their caretaking love, to learn how to love what's beholden to them. You own a dog with the knowledge that it will move through the stages of existence in fast-forward, providing you with a lesson about your own life passages, if you let it. It will die, and break your heart to varying degrees, depending. And then, when you reach middle age, you realize that one of these dogs, someday in the future, will outlive you. It's just slightly easier to imagine death if I think of Roscoe, or the next corgi we own, or the one after that, trotting with purpose around the house, wondering what's become of that person he used to know.

My Commodore

By S. B. Dogg, Colonel
Hotter–Than–Air Balloon Forces
of North Idaho

DENIS JOHNSON

OUR MISSION

We suffer incursions. I insist it is a fact. Somewhere, perhaps, remains a place in which families live at peace in the quiet woods, enjoying the sun of the day and the stars of the night, marking the journeys of a friendly moon; I daresay the Commodore would like to believe we reside there. He comports himself with an absolute indifference to fate, as becomes a great leader, and yet as enormously as I admire him, I find myself unable to condone his attitude toward the lurking dangers. No, I cannot endorse it. He is, at best, cavalier. We live in a region at war. When I hear the enemy's camouflaged steps I leap up and race forward: "This is an outrage! I shall violate the cease-fire! I shall rend you, sir!"

Just over the border lies British Columbia—British! But we serve here. I guard the perimeter. But where is it? From the mountain on the east to the mountain on the west, how many thousand leagues of wilderness? The last bastion against the Antarctic hordes. Or perhaps the Arctic. Yes, we've been driven this far north. Or south.

OUR BREAKFAST

The Commodore strides forth in his short khaki pantaloons. Fellow omnivore! He finds me already in uniform. The camp wench distributes our bowls. I breakfast alone in the open air, on the porch. As well I ought. I fear I rather gobble my meals. May I confess with no little embarrassment that I'm prone to drool? My Commodore shares his breakfast—a sausage.

As you know, his refrain is, "We are jazzmen, and balloonists." Or perhaps it's mine. Others serve with us here, the camp wench, the flat-faced, feline corporal, but we two alone belong to the officer class, we alone have seen campaigns. It binds us indescribably.

And the penguin—our POW. I shall break him yet.

OUR MORNING

After our bowls, an opiate contentment overtakes us. I nap, pursuing reindeer up waterfalls indefatigably. As the good poet Browning once said:

> *Dog's in his Heaven,*
> *All's right with the world.*

This is the hour when the camp wench makes her notations as to our supplies, and then reads from her books. The corporal curls at her feet. She reads to him aloud from the journals of Kierkegaard. (Those two are not like us.)

Flung so far into the hinterlands we never fear inspection and so go about our grooming willy-nilly. Each third or fourth day the Commodore scrapes the fur from his face—scratches it away, in fact, with implements—and he engages in a penitential ceremony that hints, I believe, at the depths of his nameless misery, stepping into a narrow chamber and calling down streams of water onto his nakedness. As for my own ablutions, I attend to them according to impulse, when struck by an abluting sort of mood. You won't find me paralyzed before the mirror. Whereas most military men possess what we call "chiseled" features, the result of desperate weather and hard rations, mine, despite my experiences, belong to the "mushy" or "squishy" categories.

His self-bullying . . . It might have to do with his pitiful condition, his extraordinary affliction. In the time I've known him he has shrunk. Once he could lift me up in his two hands. Now his waist goes no higher than my shoulder, and if he were an enemy I could easily take his head in my jaws.

So much of our world is like that, isn't it?—smaller and smaller. Over the years my chair on the porch has been replaced with a succession of less sizeable ones, this latest laughably tiny. I can scarcely squeeze in.

For the better part of the morning he labors over his memoirs. I interrogate the penguin ruthlessly. I shall wipe from his beak his infuriating Mona Lisa smile, you may depend on it. As the Commodore says of me: "There's no Quit in him." The Commodore jokes that I'm a "bullmastiff" come from English bulldogs on one side, English mastiffs on the other.

I doubt the Commodore will publish. Had either of us glories to rehash, surely Her Majesty wouldn't have banished us here.

OUR DUTIES

And then to our respective spaces to check our messages, he his e-mail and I my pee-mail. Nothing much comes to us. Most of the messages seem to be my own, cast out and then washed back to me next day by the same tide that obliterates our footprints on these lonely shores. I speak of course not literally. The only shore is that of the small fishing-pond.

We might go down the hill to his office, where we prepare for our documentary film *Ballooning to Andromeda*. And yet of late his unnamable burden distracts him, and our project lags, and many mornings he only listens to his phonograph, his crackly, hissing recordings of Negro jazz from Dixieland. The rhythms take me back—a reminiscence stirs within—the Boer War . . . but another time for that.

On impulse I may pop down and slurp a little something from the pond. I won't wade in past my ankles—I'm not mad, you know—but I do love a good drink. I don't forget the African desert. There was a war! Once it rained, and we held out our helmets to this gift, and they melted in the sun; for on the Sahara it never rains water; only madness and mirages. I nearly captured General Rommel, you know. I had him, had him—but another time for that.

It's now, when we're alone together, that the Commodore sometimes shrugs aside the mantle of rank and speaks playfully. He describes my face as belonging to the hippopotamus-gorilla-walrus type; he calls me his "boolmasteef," he calls me his "big ol' dog," and I indulge his methaphor making, as I do any of his whims, so long as they raise in him a bit of cheer. I communicate to him certain of my fond opinions: "Cheetos are wonderful." "I like hot-dogs." "Let's eat." The core of my philosophy: Food is good. Often he speaks to me of his own ideals, although his words mean next to nothing. He does not reveal what brought him here, what misstep or defeat, or in what way he must have dishonored himself. Sometimes we perform an American military calisthenic called "squoogling," which consists of his manipulating my features energetically with both his hands.

When he calls me "Co-lo-nel" I'm reminded of France—but another time for that, when no ladies are present. They called me "Co-lo-nel . . ." It was there, in fact, in Paris . . . ah, well. Another time.

Rommel? I make no secret of it. Nearly had the blighter. Nearly had him. Had my jaws round his left ankle. Or the right. One of the two, in any case.

There was a war! And there was a desert. We thirsted, and we drank sand. The heat—I was used to it, I'd seen many a campaign in many a clime, and I'd seen what the sun can do—but the younger lads, some of them . . . the eyes boiled in their heads, I tell you, boiled like eggs, I saw it myself, and when they went down onto that sand the heat of it set fire to their insignia.

OUR LUNCH

Hard rations here: soup in a single bowl, or a sandwich on a plate. The Commodore eats his share first, then hands down mine to me. Hard rations!

On occasion, a biscuit. How fond I am of them! Anything you care to present to me—I'll have a go. The deceptively banal banana, the evocative avocado . . . under the skin, they're all wonderful. And the skin, you know, is edible, too. I fall to my snarfly repast. Not all our lunches are glum. After, I take a nap: gazelles, coyotes, panda bears.

OUR AFTERNOON

A rainy afternoon. No maneuvers today. The Commodore reads: perhaps a history of the Great Game, as we called the competition for High Asia. Never saw the place myself. Not my desert. Mine was the Sahara. Rommel was a fox. Earned his name.

While my Commodore enlarges his understanding of warfare, I play with philosophical conundrums. For example: faced with several Tater Tots on the one hand and on the other a Ritz Cracker covered with peanut butter, what course would you choose, which would you tackle first? We have to conclude—I have to believe—you'd simply know. You wouldn't have to question. You would know what to do. A soldier knows.

I adore condensed milk . . . lasagna . . .

On good days we go on marches through mountains he believes to be unpopulated, and he ambles, he whistles, "riffing" on the melodies of old standards, "Summertime" and "On the Sunny Side of the Street"—blithe hero! filler of bowls! author of the Cheeto!—

ignorant of the ten million eyes fixed upon us in terror, lust, and rage. They are no jazzmen, sir! One day I shall grip their throats in my jaws as I gripped the delicious ankle of Lieutenant General Erwin Johannes Eugen Rommel.

And those most special days, when an energy fills the air and catches up our hearts! Then the doors to the gondola open wide. I am admitted within. The Commodore climbs into the pilot's seat. The many engines rumble, and off we go on a fine new undertaking. He presses a button, the glass slides down, we're awash in aromas, topography in a tumult! A day for sticking one's big velvety head into the breezes! I do not tell the Commodore that our gondola runs on wheels, that these wheels never leave the ground, that ours is not a true balloon. He has an altimeter and a compass, and he is happy.

We land at the settlement for supplies from the Commissary—nacho Doritos perhaps—or we pay an unpleasant visit to the Dispensary, where I'm told that I've gained weight, or that this old soldier's bones aren't quite sound. These medical interludes are for me alone. The Commodore enjoys unblemished good health. Often, he may chance on a former comrade-in-arms. I enjoy becoming acquainted. This old soldier at times falls prey, he confesses, to fits of agitated sentimentality. "Colonel Dogg doesn't actually say anything specific about the Boer War," the Commodore tells his friends, "but everything seems to remind him of it." Yes, everything—the nights wild with thudding drums. Those Zulu girls! I'm not sure I remember it in any of its details, to tell you the truth. I'm only five years old.

When he escorts the camp wench into the Commissary, I remain in the gondola. The Commodore appreciates my patience. May it ever be thus. We set for our superior officers an unattainable example in our manner of instantly forgiving and forgetting their small blunders—the slights, the devaluations, the utter rudeness. Every outrage and humiliation. The persecutions.

OUR SUPPER

Glorious camp wench! Doggess! Large-hearted matriarch! Pile it to the heights! Shall I show you a bowl needs no washing? There's no Quit in me.

The Commodore seems to have grown fond of the camp wench. It happens. Men are men. Following our supper the two of them linger at the table discussing, one hopes, tomorrow's menu. I change from my fawn-colored velvet uniform into my fawn-colored velvet pyjamas and commence my ablutions, the sounds and outbursts of which have been likened, I admit, to those of "siphoning ice-cream."

Immediately as the sun falls behind the western mountain, the valley grows cold. The coyotes cry from the peaks. Even the Commodore hears them. The souls of vanquished enemies.

But Rommel, you say. Well, it was bound to happen. He surviving, I surviving; eventually we'd meet; it had to be. In the smoke of war we came face-to-face. And in a forest of exploding artillery barrels and upended Panzer tanks I grappled with him, with Rommel himself. The Desert Fox!—yet he had much of the aspect, and some of the scent, also, of a weasel. He dodged right, but he dodged wrong, and betwixt my jaws I trapped a flying ankle. Shall I tell you what I tasted? Chicken. I'm not allowed to have it, but I know the taste. I know it instinctively. And General Rommel tasted like chicken, sir.

What did Rommel say to me? Never a word. He only smiled a penguin's smile and reached a hand into his tunic—Will you shoot me, Sir? Then you'd better have a howitzer; this is the head of a bullmastiff!—and drawing that same hand from his lapel presented me not with a weapon, but with a dilemma.

That Fox! He knew his man. Onto the desert floor he tossed a biscuit.

And just here let me say I make quick work of biscuits. I calculated I'd have this one down my spout and my jaws about his ankle again before he'd even thought to make his getaway. A fine gamble!

Well, sir, I took his challenge and loosed my hold, nipped the morsel down—the Desert Fox! The chase was on! And he was quick, quicker than any I'd seen, quicker than any fox, I'll tell you.

I gambled on my skill, my vigor, my youth. A better man, I suppose, would have known not to do it, would have stayed the course, would have steeled his nerve and dragged the villain over the English lines, would have stood before the chorus of applause, borne the medals home, lived a hero's life, filled an honored grave beneath a shrine to which the pilgrims came . . . But you see, I'd never had a Nazi biscuit. Shaped like an Iron Cross, weighty, a little doughy, and very pungent, pungent with—I couldn't say "with evil." With a primal destitution. Pungent with moral ruin. Pungent in that way, you see. And he got away clean. He lived to fight another day, did Rommel. And though we won that war, somehow yet the Empire faltered, the Empire faded, and the sun set on it. Yes. Cheetos are wonderful. Nothing shall ever dim the lustre of a Cheeto. But the Empire, however much we might have wished it, had not quite the indomitable character of a Cheeto.

The summer evenings are long and melancholy. Perhaps we go down the hill again. He starts the phonograph again. He opens his office windows, the better to hear it outdoors. Curious, in this light, how plaintive, how torn, the Dixieland.

And the balloons . . . the balloons never rise.

We know this place at the bottom of the hill. It is ours. Here, away from the eyes of men, we allow ourselves the deep fact of our exile, sitting on a bench—he on the bench, I beside—overlooking the water, and we contemplate the moonlight reflected—or the pink and pewter sunset, or the green and silver dawn reflected—on the fishing-pond in which we never fish.

That Fox! We shall meet again on the road to Glory, and share a bit of a laugh at the wretchedness of our histories.

I have my memories. The desert of the Second War, and the blood red trenches of the first one, of course, the Great one, and the Boer War, too—another time for that—such memories as an old soldier carries in his heart. You can see them in my face. Little children come to me and squoogle my jowls, crying, "Good dog! Good dog!" and the Commodore speaks to them in his friendly, unintelligible way, and like some murderous feline Time toys with our triumphs.

My Commodore begins to shiver. We go inside. He turns on the lamp, and in the bounds of its illumination against the tremendous dark, he looks at the pages of his books—Tennyson, I suspect, or Kipling, though I don't stand tall enough to peer over his shoulder— while I take a tiny nap. Kipling! You won't find better. Siegfried Sassoon, there's another. A real poet. Shared a biscuit with him once. In a muddy trench at the Battle of the Somme. Nothing like a good English biscuit, nothing in the world. From the knapsack of Siegfried Sassoon. I gobbled it right down, and he—enough. Enough!

Mercy: A Friendship

ROBIN ROMM

I recently moved with my boyfriend and dog eleven hundred miles from home, from a bungalow near the San Francisco Bay to a converted barn in the desert hills that fringe Santa Fe. Soon after we arrived, Don took off for a writing residency in Tucson and a thunderstorm came crashing down, shaking the walls and pelting the tin roof with rain. After a few minutes of this—the thunder and the shaking and the loud boom of thick drops on metal—the roof began leaking. An abandoned stovepipe over the bed served as a funnel, shooting water onto the pillows. A sheet of water slid beneath the big glass doors, leaving a large oblong puddle in the entryway. The wall vents spit drops out into the rooms or, in one case, allowed a small muddy river to sweep across the study's floor. The house that had seemed so charming when we visited in May—lots of windows, sun-streaked wood siding, a redbrick bedroom floor—revealed its many problems, most notably its holes and gaps, its exposure to the wilds.

The night after the flood, as I was walking to bed, I noticed a giant spider, the size of a baseball, shivering near the dishwasher. I yelped and called my boyfriend.

"I don't know what to tell you," Don said. "Put a cup over it."

"It's too big for a cup," I said.

"Stamp on it."

"*Stamp* on it?" I peered back toward the kitchen, flinching. "I can't *stamp* on it. It's bigger than my heel!"

"I don't know what to tell you," he said. "I'm in Tucson."

So I cried and woke the landlady, who groggily told me to sleep with all the lights on.

After I hung up with her, I shook out the sheets and pillows, checking for more spiders. I could feel them, their sneaky intent to climb up my neck and suck my bright, uninitiated blood. I shook out a pair of jeans that had been lying on the bed and heard a small sound, like a bean hitting brick. I squinted but saw nothing. The dog, Mercy, stood. She walked over and cocked her head, pointed her nose at the floor. I followed her gaze.

It was a dull pinkish brown, maybe an inch long, with a striated back, like an armadillo. Its tail lay flat behind it, and on the tip was a bulge. At first I found it pretty. The color seemed natural and soft, red clay left to dry. But this time when I called Don, he was less measured.

"A *scorpion?*" he said.

"It's sort of pretty," I said. "Almost elegant." He said nothing. I began to get nervous. "Can it kill me?"

"Um," he said. "No. No. I don't think so. But, Robin, don't let it get away. You have to catch it."

When I went into the kitchen to get a cup, the thing vanished.

I was raised in the Pacific Northwest. I understand slugs and snails and worms. I can handle occasional snakes, predatory birds, rot and fungus. But out here in the desert, things are different. We fall asleep to the coyotes making their scalded-sounding racket. Jack-rabbits walk, foot over foot like humans, their large flanks rippling. Every once in a while, a centipede will slither across the floor, its six-inch body like a necklace strung of marbled onyx. It's interesting out here, but it will never be home.

When it became clear that Mercy and I were not going to find the scorpion, I stripped all the covers from the bed. The tunnels and caverns of twisted blankets felt dangerous, now that a scorpion was on the loose. I inspected every granule, every speck of dirt for pincers. Satisfied, I patted the mattress, and up Mercy flew, collapsing beside me, spooning me in the way she does, her body curled into mine but with her belly slightly up, her feet apart. Though she's not much braver than I (when we're hiking the horse trails out here, she circumvents the large beetles), I rubbed her tummy and felt a little safer.

Mercy has been with me for more than three years now. I got her from the Merced County Animal Control in August of 2004, three months before the death of my mother. Before the Berkeley bungalow, Mercy lived in a cement cage full of barking dogs, behind a portable office that served as the adoption center. Merced has one of the highest kill rates in California, and most animals that wind up there wind up dead. I wasn't looking for a Queensland heeler; I wanted a city dog for that bungalow by the bay, a dog that would sit near me when I wrote, a squat urban canine that I could tire out by a walk around the block. I'd driven the three and a half hours to Merced for a small, puffy golden dog that resembled a shrunken fox. I'd seen this dog online, called and interviewed the adoption coordinator. "Is he cute?" I asked. "Yes," she replied. "What's his personality like?" The woman on the phone tried to answer. She said he seemed playful. A little shy. I didn't listen to the hesitation in her voice.

For months before this trip to Merced, I trolled Internet dog-adoption sites until long after midnight. I bookmarked pages, decorated e-mails with JPEGs of weird pug mixes. I salivated over the bright puppy eyes of corgis, read about Jack Russells, Chihuahuas, fox terriers, beagles, rat terriers, papillons, Pomeranians. Most of the time, I simply ogled, but that little fox dog woke a new urgency in me. Not only was he handsome, he had the distinction of being a mutt, usually the most stalwart of dogs. And if I had to travel, he'd be small enough to fit under an airline seat. I imagined that when I got called back to Oregon for my mother's final days, this dog could accompany me to the grocery store. He'd sit calm and regal in a messenger bag, just like he sat in the JPEG, and I could reach in to give

him a pat every time I grew despairing. I gave him traits: He'd be a
licker, but his breath would never be bad. I'd be able to tire him out
with a small ball in the yard. Maybe he would mimic the sirens on
police cars like another small dog I'd seen, bringing hilarity to every
outdoor café.

But when the adoption coordinator brought the shrunken fox out
of the cage, he didn't look at me. He began to sniff the grass, every
once in a while glancing up furtively. Instead of animal wisdom, he
embodied paranoia. His little black nose worked over that grass, as if
he wanted to burrow into it. Around in circles he marched. The
adoption coordinator waved a plastic duck at him, but he didn't take
to it. The bark of a pit bull caged nearby got his attention, and he
barked back, shrill and obsessive. He barked and barked and barked.
The woman waited for me to say something. After all, I'd already
paid the shelter fee by credit card to hold this dog, to prevent anyone
else from taking him home. I must have looked crestfallen under the
big elm tree, my hands shoved into a sweatshirt pocket. I'd hung my
heart on returning with a dog that day. I'd woken with a happiness I
hadn't felt in months. Despite my mother's metastasizing cells and
dark prognosis, I trotted to the car that morning feeling like all my
joints had been oiled.

The dog gave a few last barks before starting on the grass routine
again. I shook my head, aware of a heaviness seeping back into my
bones. "That's not the right dog," I said.

The adoption coordinator squinted at me. Her brown hair looked
singed at the tips, her wide face affected by small red patches. She
scooped up the shrunken fox. "What are you looking for, hon?" she
asked. I told her I wanted an excessively loving dog. I saw her turn
toward the large-dog area where beautiful German shepherd or rottweiler mixes pressed the sides of their heads against the grates. "But
under thirty pounds," I added. She moved her jaw to one side and
nodded slowly. "Wait here," she said.

Within minutes a speckled dog with a pea head and barrel chest
came squiggling out of the medium-size-dog area, her entire body

electric with joy. She leaped onto me, licked my hands, and dropped to the ground, rolling belly up. I knelt next to her, and she looked at me, pointing her narrow nose at my chin. At first she simply seemed frantic, but then a dullness flickered in her eyes. It remained only briefly, then disappeared back into the puppy brightness. A kinship so intense and so irrational surged—how do I explain it? I named her Mercy, for Merced and for what we all needed that year, the horrible year that followed.

"That dog's going to have to lead you through this," my mother said, a few weeks before her death.

The night of the scorpion, Mercy and I shivered together on the blanketless bed, staring at the brick. I try not to discuss things with the dog. I'll croon to her and give commands, but longer conversations I reserve for friends or for Don. But it was so late, and we felt so far from home. Besides, Mercy seemed unusually attentive, aware of her importance in the moment. I ran a finger around the soft fur behind her ear.

"This move might have been a bad decision," I whispered. She flattened her ears to her head and gazed at my face. She pushed herself even flatter against my side. *I can give you me,* she said, as she always says. *Me me me me me me.* And she got me through another night, leaving the bed only to bark like crazy at something creeping outside the big windows.

All relationships are complex. I have a friend who believes that the minute a relationship becomes nasty or deceitful, more of a struggle than a joy, you should get out. She has rarely been in love for more than a few weeks. I don't argue with her, but my boyfriend and I agree. If we'd used that criterion, we'd have been history years ago. We have gotten through some ugly months, hissing and slamming doors. But when he returned from Tucson, he took the entire bedroom apart looking for my scorpion with a cheap plastic flashlight. He made me dinner and listened to me reconstruct the whole

affair—from the leaking roof to the bugs—and never said one un-
kind word.

One morning, after my mother's death, I took Mercy out to Fort
Funston, a piece of beach that sits below dramatic cliffs in San Francisco. Men and women attached to synthetic and metal wings jumped
from the tops of green cliffs and sailed out above the open ocean. I let
Mercy off the leash, and she bounded down the perilous steps to the
water. She loves the beach, the way it stretches, the way sand feels between her paws and in her coat. She bows to it, nips at shells and
kelp, chases the balls of foam that roll on the darkened edges of the
water. She runs into the waves, curling away from them, chomping
at the surf. She pounces after the seagulls, pleased to make them fly.

I sat on a log and watched the stillness of a barge situated somewhere between the city and the Farallon Islands. The clear sky
seemed nearly turquoise before it disappeared into the darker sea.
The sun caught on the ripples of the water, creating glare and glitter.
My body filled with it—the wild beauty of a California beach in the
middle of a weekday. I listened to the tremor of waves, the squawk of
birds. I thought of the beaches in Oregon, how my mother loved
watching the kids dig holes. How much she longed, in the final
stages of her dying, to see the dogs chase birds against this very back-
drop. We might drive out to Yachats and park her wheelchair at the
craggy shore and sit, muted by the things we couldn't understand. I
began to tear up. I hadn't come to mourn, but now that all this world
unfurled before me, I felt I needed to absorb it, send it out to my
mother, so she could see it, send it out to that world she inhabited
now, a world I couldn't be sure of. A smarting sensation spread
through my chest.

Mercy, intent on terrorizing every last shorebird, had vanished
into a dot. I stood and brushed off my pants, took a deep breath, and
started after her. She was enjoying this experience to the same degree
as I felt the pain of it. Look at her go, down down down, frolicking
in the ocean, unaware of death and survival. Aware only of the sun

and the dark water and the rhythm of the ocean in her blood. So absorbed was I in all of this complicated oneness that I didn't notice what she was *really* doing. That my dog, my furry anchor, port in the storm, had seen an intriguing sight in the distance and was wading into the water after it. I tried to make out her destination, but a sheet of fog draped that side of the cliffs. By the time I made out her intention, I could do nothing.

"MERCY!" I called.

The naked man emerged from the sea. His skin puckered by the wind, his bony shoulders stooped. I called her again, but Mercy didn't turn around. Instead she leaped up, licked his hands, then collapsed in front of him as he came toward me, entwining herself between his ankles. The white of her belly matched the white of his leg hair. He stopped and leaned over her. *Me me me me,* she seemed to be singing. *I'll give you me!* I glanced down the beach behind me. The man had chosen this part of the sea for its relative privacy. The cliffs came out at an angle here, creating a little barrier. No one else had come this far. I noticed a blanket and a garbage bag in some rocks. My heart beat in my nose and cheeks. No one knew where I was. I smiled at the man. He must have been sixty, his face weathered by the sun and cigarettes. He wore his receding hair in a ponytail. He smiled back, revealing jagged teeth. His eyes filled with disoriented delight.

"What a nice puppy," the man said, his voice a deep, rocky bass.

"Mercy, come!" I said. "Sorry." The man bent further over the dog and scratched beneath her collar. I thought of turning around, leaving her there, but I couldn't. "She is really, really friendly," I stammered, walking over the wet sand, kneeling down. I tried not to breathe in, not to look at the wrinkled body parts staring back at me. Careful not to hit the man's privates with the leash, I pulled Mercy away. The man waved and grinned.

We walked back to the car in silence.

"Bad," I said to her as she hopped into the car. "Bad dog." But she smiled with her jaws apart and steamed up the side window.

———

Elasticity is a crucial part of relationships; one must be willing to bend and stretch. But naturally there are limits. While I might forgive Don for perpetually leaving the toothpaste tube mauled and bleeding by the bathroom sink, some behavior would inevitably lead to separation. For instance, if he lit up like a neon banner every time he saw a dead rabbit—if he jumped into the air at the sight of it, situating himself so he could grind his shoulders and spine into the tearing flesh—I would cast judgment. I would tell him, later that night when he turned toward me in bed, that my feelings for him had shifted, that I couldn't run my hand along his spine without thinking of the other places that spine had been.

Of course, a few months back, Mercy did just this. I was with my friend Liz, deep in conversation, both of us studying the dirt of a trail, our heads tilted down. We'd come to the Berkeley Marina. Trim, athletic moms jogged babies around the park in expensive strollers. We stopped to admire an owl, sunbathing on a rock. I didn't see Mercy at first, and then when I noticed the commotion off to the side, it took me a minute to register the unhealthy glee that laced the regular dog joy. Mercy, leaping up and collapsing on a patch of grass near a storm drain, had dressed herself in old gray entrails.

And she eats cat shit, too.

Don quit his day job to move with me to this old barn so I could teach at a college. He's got a new job lined up, but until it starts, he spends a lot of time alone with Mercy. I'll walk in the door from work, swing my book bag down. Student manuscripts slip across our cement floor along with paperbacks and wadded muffin bags. I'm exhausted from giving and giving, keeping my students on task. I want to dive into the bed, this time with the covers on it, and hide in the dangerous folds. But usually Don's eager to see me, to have a conversation with the one person he knows in this town. And often, when I sit beside him on the sofa, he'll glance at the dog curled in her little fleece dog bed. "Look at her," he'll say. "Mercy!"

We both do this. Like the worst new parents, we wake our dog up just to prove that she's still cute, still alive, still fun. "Come here," he'll say. Mercy opens her eyes, stands up with a groan, marches toward us. We don't allow her on the sofa (it was expensive! an adult purchase!), so he'll race down the two steps into the bedroom and hop onto the bed. The dog chases him, following with an athletic leap. He'll catch her—all of this is as choreographed as a circus routine—and flip her upside down so that her head hangs over his elbow and she's a limp fish in his man arms. Mercy will heave a sigh, like a perishing maiden, and Don will press his nose into her head.

"What do you think she thinks?" he'll ask. I usually say, "I don't know." Or, "Probably she's thinking about dinner." Don will get huffy at this and remark that *he* thinks she's thinking of *him*.

The other day I stopped to consider it. What *does* Mercy think of all this? Is she really, as animal behaviorists say, just caught in the here and now? Does she experience sensations and repeat the actions that seem to lead to pleasurable ones? Or is she conniving, strategic? What organizes her world?

When Don went to Tucson, Mercy had to spend many hours alone in the house. I had time to take her for a long walk only every other day, if that. When I came home she'd stretch and howl. I figured she must be excited for companionship, but maybe she just thought that out that door sat piles of steaming horse shit, loads of dead rabbits. Maybe she saw only my ability to open the door.

Sometimes she looks at me with great concentration, and I think she will bust out with language. I have even scolded her for this. "You *understand* it," I will say. "Now just *use* it." She just continues to stare with her bright eyes, sometimes cocking her head and shifting on her hip. "Get in your bed!" I tell her. Dutifully she will get up from wherever she is and walk to the bed, crawl in, and continue to stare. Proof, of course, that she's fluent. Just insolent.

———

There were a few weird days between my mother's death and her funeral, and many of my friends came from New York or San Francisco to be with me. No one thought it a good idea to sit around the house, and so we headed for the nearest mountain. We hiked up the yellow, grassy hillside, watching birds overhead, watching the rhythm of one another's heels in the dirt. My father's dogs chased Mercy relentlessly, the biggest one, Sol, jumping on top of her to best situate his jaws over her snout. On the way home, I held Mercy in the passenger seat of Don's car. My friends, heaped in the back, tried to make conversation, tried to find the right words. I felt remote and empty. I squeezed Mercy to me, holding her as if she were the only thing I could count on in this world. *Never die, never die,* I repeated in my head. And then the dog began to ripple. It seemed to begin in her legs. They wobbled, and then her stomach started to shiver, and then that barrel chest of hers heaved twice, and within seconds I was covered in hot, brown dog vomit. She threw up three times as we hurtled along that highway. She seemed to be aware that she shouldn't barf on the seat covers, and so each time she barfed right down my neck, over my chest, and into my lap.

Everyone started talking at once.

"PULL OVER," I said to Don.

"Do you want me to just go home?" he asked. The stench was fantastic. I felt the throw-up through my shorts.

"PULL OVER," I said.

Don pulled over and ran to the back of the car. He dug through his trunk and located an old Mexican blanket. There, on the side of the highway, I shimmied out of my wet shirt and shorts. A semi slowed and honked. I wrapped the blanket around me and settled into the car again, pulling Mercy back onto my lap. My friends giggled nervously. Mercy looked relieved.

———

All through my childhood, we had vizslas (many many vizslas) who pissed on the rug. Both my parents worked, and no one really had time to walk them as often as they needed to be walked. We had a husky once—bought off an Iditarod racer in Alaska—who took a corner of wallpaper and ran to the end of the hall, stripping it bare. I can't remember a period of my life that didn't involve kneeling to scrub down a soiled rug, pushing a dog nose out of my crotch, yanking a leash to prevent a dog fight, wiping dog vomit off my neck. It's a little nutty, if you stop to consider it. But no one in my family would dream of being without a peeing, barfing, carcass-rolling friend.

I asked Don why he thought we put up with the dog's antics.

"Because she's not human," he said, then looked at me like I was dumb.

It's a good answer, really. As good an answer as you can ask for. The night my mother died, I shut Mercy in my childhood bedroom. When I came back in, I found that she had chewed a hole through the plaster, as if trying her very best to lead us out of there, into the woods beyond—to follow my mother's proclamation and lead us past it.

We love Mercy for her companionship, for the way she mirrors the size and rawness of our feelings. At times she seems to know us the way we wish to be known. But perhaps we love her even more for her inability to know us, to talk back, to tell us not to wake her up when she's sleeping in the dog bed, to say she hates the organic kibble we've purchased so that she will never die, to say she only chewed through that wall because she was bored. Maybe it's a relief to be able to invent her feelings. To decide how much she loves us. Maybe that is the trade.

"Why do I put up with you?" I ask the dog. I'm sitting before her on the cement floor. She makes her ears stand out like little wings and tilts her head. Her black nose shines. Then, as if she cannot help herself, she shifts her weight back so she's on her haunches and rests her paws on each of my shoulders. And, as if choreographed, she faints, limp fish, into my arms.

The Leash

TOM GRIMES

The neighborhood knew him because he walked its streets every day, up to ten miles, unless a thunderstorm, a hurricane, or a blizzard had driven everyone indoors. As soon as the weather cleared, he was back on the pavement, ice or no ice, snow or no snow, his leash's collar slightly loose. The old man's hand held the leash's leather handle, which, over the course of a dozen sweltering New York summers and frigid winters, had been worn smooth and darkened until it was nearly black. The slender old guy wore a floppy engineer's cap and a gray fishing jacket—the kind with a dozen pockets. He always had a walnut-colored leather pouch slung over one shoulder and a dented silver canteen hung on a twill strap draped over the other. His shirts were flannel or cotton, depending on the season, his pants never anything but beige chinos. His boots were ankle height with thick rubber soles and rawhide laces. A thin but bristly mustache straddled his upper lip, and I noticed, by the time I was ten, that he scratched it contemplatively, not because it itched. I lived around the corner from his house, and my curiosity about him led him, in a way, to adopt me. This earned me rare privileges, denied to the rest of my friends, such as the summer day he saw me having trouble spinning my wooden top on the street's soft tar. He tilted his head, as if to say come on, and I followed him to his garage, which was his sanctuary. There he placed my top in a vise clamped to his dusty workbench, took a file, and rounded the sharp metal point of my top so that it would spin longer, which it did.

He was Mr. Whalen. His dog, Charlie, a beagle, purebred, classic black, tan, and white coat, twenty-odd pounds, sweet-tempered, which is a beagle's natural disposition—"merry," according to beagle experts and enthusiasts. He considered it his job to let people on the street stop him at any place and time to pet him while Mr. Whalen stood patiently by. One evening, as dusk settled and the streetlights came on, they seemed to me to fuse into a single spirit: one being split into two bodies, two species. Charlie wasn't Mr. Whalen's dog, and Mr. Whalen wasn't Charlie's owner. Afterward, I never thought of them any other way. When my friends and I stood on the street corner waiting for the local ice-cream truck to appear on its route through the neighborhood, I often watched them approach, familiar in the distance but barely visible. When they stopped, we petted Charlie, and he accepted our fondness nobly—neither eager, indifferent, nor short-tempered—while Mr. Whalen told us where they'd walked in Queens that day.

Their hikes became a mystery to me, treks that in my boy's mind gradually took on the quality of myth. And hoping for an initiation into a secret world, I asked if, on my days off from school, I could come with them. "They" said yes. Afterward, when we tramped along Jamaica Avenue, the street below the elevated J-train tracks whose ties, in sunlight, laddered the pavement with alternating gold and black bands, we stopped in the usual places: the hardware store; Heinz's delicatessen; the butcher's shop; Dilbert's, the dim grocery store with its grimy tile floor; or Lewis's, owned by the madman Al Lewis. All the stores on Jamaica Avenue were one story high. Above them were two stories of small apartments. The top-floor apartments stood so close to the train tracks that during the summer kids standing between the stopped cars could spit out pearl-size gobs of phlegm and watch them sail through one of the open windows. Lewis's had maybe eighty feet of sidewalk selling space, and every morning in a maniacal rage, forty-going-on-a-coronary Al Lewis crammed into it cardboard bins he'd stuffed with bundles of brown, orange, and sky blue wool for the hordes of neighborhood women who knitted, some of whom made blankets for Mr. Whalen's and Charlie's beds and doilies for their living-room armchairs. Inside, Lewis's was the demon seed of Wal-Mart with everything from flathead nails by the pound to beef jerky at the cash register. No product was too lowly or obscure not to warrant space on the packed shelves—doll carriages, power drills, bow-and-arrow sets for real and for play, and, of course, cans and thirty-pound sacks of dog food. Braving the crowded aisles of Lewis's, Charlie cleared a path for us through people who said hello to him in varying tones, from happy, "Hi, Charlie!," to deferential, "Charlie, good dog, yeah, good boy," to hip, "Hey, Charlie, what's going on?," to high-pitched, borderline-hysterical four- to five-year-olds, "It's Charlie! Yay!"

Mr. Whalen seemed to be a perpetual sixty-five, but he was lean and wiry and could haul a thirty-pound sack of dog food and still carry his canteen and leather pouch while holding on to Charlie's leash. I was eleven by then and could carry a case, or maybe two, of canned food on my shoulder. When we reached the house they shared with Mr. Whalen's retired sister, I'd get a quarter, good, in the early 1960s, for a bottle of Coke and a Snickers bar, or a pack of baseball cards. Sometimes, if it was noon and lunchtime, which he and Charlie were punctual about, I'd be invited in for a sandwich.

In the spare living room, a hooked, oval, multicolored rug lay on the maple-stained wood floors. Around the rug stood three armchairs—Mr. Whalen's, his sister's, and Charlie's. Also a vintage radio, honey-hued, about four feet tall and stout as a trash can. Two panels of mesh fabric ran from its pedestal to an inch below its wavelength band, a ruler-long piece of ivory-tinted plastic notched with black hash marks that indicated numbers from 94 to 108. When you turned the tuning knob, a red needle slid over them, finding music, voices, and recurring patches of static. The Whalens didn't own a television set, and since at home I watched TV before school, dinner, and bedtime, stepping into their house was like stepping into a world in which the clock had stopped ticking twenty years earlier. Next to each armchair was an oak table with a round coaster, on which they set their cups of tea and coffee. Beside the coasters were framed pictures of Charlie and Mr. Whalen, either seated on the front porch or posing in Forest Park, a sprawling, heavily wooded green space, laced with miles of hiking trails. The Whalens had an immaculate, never-used dining room, its breakfront filled with perfectly nested china, and crystal wineglasses lined up like cadets. The kitchen was snug, the life force of the house, its spotless white stove topped by three gas burners and one cast-iron griddle for making pancakes on. The white refrigerator was an older, single-door model with a silver latch handle. Charlie's dinnerware sat on the floor, two elegant silver bowls, one filled with fresh cold water, the other, at mealtime, with gelatinous meat-related canned food or dry, pebble-size kibble. We ate at the Formica table beside the window overlooking the ten-by-fifteen plot of backyard grass and the garage. Lunch was usually tuna-fish salad mixed with real mayonnaise; my parents were always broke, so at home we used Miracle Whip. Mr. Whalen's sister also chopped up celery and stirred C-shaped bits of it into the salad before she laid it between two slices of Wonder bread.

Like a Zen monk, Mr. Whalen never had much to say. Weather talk was superfluous. He didn't follow sports teams, but because a copy of the *New York Daily News* turned up on his porch at seven each morning and a *Long Island Press* arrived each afternoon at four, I knew he read the paper. But the Cold War and the vague, far-off war in a country named Vietnam never seemed to interest him. Maybe years earlier someone he loved had died, and afterward the world and nearly everyone in it seemed ghostly and diaphanous. I don't know. I do know that mainly he liked sawing wood in his garage, a place as tranquil as a church with only a few people kneeling in rows, praying silently. He had plenty of space for his tools, because he didn't own a car. One time he built an airplane with a wingspan of eighteen inches for me, and then whittled a figure of a pilot wearing a leather cap and goggles into its cockpit. He enjoyed repairing things and could sometimes reflect on the nature of a screw for up to a minute, as if he were testing not only its usefulness, but also its reality. Meanwhile, Charlie sat at his feet, ready to spring into action if necessary but mainly watchful, as if he knew that the old man needed long stretches of solitary puttering. Then, at one o'clock sharp, they began their five-hour afternoon walk.

Each outing was a zigzagging, semi-Homeric journey. One afternoon we changed direction to avoid a gang of local teenagers who wandered through the woods of Forest Park, carrying switchblades and drinking three-dollar strawberry wine or green schnapps until they were delirious. Another day we walked past the mansions of Forest Hills, its streets car-free and quiet except for the sound of an electric or gas-powered clipper trimming hedgerows along the leaf-swept sidewalks. Charlie dictated our route, it seemed, as much as Mr. Whalen did. Charlie had minor interests, like standing on an overpass and watching traffic on the narrow-laned and serpentine Interboro Parkway, known for its stupendous car wrecks. He also seemed obsessed by kites. In the park he'd watch them circle over-head, his snout in the air as he pranced beneath them. If one drifted away or sailed toward the ground, Mr. Whalen might let go of his leash. Then Charlie would bolt in the direction of the kite, mesmer-ized, creeping toward a downed kite as he would a dead rabbit but respectfully keeping his distance from the owner, usually a boy though sometimes a man with too much time on his hands. Charlie would sit ten feet away to prove his benign interest, and after a while Mr. Whalen would call him and we'd move on. Mr. Whalen sched-uled our market stops. We started at the butcher's place, which, like Mr. Whalen's garage, had a floor covered with sawdust. Blood from raw meat dripped onto it, dried, and then stuck to the shoe soles of the butchers as they moved around behind the counter, plucking pork chops, shell steaks, and necklaces of linked sausages from glass coolers. The butchers—three cleaver-wielding, relentlessly cheerful men in bloodied white shirts, pants, and aprons—seemed to enjoy the primal pleasure of hacking apart raw meat every day. They treated Charlie like a prince, making a game of skill out of feeding him. They'd toss scraps of prime-cut beef over the counter so he had to leap to snare them between his teeth, and they kept lobbing them until he missed one and lost his right to more. If he didn't catch the first one, he got pity scraps and was told he'd do better next time. When he was on a streak, they said, "Okay, that's enough." Next stop was the German delicatessen, a glacially air-conditioned place owned by a chubby-faced man named Heinz who ran it with fascist ardor and precision. Heinz was a legendarily cheap bastard who disliked me because one night my mother sent me to buy an overpriced quart of milk and a loaf of bread from him, since we'd run out at dinnertime and his was the only open market. When I stood on my toes and laid the item on his chrome countertop he yelled, "Is that all?" I mumbled yes and then paid him with nickels and pennies, which he glared at as if they were diseased. Yet as soon as Charlie set paw on the deli's black-and-white ceramic-tiled floor, even before he passed the Ring Dings and Devil Dogs stand, the exotic Pepperidge Farm cookies, and the trays filled with cold coleslaw and potato salad, Heinz, the miser, stood at his slicing machine with a torpedo-size log of balogna, shaving off tissue-thin slivers of it, and then limped around the counter. (I was shamefully but secretly glad he limped, although in my more empathic moments I considered that his limp might be the root of his bitterness.) He bent forward, dangling a slice of balogna centimeters from Charlie's nose, and said, "Und how are ve today?" Charlie's good manners restrained him from lunging at the treat. Instead he took it politely, almost reverentially, allowing Heinz to place it in his mouth like a priest laying a Communion wafer on a believer's tongue. At our final stop, the bakery, Charlie was treated to sweets—a chocolate-chip cookie or a chunk of napoleon. But he never got fat. The daily ten-mile hikes kept him and Mr. Whalen fit until, unexpectedly, Mr. Whalen died while walking alongside a busy eight-lane road in ninety-degree heat, returning from the hardware store.

I never learned whether Mr. Whalen fell facedown on the sidewalk, crumpled to the pavement after his knees buckled like a pair
of snapped drinking straws, or after dropping the two gallons of
house paint he'd been carrying, sat down, reached inside his fishing
jacket—which he wore regardless of the temperature—and placed
one hand over his quivering heart. I also don't know if he asked
Charlie to bark for help or if he searched his expression for a sign that
he understood what was happening. Still, I always pictured Charlie
as the hero of the event, circling Mr. Whalen's body, nudging his face
with his snout and pawing his shoulder, trying to revive him, and
then dashing into traffic, dodging it as he barked, imploring some
driver to stop. When one finally did, Charlie patiently let the person
examine the old man's body, feeling for a pulse as Charlie looked on,
pacing, or perhaps sitting quietly, hoping his world wouldn't end.
When the police and paramedics arrived, their vehicle lights whirling as their sirens whooped, Charlie backed away, giving them room
to work. He even permitted one of the officers to pet him because
this was still his purpose, to make people who were nice to him feel
good about themselves. Then he allowed the ambulance to carry
away Mr. Whalen, and he rode home in the back of the police car
with Mr. Whalen's leather pouch, dented canteen, and the two gallons of paint beside him. The officer in the passenger seat studied the
contents of the old man's wallet, looking for an address, and found it
on Mr. Whalen's library card. Charlie waited to be asked questions.
What happened? Did your owner show any signs of a heart attack?
Shortness of breath, chest pains? Why didn't he take the bus? In my
childhood fantasy, Charlie could feel human emotions and think
human thoughts; he simply needed a chance to prove it. But the
questions were never asked.

And Mr. Whalen's funeral was never announced. He seemed to
have simply disappeared. Briefly, Charlie's whereabouts were also
unknown, as if he too had vanished. Then Mr. Whalen's house was
put up for sale. His sister planned to move in with relatives. Yet one
summer evening Charlie returned, being walked by a cousin in the

family. I was in front of our house with my parents. My younger sister and brother called Charlie's name when they saw him, and for their sake he stopped to be adored. Mrs. Whalen's relatives, we were told, wouldn't take Charlie in, essentially orphaning him and condemning him to the pound. My brother and sister shouted—with glee, not moral outrage—that we should let him live with us. I said, "I think we ought to do it." My father said it was all right with him, but my mother balked. She liked Charlie in the abstract, as a passerby on the sidewalk, not as a member of the family. She kept a neat house and didn't want it ruined. We pleaded and she caved, but with strict limitations. Charlie wasn't allowed on the furniture, he'd sleep in the kitchen, and she wasn't walking him—I was.

We took him in that night, my father and I carrying from Mr. Whalen's house to ours Charlie's dinnerware and dog food, but not his armchair or bed because my mother said they were too hairy. Then, as if it needed his approval, Charlie inspected the downstairs floor of the house. Upstairs, my mother warned him, was off-limits. He seemed satisfied and wagged his tail. At bedtime I lured him into the kitchen with a treat and asked him to lie down and stay there. Standing in the kitchen archway, my mother said, "You don't come past this line, understand?" Five minutes after we'd gone upstairs, she was back downstairs. The rest of us had followed, and I saw Charlie curled up on my mother's armchair, his head raised, looking puzzled. My mother dragged him into the kitchen and then sent me to the basement to fetch a three-foot-high wooden gate that opened laterally, like an accordion. She lodged it snugly between the archway's molding and said, "Stay. I don't want to see you out here again." Within five minutes Charlie had pushed aside the gate and returned to her armchair. My mother, who'd been spying from the staircase, marched into the living room, turned on the light, and with the rest of us hovering behind her like a Greek chorus, said, "What did I say? What did I tell you? I said stay in the kitchen. Did you stay in the kitchen? No. You want to be out on the street? Huh? You want to live by yourself?" Rather than hanging his head during her tirade, Charlie seemed genuinely concerned, almost worried about her. My mother yanked his collar and dragged him off the chair. As she led him back to the kitchen, I volunteered to spend the night beside him on the floor. "Just until he gets used to us," I said. I also looked forward to comforting Charlie during his period of mourning. But he never seemed to have one. He didn't sulk, pine, or plague us with grief-stricken sighs. Secretly this disappointed me. Then I refashioned my disappointment into appreciation. It was obvious. He was sparing us months of canine lamentation, a woeful hunger strike, endless midnight howls and sorrowful whimpering. For our sake he was pretending to be content to eat, be walked, be petted, and, every evening, to lie at the foot of the couch—my father's territory, therefore his call—and watch television with us. If Charlie missed Mr. Whalen and his radio, he was kind enough not to burden us with his anguish.

When I turned fourteen, I ran for my school's track team, and each fall was cross-country season. I was expected each summer to run three to five miles a day to train for it, so I began to take Charlie with me to keep him in shape. Whenever I appeared in my tank top, shorts, and running shoes, Charlie worked himself into a frenzy while I attached his leash. Then we'd bolt out the screen door and run flat out until we reached the road where Mr. Whalen had died, stopping if the light was against us, sprinting across the eight lanes if it wasn't. Once we were in the park, I'd let go of his leash and we'd race across the meadow where kids flew their kites. Then we were into the woods, streaking along a rutted dirt path, the air cool under the trees, a quilt of bright sunlight and shade ahead of us, the world silent except for the scuffle of leaves beneath our feet and our breathing. Charlie grew winded faster than I did, and after a mile he'd slow down, look at me, and raise his eyebrows, suggesting a breather. But I kept going. It never occurred to me that he was getting old. His Charlieness was a fixed point in my tiny universe, as stable as true

north. I'd known Charlie before I knew that each of us—all of us—
would one day die. So to me Charlie was immortal. But as he aged, it
became clear why he hadn't mourned Mr. Whalen's death. Charlie's
fate was to allow us to practice *our* mourning on him. To prepare *us*
for unbridled desolation and grief without end. We had it backward.
We weren't here to take care of him, he was here to take care of us.
To be our guide and our consolation.

I didn't understand this the day my father and I took him walking in the snow. Half a mile from our house was a bleak, deserted
field where, during the week, factory workers parked their cars. But
it was a Saturday, and the late-afternoon light was graying into dusk,
the world stilled and weirdly quiet. When we reached the field, I
dropped Charlie's leash so he could wander off while my father and
I plodded along, our noses dripping, talking of things I can't recall.
As the snow fell harder, we kept our heads down. Ready to start
home, we turned to look for Charlie. He stood fifty yards from us,
amid whorls of snow.

"Come on!" we yelled, but he hardly moved. We called his name,
and he barked at us. Again we called come on, and again he barked,
ignoring our arm waves, maybe defying us or maybe playing. My father said, "Let's hide," and the two of us slipped behind the factory
wall, pressed our backs against its red bricks, and listened to Charlie's barking. His tone had grown earnest, even a bit worried, possibly
terrified. My father peeked around the wall. "He's still standing
there," he said, pleased with our mischief. We waited a while longer.
"Is he coming?" I said. My father poked his head out. "No."

Charlie barked intermittently now, his voice softer, as if he'd given
up hope of being heard. The silences became longer, and I finally
stepped past my father. Charlie hadn't moved. I started toward him,
and he barked, making sure I could track him in the dusk. When we
were halfway across the field, I said to my father, "He's stuck." Charlie's leash was caught on a fallen branch too heavy for him to drag. I
heard his high-pitched whines, and he danced frantically from side

to side as I knelt down to free him. "It's okay," I said, letting him lick my face and feeling ignorant and ashamed for frightening him.

At times I lie awake now and recall my disgrace, and I'm inclined—because Lassie books, *Old Yeller,* and Walt Disney movies have taught me—to trace childhood's end to the day my dog died. But it's a syrupy, maudlin cliché, and so I don't. Childhood ends, of course, although in ways too complicated and fluid to explain, and yes, our dogs die when we're children.

One year we gave Charlie a gift-wrapped Christmas present with a snowman sticker on it that said, "To Charlie, with love from everyone." Inside was a tartan plaid coat, which we draped over him and secured with a matching belt below his chest. "It'll keep you warm," we told him. Then we put a Santa Claus hat with a white pom-pom on his head, took his picture, and slipped it into our family photo album, which naturally, over time, yellowed and will one day disintegrate into ash. Such a day will come for me, too, and although I'd like to be a lot further from death than I am now, I don't want to return to childhood either. I imagine that I'd like to live outside of time. Maybe that's how dogs live. Complete. Egoless. The moment and the infinite undifferentiated.

But this, too, is a fiction, this is romance. Charlie felt abandoned that day on the field. He was frightened, a creature no more or less unbound by time than I am. The story was never about Charlie, or me, or time, or mortality, or the ashes we're all destined to become. The story is about the leash, the leash worn smooth and darkened until it was nearly black. The leash Mr. Whalen attached to Charlie's collar when he walked him, the leash I inherited. The connection between us. That's the story. And in the universe of stories, this is the only story worth telling.

Odin, King of Hearts

MARY OTIS

I like to say that Odin was fifty-five pounds heart, five pounds as-sorted dog parts. He was a pit bull, my neighbors' dog. At first. And then for a time he was mine.

Odin's chest was the width of a small bureau. Odin got stoned on sunshine. Odin caught bees in his mouth. Sometimes he spit them out. Odin drank tuna-fish water like it was fine wine. Odin wagged his tail so hard against chairs, tables, and walls that he knocked his fur off. Odin had a big handsome head, so handsome it could have been on a postage stamp.

Some were of the opinion that Odin was a little thick in the skull. One time Khaki Swings, the lady down the street with the pink stucco house where the shades were always drawn, used those very same words. And yes, at that moment Odin was trying to drink from my neighbor's sprinkler and getting whacked in the head, and yes, I was aware that Khaki had recently given her dachshund, Dirk, a dog-IQ test and Dirk scored 121, but Khaki was hardly in any posi-tion to weigh in on matters of good sense. Given that she ran a porn-film company out of her house. Given that sexy but tired-looking people were coming and going at all hours. But I digress.

Odin's owners, my neighbors Sylvie and Frank, were retired and consumed by activities of which I could never make sense. Sylvie

wore bejeweled caftans and always seemed on the brink of leaving
their house to attend an important meeting or event. I pictured exotic women's clubs, strange and secret ceremonies. But her car never
left the driveway. If she ever attended a single meeting, I couldn't tell
you how she got there. Frank spent his days loading and unloading
small green Styrofoam boxes in and out of his orange minivan. I
imagined a cheese or jam mail-order business.

My apartment, a small cottage, was next door to their house, and
our windows faced each other. I saw them, they saw me. I had only
ever talked to Sylvie and Frank in passing, and I suppose they thought
I was a strange girl who sat all day at her kitchen table, which was
where I wrote. Sometimes I imagined us as characters in a kind of
existentialist performance piece—Frank packing and unpacking his
boxes, Sylvie running to the door only to never leave, and me sitting
there at my kitchen table waiting for ideas.

I'd lived in my apartment for about a month when one morning the
Santa Ana winds whirled in. This wasn't unusual for mid-October
in Los Angeles, but there was something strange about the sun that
morning. It lay on the horizon like an egg that didn't break right.
Warm air frothed the palm trees in a sinister way, and there was a
quality to it that was not unlike sitting next to someone who is about
to burst into tears.

And then my mother called. She said she had some bad news.
Bad news that was also wrong—as if there were a right kind of bad
news.

"I'm sorry to say this, but he shot your dog."

"Who? Who shot my dog? You mean Ringo?" I said, even
though there was only one husky that lived with my parents back in
Massachusetts, only one husky that I'd left behind when I moved to
California. And that's when he started to go "off"—busting out of
our yard, charging for miles, fighting with other dogs. My father was
paying vet bills, sending out "I'm sorry our dog went nuts" cards. It

was a real problem. This time Ringo had broken out of the yard and cornered a neighbor's corgi under the patio.

And so the neighbor called the police department, and an officer was dispatched. But not just any officer. Officer Clarence Feeney, well known but not well liked in the small town where I grew up.

"He had it in for Ringo," my mother said, "besides which, he may have had a flashback." Around town Officer Feeney often alluded to being in an indeterminate civil war. A civil war that didn't go with any country. Sometimes the soldiers in his war trudged through snow, sometimes they died of heatstroke. Sometimes the year of the war was 1977. The Disco War, people said behind his back. Perhaps Officer Clarence Feeney did not get the respect he deserved. Perhaps this drove him mad. Perhaps instead of a husky with his head jammed under a redwood plank, he thought he'd captured the enemy from behind. But in any case he took out his pistol and shot my dog.

I did not cry. I thought of Ringo as I had last seen him, standing by the door to our house, watching me pull out of the driveway. Then he suddenly turned, sat down, and stared in the other direction, his back to me. As if to say, *You want to leave, leave.*

"Are you there?" my mother said. "Because there's a little more to the story." I heard her turn down the evening news, and then she cleared her throat. "Officer Clarence Feeney is also dead."

"He shot himself, too?" I said, and I must say that for a second I thought it served him right.

"No, he had a little accident with a noose." My mother paused. "When he got home."

"What kind of an accident?"

"Well, a sort of unplanned accident." She sighed.

"What do you mean, an unplanned accident?"

"Well, a bit of a sexual accident, you might say."

I looked out my kitchen window, and I saw Odin's big head staring back at me from what I thought was Sylvie and Frank's bedroom, his head framed by a royal blue satin headboard. As if he knew. As if he'd heard the entire story. His expression was resigned, world-weary. I thought of Anubis, the mythical Egyptian dog who weighed people's hearts at the moment of death—weighed them for goodness and decided who got into heaven and who didn't.

I thought of Officer Clarence Feeney's pistol going off. Of Ringo being "off." Of getting off. And what some people won't do. Isn't that the phrase a person might use in this situation? *What some people won't do.* And why did he have to shoot my dog? I looked out the window again. And still Odin was staring at me, unmoving, un-dog-like, considering, it seemed, the weight of things.

That night I couldn't sleep. A gust of hot wind blew in my window and funneled around me. The air smelled like pennies and burned sugar. It was enough to make a person go crazy. In fact, there had been a story in the paper that day about a man who killed his wife and used the Santa Ana winds in his defense.

A parade of dead dogs trudged through my mind. I remembered my first dog, Darby. Darby was a beagle my father found wandering outside a filling station. He seemed to have been trained as a hunting dog, but it just wasn't in him. Or whoever taught him to point scared him so much that he just never got it straight. Darby shook a lot. He pointed constantly, but at all the wrong things—the school bus, the hair dryer, a photo of JFK. A hundred foxes could have blasted through our living room. No dice.

I got up and drank a glass of water. I looked out my kitchen window and saw a solitary light on in Sylvie and Frank's house. Occasionally I heard them laugh or argue. More than occasionally I heard them watching a local cable-TV program called *The Universe Is Saying Yes.* I suppose they knew my habits, too. Yet we all kept our distance. It's not that we were impolite. We weren't. Once Sylvie left me a note on my door that said *"Watch out for bees!"* A couple weeks later, when the bees had departed only to return, I taped a note to their door that said *"Watch out, bees are back!"*

The night was even hotter than the day, as if the crazy winds had blown the earth in reverse. A bird sat outside my window and wailed. I sat down at my computer and researched Officer Clarence Feeney's sexual mishap. Popular slang included "airplaning," "scarfing," "hangman." And then I thought of Officer Clarence Feeney standing on a chair, stepping to the edge, and then whoops, just a little too far. Or maybe the error had been in the length of the rope. Just a little too tight. Or maybe he'd been off by a split second. And it appeared that if there was one thing hangman was all about, it was about timing. I wondered if Officer Clarence Feeney left a dog behind and what would become of it. I recalled reading about dogs in nineteenth-century France who committed suicide upon their owners' deaths by jumping off bridges and throwing themselves under carriage wheels.

Dead dogs. Dead people. I was no closer to sleep. It occurred to me that if there were some kind of conveyor-like contraption that transported Officer Feeney and Ringo to the great big ever-beyond, they'd arrive on the very same night.

Then I heard someone softly kicking my front door, if someone without much aim could kick a door. If someone had a paw instead of a foot. I looked out my window and saw Odin. I opened my door, and he bolted in. He did one quick circle of my place, then another, like someone about to leave for the airport. Then he ran to the side of my bed and jumped on it. He stood completely still before suddenly collapsing, and I would become very familiar with his crash-landing method in days to come. Odin's big, beautiful head lolled over the foot of the bed, and he had a dreamy, disconnected look, like he was listening to distant dog radio. I noticed that he had little blond eyelashes. He fell asleep within seconds, and I let him stay there. I heard Sylvie and Frank's back door shut, and I realized that they knew he was there, and that maybe they'd even sent him.

Well, let's just say I fell quickly. Let's just say Odin started coming to my place every day. Sylvie and Frank didn't appear to mind. In fact, one day I saw them sitting on their front stoop, and Frank said, "Odin likes you."

Sylvie said, "Odin is like you." I took that as a compliment and felt she was precisely right. I was never a big gabber, and Odin would have been a man of few words if he could speak them.

"Thank you," I said, and I thought about asking her what time Odin ate dinner, because some nights he was at my place during what I thought might have been that time. But then I decided against it. No need for them to know at that moment I had a bag of dog food, really good dog food made with special dog vitamins, which I'd purchased that very morning, sitting in the trunk of my car. Just in case.

But the very best part of my burgeoning relationship with Odin was that when I wrote at my kitchen table, he fell asleep on my foot like a drunk with his head on the curb. Let's just say I did absolutely nothing to stop this.

And did I mention the color of Odin's fur, which changed in the light and which might be described as champagne, or the color of a milk shake with a shot of caramel, or bamboo that's been in the sun a while, or the color of white sand when it's wet, or even, on occasion, pig-colored?

One morning while I was at the pet store buying Odin presents, I found myself wondering what he was doing back at my apartment. It was a pleasant thing to ponder. And basically I knew what Odin was doing. He was following the sun around my hardwood floor, dozing as it moved with every passing hour from the rug to the kitchen table to the bookcase to the back door, upon which each afternoon it appeared to slowly melt.

Odin's schedule fit perfectly with my own, which involved writing in the morning, then eating, then writing and drinking tea, then writing and washing the dishes, then writing and standing by the kitchen door to read out loud what I'd written that day. It wasn't exactly like I read to Odin, but I'd be lying if I said he didn't appear to listen. If Sylvie and Frank ever missed Odin, they kept it to themselves.

Though Odin's napping habits dovetailed with my writing, I began to fret that he wasn't keeping fit. Sylvie and Frank had a small yard within which he could roam, but his main source of exercise involved planting himself directly under the power line that ran from the roof of my cottage to the street—the domain of particularly taunting squirrels. There Odin would sit in amazement, his head going back and forth, back and forth, while the squirrels appeared as if by magic on one end of the line and then the other. He never thought to look straight up.

And so the next night when Odin was at my place, I tried to walk him. I'd bought a leash earlier that day, a good, sturdy black one that I thought would complement his fur. I didn't mention this to Sylvie or Frank, because really, who would mind if their dog got a free walk? Besides, he could use it.

Trying to walk Odin was like trying to walk a Fiat. I've since read that you should multiply your dog's weight by 2.5 prior to attempting a walk. And if that weight is more than your own, you're in big trouble. Because that's how much a dog can pull, and by my belated calculations Odin had me beat by the weight of a first-grader.

Though it was seven o'clock that night, it was still eighty degrees. The Santa Ana winds had yet to pack up and leave, and red bougainvillea leaves and dust swirled around our legs. Odin dragged me past Khaki Swings' pink house of porn, past a pack of "cheerleaders" smoking cigarettes in her driveway, past Dirk the dachshund, who waddled at a diagonal across the yard at us, and for the first time I noticed that while Dirk could have been a member of doggy Mensa, that was nothing compared to his physical endowment. Let's just say the image of an anchor came to mind. Let's just say I hope he wasn't working for dog food.

Odin and I picked up speed as we headed down a hill, crashing through stacks of fallen palm fronds. We went three more blocks, as far as a dilapidated mansion that was rumored to have once been owned by Chuck Berry. The only vestige of finer days was a metal deer on the lawn, rusted but still standing. We're talking lifelike, as far as cast iron goes. This was a deer not to be messed with. Odin came to a complete stop and then stared at it. If he had an internal dog clutch, then he downshifted and popped it into first. And then Odin rammed the deer. Hard. And there the deer lay, its flat metal deer eye peeking up at me, as if to say, *It was bad enough already. Why do you treat me so?* Odin tried to push the deer up with his nose. I tried to rock it up, pull it up, lift it by its legs. No go. I remembered a time I found Ringo the husky curled up in a snowbank and thought he was gone, but of course he was only sleeping. Odin sat down and contemplated the deer, as if the deer were a very special case. Dead-like, but not dead. And how could the heart of such a thing ever be weighed?

Time passed. The Santa Ana winds blew out of town. One day my friend Drea stopped by on her way to work. Drea was a food stylist, the person at a photo shoot who sprays Aqua Net on fruit so that it looks wet and shiny. I realized I hadn't talked to her in a couple of weeks. Or any friends for that matter. She stood in my doorway, and I realized I was reluctant to let her in. Odin was napping in the kitchen, and I didn't want to disturb him. I hadn't seen him the previous day, and I was glad to have him back.

Drea stood in my doorway, lit a cigarette, and blew the smoke out in one short stream, pursing her lips in a way that always reminded me of someone about to play the trumpet. "How's your dog, Otis?" she said. My heart leaped. *Your dog.* Then sank. As if. As if I had a dog I'd give it my own name. What did she take me for? My God, did she think we were married? Did she think he was my dog husband or something?

"It's Odin," I said. "Odin. And he's not my dog. Okay? He just visits me sometimes, okay? Not my dog. Not mine." Odin lifted his head from the floor and looked at me. "Maybe we should step outside to talk," I said.

"Look," said Drea, "I think you're getting a little strange about this dog. She took another drag of her cigarette, exhaled. "I think you're getting in deep."

My phone rang, and I said we'd have to chat later.

"Sure. Sure we will," she said. She shot a look at Odin, as if he'd placed the call himself.

I picked up my phone and heard the sound of a power drill. My father didn't like to waste valuable work time when placing a call.

"I'm on!" I shouted. The drill stopped.

"How's the writing business?" said my father. I could picture him in the barn at his worktable, Frank Sinatra playing on the radio.

"Fine," I said.

"If a person were to ask you to write about a specific thing, could you?" he said. I knew he worried about the logistics of a writer's life.

"Are you saying you want to hire me?"

"Just curious," he said.

"Well, if I were to write a story specifically for you, what would you want it to be about?" I asked. I watched Odin move from the patch of sun by the rug to the patch of sun by the bookcase. He sighed. I felt that he understood the difficulty of claiming oneself a writer. It was like telling people you were psychic. Events could take a while to shake out. "I mean, if it could be about anything at all, what would you like it to be about?" I added.

I heard my father pull his chair back from his worktable, and I knew he was giving this real thought. "I like to read about dogs," he said. "Dogs and the Mafia."

"One day," I said, "I will try to write you a story about dogs and the Mafia." But I knew it wasn't true, because really, the only dog I wanted to write about was Odin. A series of linked stories featuring Odin as the protagonist in every story. But I didn't want anyone to think I was getting *strange* about Odin or that I was *getting in too deep,* so if I were to ever write said book, I'd give the dog heroes (that were actually all Odin) other names, like Bill, Scooter, and Jake.

Outside, I heard Frank calling Odin. Odin opened his eyes, though he didn't move a muscle.

A few days later, I didn't see Odin. He hadn't been out of his house all day, and I thought maybe he was sick. Though later that afternoon, I saw him sitting under the telephone line as usual, watching the squirrels like they were the Cirque du Soleil. I propped my door open, and about an hour later he came through it. Since it was almost dinnertime, I gave him some dog food. Then I heard Frank whistle, one of the few times I ever had, and Odin bolted out the door. I stood in my doorway looking after him, and when he ran into his own house, I must say I felt a pang of jealousy. Then I saw Sylvie in profile, a rhinestone-covered aqua caftan, a hand on the doorknob. "We would appreciate it if you would not take it upon yourself to walk our dog," she said. She never turned to look at me.

I thought, *Give him back, he's mine, and besides, he likes me better.* Although instantly I knew that might not be true. And then I realized that in some way they'd been trying to wean me off him. Maybe they never meant to let things get this far. Maybe they didn't know what to do. Maybe I could steal him. Maybe Odin and I could move to Nebraska, and I could buy a place with a field for Odin, because I was always reading articles in *Parade* magazine about how in places like Nebraska or Iowa there were affordable homes with porches and shade trees that one might purchase. *I could do that,* I thought. *I could do that with Odin.*

But in the end I had a problem, and the problem was that Odin was a dog, not a person, and he couldn't cash out his stocks and run away with me. He continued to come by my place in the afternoons, but I was careful to put him out before nightfall. Some days, before his circuit of the sun was complete, he would abruptly get up and leave. It almost seemed as if he understood our dilemma and didn't want to get either of us in trouble. I let him in, I let him out, my head and heart in civil war.

Shortly thereafter Frank pulled off the white shutters next door, repainted them in what I considered an overfriendly shade of yellow, and put them back up. I heard vacuuming. I heard hammering. A professional window cleaner made an appearance. And then, a few days later, Sylvie and Frank put up a For Sale sign. The house sold that week, and off they went with my dog. Because, after all, he was their dog.

I received a Christmas card from Sylvie and Frank the next year. I imagined Frank saying something like, "Maybe we should tell that girl who liked him so much."

"Oh, the one who sat at her kitchen table staring into space?"

"Yes, that one. I think she was a little off."

"I think she wanted to run away and marry Odin."

"Yes, I think she did."

"What some people won't do, given half a chance."

"Yes, what some people won't do."

The card said that Odin had died on his birthday, June 10.

I still think of Odin and his big dog head, and his heavy heart, and how he appeared to me like Anubis that first afternoon. And like Anubis, I can imagine him conducting similar business in that great big ever-beyond, weighing the hearts of both people and dogs, and in the end allowing one and all to enter, those that were good and those that were bad, and even those, like Officer Clarence Feeney, who didn't mean to come to the party so soon. I see him forever leading his troop of the dead and gone—dead dogs, dead people, the line extending back and back and back until finally one day he turns his head, and I, too, take my place.

Nightmares

PAUL WINNER

I

I am traveling with a dog named Bill. We are on a highway, driving east, one hour from New York City. He is spread over the length of the minivan's nearest backseat like an afghan. He has been in this position for a hundred miles, asleep, only his rear left paw twitching a bit, which could be a dream. Apart from a lifelong habit of twitching in his sleep, Bill has always possessed what complete strangers have remarked upon as extreme mellowness for a large dog. Over the years those strangers appeared and stood grinning in front of Bill as he reclined on the grass outside our apartment in St. Louis. They would pat his head, ask his name, and then, perhaps because there was little else to remark on aside from mellowness, tell me how pleasing it was to meet a dog with a real name, a human name. *Bill,* they said. Oh, hello, *Bill,* searching his eyes for signs of Billness, which they believed they could see. When he first came into my hands, barely a month old and the size of a small handbag, I chose his name from the world of man and naturally believed that a certain soul of man came with it.

Bill tends to look at most things sideways, like a disapproving manservant. He is a soft brown mix of German shepherd and Rhodesian ridgeback and has accepted from each breed gifts of size and disposition. His default expression is . . . unruffled. He never barks, never fights. He taps the doorknob with his nose when he wants something to happen with the door. He politely allows the drift of a crowd to guide him as he walks, moving to and fro, though he hasn't been able to walk farther than a square block since the last diagnosis, degenerative myelopathy, three months ago. The nerves in his hind legs are failing. More specifically, the smooth, flexible casing of each nerve in a certain region is breaking apart and taking with it any intelligent feeling. Very soon, I have learned, he will have what amounts to MS for dogs. The left hind leg has begun to rise and dip like a pedaling cyclist's whenever he waits at a curb. I think maybe he is trying to shake life back into it, as if it's only fallen asleep.

This would be his second diagnosis. The first concerned his mysterious twitching. That appeared several years ago and has increased in force and frequency due to the genetic admixture of shepherd and ridgeback, which produces, in random litters, a dog with a progressive form of epilepsy. Now a single tremor can lead to a complete grand mal seizure, if not several. He suffers clusters of them once a month. The nerve degeneration is apparently unrelated to his ongoing condition. This is what the last doctor told us. The doctor before that tried to combat the epileptic condition with a holistic regimen (antioxidants, boiled greens), which did little except make Bill have to urinate at inconvenient hours. The doctor before *that* was adamant about expensive testing at the state university's neuroscience wing to rule out the need for an MRI. Then the doctor prescribed an unusually large dose of phenobarbital to blanket the seizures all at once, like a great tarp against the torrent of brain firings or misfirings that make up the condition, in hopes of erasing the seizures once and for all. The seizures were not erased, and Bill became dependent on the unusually large dose. He will soon be eight. He has been epileptic since one. Billness—this sidelong, placid expression—could thus be the result of a grown addict's dependence on barbiturates as well as the overwhelming fatigue that comes from eating them every day.

The last doctor, the doctor we left, was a fifty-something woman with bristles of white hair and no patience with eye contact. She gripped a pen and stared at the floor and listened to details of his most recent attack. Bill had been stabilized on a steel table with two shots of diazepam. The previous night's cluster of seizures had struck hard, one after the other, enough of them (nine) that I was certain he'd suffered brain damage. The first hit after midnight. I heard him moving in the next room, stepping in an uneven rhythm and crying lightly as his body pushed through the stage known to human epileptics as the aura. He collapsed to one side and shook his head and chest, first mildly, then violently. I knelt and cradled his head to prevent a broken fang or concussion. He pissed himself. Spit flew out of his mouth like a spray of fountain water. He thrashed and pedaled four legs in wide circles until I sat on the floor and wrapped my arms around him from the back, like I was trying to heave his body out of water, pulling him onto me after a nail on his flailing front paw caught on a loose kitchen tile and ripped, exposing the cream-colored quick, blood spattering the floor. There was noise, too— furious scratches, the clink of collar metals, shoulders and limbs slamming repeatedly down, over and over. Finally the seizure's worst moment arrived, the apex: jaws open, fangs bared, eyes tightly shut, his face seeming on the verge of collapse, shaking so rapidly it doesn't seem to move at all. The seizure broke. The second phase leveled, and I ran to the closet and found a semi-clean towel to wipe the floor, wipe his body, his face. More attacks followed, often spaced apart by less than a full minute.

The doctor asked if I would back up and describe the post-ictal phase, the period following an individual seizure, when an epileptic dog attempts to reconcile with his senses, standing, circling a room's perimeter, despite unsteadiness in all four legs as well as a kind of sensory blindness that seems to fade according to whim. In order to block further injuries, I wanted to prevent this circle. I tried holding Bill down with my entire body, like a wrestler—he weighed 110 pounds—until he strained and cried and angrily pushed himself up.

He was panting and delirious. He looked crazed. In this phase Bill does not remember who—or even what—I am, and he fights the sense of confinement as a wolf might, overcome with a natural fear of being hemmed in, a fear that means he is about to be killed. He slid over the kitchen tiles trying to steady himself and smacked his face into a wall; he didn't seem to feel it. A smear of white wall stain rubbed onto his nose. His exposed nail tracked blood. He drifted backward. When I called his name, he followed the voice, not sure of the role it played in all this and whether that recollection was relevant. Gradually his pacing slowed. He slid into a sitting position in the front room, by the door, as if preparing for a trip. All the apartment lights were on. After an hour he shut his eyes.

I found another towel and sat down, facing him. It was close to four in the morning. I concentrated on a collection of objects I had accumulated over the years as a kind of proof that I had grown older, half settled: there was the good couch, the antique mirror, the tasteful framed thing, a pine worktable that looked like a butcher's block, and a surprising number of books that I had not gotten around to reading. I tried to sleep. Sometime later I rubbed my neck and moved to the bedroom. By morning Bill had ended up beside my bed in a hard slumber, the kind that produces the most storied, narrative dreams. That had been the last seizure. There was nothing to add. The doctor kept writing. Her smock was a vibrant purple with brightly colored paw prints walking all around it, up and down.

Bill and I would soon be moving from St. Louis to New York. She examined each of his limbs, one after another, asking what for, how long a move it would be, pressing with two hands on muscles that under normal conditions produced involuntary reflexes but did not just then. His myelopathy, she told me, had clearly progressed at a common rate for a dog his size. Both diagnoses now seemed to take up equal space, sharing the range of his nervous system. She took Bill's face in her hands, peering into his eyes, seeking signs of Bill-ness. He did not object. He sat in his usual state of obedience and returned her professional gaze, rather graciously, I felt. I told her that we would be living in New York for at least three years. Now she looked at me. She said Bill, living with these particular prognoses, would die there.

That was two months ago.

He has no doctor now. He has a seven-year case history showing several doctors' scribbled notes and erasures and corrections of earlier diagnoses. He shows flexible yet manageable toxin levels in his blood and liver. He has his many expensive prescriptions, precious things, without which he would fall into *status epilepticus,* the unending seizure, his last.

> 3 bottles phenobarbital, 99.5 mg tabs, 250 count
> 3 bottles Potassium Bromide (KBr) 250 kg / 250 ml
> 2 dispensers Belladonna 6a
> 1 bottle Soloxine, 0.8 mg tabs, 250 count
> 1 bottle large animal antioxidant pills
> Otomax
> Styptic pencil, broken
> Prednisone tabs
> Children's Tylenol
> Hydrocortisone
> Off-brand Neosporin

The stash is wrapped in a plastic sack and hidden under the far backseat in case I am pulled over for speeding and the patrolman spots a plastic bag of multicolored pills. There is enough medicine to last one month, and then we find a new doctor. There is an official-looking paper signed by the last doctor explaining why Bill has not been immunized against rabies or distemper, because of the adverse effect such immunizations have on an epileptic's neurological system. She had warned me that without proof of immunization dogs can be quarantined upon entrance to New York City. This word— "quarantined"—scared me awake last night. Bill's disease has always given me nightmares, vividly photographed stories of awful logic elaborating a simple theme: how or when will I fail him? The theme produces what feel like emotional cataracts, night after night, and are difficult to distinguish from waking consciousness, since I manage to hear everything at all hours. If he turns his head. If his bed is too warm. If his leg is in pain. If he's bored. If he's thirsty. If he's standing at the toilet. If he's staring at the wall. If he feels another attack on the way. Bill turned me into a light sleeper years ago.

It is a misty Sunday morning, just before ten. New York City is set to begin hosting a political convention the following night. A voice on the minivan's radio explains that bridges into downtown and midtown and uptown have been militarized and that MPs, along with traffic policemen, are searching vans on bridges and along random points of interstates as far out of range as Philadelphia. All motorists are potential terrorists.

Because I am relocating to a new place in the dead of summertime, because the minivan is overloaded and dragging its bumper, because I don't know all of a sudden where any of the documentation is that confirms I'm supposed to be in New York (welcome letter from school, apartment lease), and because Bill is still twitching—now both paws on his left side—I try to anticipate what could conceivably go wrong on the bridge, at the toll, at the inspection, with a city policeman whose job it would be to stand at the ready with a choke chain. Recently I saw footage on the national news of a state trooper who stopped a van for speeding. When the driver's overheated German shepherd leaped from the backseat and squeezed out the passenger window to greet the state trooper, the trooper thought he was under attack and shouted and drew his sidearm and shot the dog through the head. The shooting was captured on black-and-white police video. Half the incident is out of frame. The trooper jerks to the left, grabbing the sidearm, opening his mouth—then only the owner's face can be seen as it lights up with pain.

If Bill were to choose this moment to seize, the tremors would start in the rear paw and travel up to his chest. He would open his eyes and rotate his head, curiously, as if trying to locate a peculiar smell—human epileptics often describe the aura before the grand mal as an intense impromptu stench, as if fruit or rubber were burning—and then his legs would stick out straight as furniture before starting the frantic pedaling, a trip to oblivion, the long paddle there and back. State troopers and MPs are up ahead to one side of the bridge, waiting, rifles pointed down, ordering the inspection of unmarked vans and rigs with Nevada or Georgia plates. The toll man is a Puerto Rican–looking older gentleman who lifts up his glasses to rub his face. He does not look at me. He does not see Bill. He takes his money, and the bar rises. In less than a minute, we have crossed the Hudson River. The fog has disappeared, and an ailing, silver sunlight is reflected within the city's scattered damp surfaces— on car hoods, windows, and gutters. I locate the address and park the van and wait for Bill to notice we've stopped, which he does not. His twitching has paused, it seems. Bill? I call his name. Hello, Bill? He does not wake, not immediately. He makes a sad grunt that tells me he's not going to seize today but is instead pleading with someone or something in a dream.

II

The long nail that ripped on the kitchen tile made several tear-shaped bloodstains, which needed bleaching. Very old hair appeared everywhere—behind the sofas, in corners, stuck to the base of a floor lamp. He had scuffed the hardwood. A disgusting spot above his dish needed some attention. His big black nose had rubbed the wall, probably thousands of times, making these skidmark-looking spots in a little arc. I covered the area with white paint. I swept the corners and rinsed the floors with boiling water and used a broom to push the excess out the door, saying to the excess, *Take that.* I was sharp and focused on cleansing and removal. I was moving to New York to attend seminary. The ascetic seminarian life, or what I had imagined being the ascetic seminarian life—silent meals, a humble bed, common prayer, a luxurious and restorative dark falling over the grounds at compline—had moved me into an obsession with ridding myself of burdens, actual and imagined. Here was the ridding phase. I sold every piece of furniture and twenty-three boxes of books and turned my attention to the apartment surfaces until the doors of perception, or something like them, had been cleansed.

Several months before this, my father Francis died. He had reached his late seventies and the end of a long retirement in which he did less and less, apart from remembering to take pills. He was losing his eyesight. He refused most trips out of the house, since either his balance or his diabetic feet had stopped a full range of function. He had been thinking of writing a memoir entitled *Old Is Hell.* On a warm July morning, he passed away from complications after a massive cerebral hemorrhage, one that left him unconscious for several hours and then gone. I remember a kind of relief at hearing the news, as if I had willed it. Surely there were things worse than dying, for him. Perhaps not for me. I had no experience with loss of this kind, the grown child's loss.

His absence became the central fact of consciousness (and whatever lives below the consciousness) for months after, months when in the middle of a day I would pick up the phone to call him. That little space between intent and perception was a four-second nightmare and occasioned the same paranoia one feels upon frightening oneself awake in the middle of the night, completely alone. I would come to believe that losing the father is one of the primal scenes; you are stripped of whatever cant or desires had covered adult life thus far until consciousness turns raw, divulged; the mind does not negotiate the facts of what feels like a promotion to an unwanted post—the fatherless life—quickly enough. No one could have explained the completeness of such a loss, even how strangely banal it could feel at times. My love for him had been enormous, hagiographic. I experienced an ongoing nausea that I wasn't able to separate from self-indulgence, worrying whether I was living a life worthy of the sort of person I had believed him to be. This lasted longer than perhaps it should have. Randomly I would ask friends, Am I good? Do I seem like a good person? This, too, was pretty banal. These friends listened with patience and tact, but rather in the manner of the wealthy, uninvested. And they *were* wealthy, rich with self-esteem and fathers.

My mother had been there, waiting beside him, in intensive care. Later she told of feeling what other wives or children or devout relatives have claimed to feel at the precise moment of death, as the threshold is crossed, of the soul quitting, the body easing its weight. To her it had become perfectly clear that he was not in the room.

The notion that her husband had gone elsewhere felt appropriate if only for the fact that he had spent a portion of his adult life as an amateur theologian (he wrote articles on the role of the bishopric in the lives of poor Catholics and was ordained, after three years in seminary, a permanent deacon in the church). This was not an unusual question. What sort of afterlife had he imagined? What paradise? To my knowledge he accepted—cautiously—the popular premise of a "heaven" where everyone he had ever loved or lost appeared, gently took his hand, and led him through storms of nourishing, diaphanous white to record his name in the Book of Life. He also accepted—less cautiously and with greater intellectual interest—the most punitive side of religious belief, of an aggrieved God who sees all, who forgets nothing, and whose vengeance disgraces human comprehension, burrowing inside every excuse and deceit until nothing is left but the soul, a beaten thing.

In a dream he stood with strangers in a large room. Low-watt bulbs were screwed into the ceiling. He looked different, in the manner of dreams. He moved among the crowd, settling his hand on this or that person's arm. I fully understood he was dead. I believed he was somehow making amends. For what? By viewing dreams as projections, this meant he was making amends with his son, proving his love in abeyance. There he walked, offering words of consolation to everyone in the room, and he did not answer when I called his name. I kept calling his name. I was sick with the most rapturous physical longing for him to notice me. Disengagement crept in—gradually the feeling was like being drunk and sensing the sober self somewhere behind you, shouting commands to snap out of it. Slowly I relaxed into a different sensation, detached from longing or fear, and felt what could be the proper end of all grieving: gratitude. Grateful for the chance to watch him stand and walk on strong legs, to watch his face betray feeling; grateful even though the emotions flickering across his dreamed-up expression had altered somehow, enough to want to belong to someone else, a father I had never met. Then I woke up.*

I remembered, as a child in the next room, hearing his nightmares. He bayed and clawed the air like a man whose tongue had been cut out. They could have summoned memories of combat, drowning, falling, having to watch his children suffer—his peculiar phobias. They could have dressed and vivified sins, no matter how distant, no matter how petty, trusting as he did the dominance of sinfulness over that of his better nature. And I believe that once in a while the nightmares intimated a separate existence, hints of the extent to which he did not possess his own mind, of his soul placed in exile after death. For many of the patristic theologians he studied in retirement, to dream was to enter the element of time, no beginning and no end, sensing traces of the afterlife or even what preexistence we might have been wrenched from at the moment of birth. A single dream attempted, with its confusion of feeling and mysterious locations, to speak for a permanent state of the God-given soul: one's conscience provided the set, the dressing, the characters, the plotline, even the offer of revelation. To this kind of theologian, a penitent soul most deeply feared an afterlife in exile—realizing too late that one had not been good enough.

Not long after the funeral, an old Jesuit friend of my father's dis-

*Rather, Bill woke me up, loudly looking around the apartment for some other place to sleep.

cussed with me the idea of formal study at a seminary. He had known me since I was ten. He had always assumed I would follow in the father's steps and spend some time looking out from the interior of faith, my faith, such as it was. The idea accumulated weight. I had no responsibilities aside from paying rent and looking after Bill. The unremarkable job I had held for three years could be deferred. I started paying attention in Mass. I started *going* to Mass. I read Milton and Dante like travelogues. I studied textbooks on the subject of soteriology, the doctrine of salvation and placement in the next existence. Notions of God drifted in and out of varied incarnations— underlying patterns of nature, the grand enclosed firmament, even the white-bearded *abba* who lived in the sky—but these dissipated, settling eventually into element: a benevolent astral knowledge, stretching over the surface of this world and revealing itself in arcs of feeling, premonitions, dreams. God was perhaps what centuries of Platonists had speculated: pure mind. And if God were in fact the Great Mind, then an individual mind (made in the image of the celestial) was a weaker, messier, broken particle of the one that superseded all. Dreams partook in whatever visions the Great Mind had, visions where our own lives might conceivably exist in toto, reflective of an existence that was, like the universe whose matter we share, infinite. I slept and dreamed a room with poor light and strangers in need—there, moving through a crowd, all of him. Looking different in the manner of dreams meant that the rest of him, even the father before I came into his life, inhabited the same space. Here stood the complete soul, disclosed and revealing all available evidence of how good a man he had been, or failed to be.

I discussed pure mind with a few divinity-school graduates, each of whom listened and endorsed the idea of applying at their old schools (interdenominational) and living with the sorts of people who would enjoy discussing pure mind. I wrote the schools and dreamed the ascetic seminarian life. That life was focused and clean, as if anything blocking one's vision into a higher existence could be swept away as easily as garbage off a floor.

In March, I received a letter telling me I'd be moving to New York.

Bill had just received the second diagnosis and was unusually watchful, lying in his corner. Now that he and I would be leaving, I had difficulty seeing us in New York. How far away was the new doctor? Did taxicabs take large dogs? The nearest park was three blocks to the north, according to the school's map—if the attacks came at two in the morning, was it safe to walk him anywhere? What if he collapsed on the sidewalk? What if I had to carry all 110 pounds of him home?

Near the end of our time in that apartment, Bill placed himself in the most conspicuous locations—in doorways, in the middle of the front room—watching. I stepped over him and hauled boxes away. He climbed on the couch to sit beside me until there wasn't a couch to sit on anymore. Then we sat on a bare wooden floor, his chin in my lap, as more objects around us disappeared. He did not enjoy being separated for longer than a few minutes. Strangely, his health improved. He even stopped seizing, for a while, as if convinced that once he had regained consciousness and began his pacing through the rooms to find me, I'd already have gone.

III

In the city Bill needs his nose blown after each walk. He will not stop catching colds. Myelopathy, I had been warned, attacks the immune system as the nerves break apart, and Bill's system (according to the holistic vet) must have been seriously depressed from a life of seizing anyway. Filth collects along the sidewalks and tiny parks. His underside turns a darker shade, coated with gray dirt. I dress him in little rubber boots to protect his paws—his canine instincts are not so developed that he would refuse to lick a layer of urban grime from his own foot and catch some other, more exotic illness—and he accepts them stolidly, with evident shame. He reminds me of my father one birthday, unwrapping the gift of a cane.

After handling the filthy dog boots for several weeks, I'm the one who comes down with an upper bronchial infection. I am devastated and useless. Bill and I are alone in the seminary apartment. I cannot get out of bed. I think he understands this, even a bit. Hours pass where he sits on the floor and watches me convalesce.

New neighbors volunteer to help. I do not lack for good-intentioned neighbors at seminary. They appear a bit nervous when I refuse to let Bill go without an elaborate set of instructions. One young woman, a Methodist from Texas, listens to me describe worst-case scenarios. Move him to one side and wait to see if it's an attack. If it's an attack, don't try to open his mouth or keep his jaws open—he will easily snap one of your fingers—but let the seizure do its work. Once it passes, you have to get him up and walking in the other direction, back home, as quickly as possible, so that he can start recognizing familiar objects. He'll be blind, he'll be disoriented, and he might walk into traffic, so straddle him with both legs on the out-side of *his* hind legs as you move forward, like you're teaching him to walk. Talk to him the whole time, until he knows it's fine, you're there, he's not to be afraid, he's going home.

During the set of instructions, he taps the doorknob with his nose. The neighbor looks into his face. *Bill,* she says, smiling, and leads him out the door.

When they return, she nervously regards Bill, who regards me. What's wrong? Nothing, nothing, she says, twisting the leash around her hand. Does Bill also have arthritis? Tell me what happened. He just had trouble walking. What kind of trouble walking. First, he tripped. He tripped? He was nosing around the base of a hedge and then his front leg tripped on something and he hit his head and smacked his chin on the sidewalk. I said Bill, did you hurt your chin? He had this sideways expression like he was ashamed. He didn't get up. He put his head down. I waited for him to move but he just wanted to lie on the sidewalk. For like fifteen minutes. People stepped over him. When I convinced him to stand it took him forever. His back legs didn't work. Each time he tried to stand it looked like it hurt. He waited for me to help.

He does that, I say.

How long have you had him? How old is he, again? Is he in pain a lot?

Bill retreats into his corner, facing the bed. He sits and stares. Once the woman has gone, he continues to stare, grave and studious, like an attentive pupil. It is as if he were curious about what happened during his absence.

Are you sick?

Are you in pain a lot?

A painting of Sir Edwin Henry Landseer's, *Attachment,* depicts a small dog, some kind of blond terrier, placing its paw on the chest of its fallen master. The master is a young man wrapped in a heavy, wool-looking shawl, lying on a rock. Evergreen branches stick up out of the rock face. The master seems to have fallen while rock climbing. A jaunty fur cap has been knocked behind his head. His right hand is livid, broken. Distant godlike mountains loom to one side of the painting, while a magnificent sunset removes itself from the scene behind a storm of black clouds. Everything in the background is doomed and vague. The most concentrated expression is found on the face of the poor dog. He (or she) stares into the face of the young man. It is unclear whether the dog knows that the master is dying, whether the dog is preparing for a future of climbing back down the mountain alone, seeking shelter, seeking a new master, or whether the dog plans to stay—I think of course the dog stays—beside the young man until the young man is dead and the dog, too, expires from exhaustion, starvation, grief.

Composed in 1829, the scene had been inspired by Landseer's affection for a few lines by Sir Walter Scott:

> *How many long days and long weeks didst thou number,*
> *Ere he faded before thee, the friend of thy heart?*

A friend once explained to me that humans own pets so that something in our lives will die before we do. He was unpleasant, this friend. He'd owned several dogs in his life and frequently dispensed hard bits of wisdom to people who he thought needed shaking out of their bourgeois even keels. He explained that from our advantage— the guardian, the party responsible—we gain a first education in dying through witnessing a creature desperate to communicate a fear of mysterious looming death, a death plain enough to us. The frantic eyes, the lung rattle, the lurch, the almost-human cry that ends with a final clip of breath, and then the pet's soul is gone and nothing is there but a body that needs to be dealt with.

And what would the pets have done, how would they take the news, if their owners died first? Landseer's terrier with his paws on the master's lifeless arm—did he think he had done something wrong? His entire life had been in service. What was he going to do with himself?

The recurring fear, in our family, was that our mother would die first. No one among the grown children could contentedly picture Dad dressing or feeding himself for longer than a month alone— removing her from his presence would be a cruel reversal of the only acceptable scenario. Yet because it was cruel, to me that meant it was all the more possible. Even though he was the diabetic, the blood-pressure victim, the pacemaker patient, the recovering alcoholic, the one who had so clearly aged faster and harder, it could still happen— anything could happen. It seems a strange thing to hope for, but I did. And it was answered so easily, shorn of announcement: only after the funeral as I was holding the widow's hand did the realization hit.

When I call her now, Mom is surviving. She is a devout woman who believes that life alone must simply be what is asked of her. She sometimes forgets to eat meals, having grown accustomed through the years to making them only for him.

She asks about New York, about school. How is school?

The school is an old stone fortress with leaking pipes and broken glass in the stairwell windows. There is no vow of silence. There are few communal meals. Because of the mixed denominations, there is

no compline, and chapel each day is like watching a pleasant television infomercial with the volume down. Dogs are not allowed in the
center court, a rugby-field-size grassed area with benches and shrubs.
We do not read Milton or Dante. There is no lake of fire to contemplate, no wandering devils. Groups of serious young men and women
organize into caucuses and demand justice, fight for an end to world-
wide poverty, for inclusiveness and tolerance and change. Naves and
towers, ancient gray stone, this shared austere milieu—an untested,
nervous energy disturbs all ascetic feeling.

So time is spent in corners of the old stone fortress reading and
debating, constructing challenges to doctrine, to conventional thought
and liberalism, these sincere and progressive seminarians shaping
curriculum as an exercise in social justice as well as a kind of desperate prayer that one has begun setting down the clearest path to revelation. (Am I "good"? Do I merely want to *seem* like a good person?
Am I rational, therefore good? Will that save me? Who or what am
I being "good" for?) The energy pushes outward and hits the seminary walls; it returns to the students, all of whom make a habit of
testing each other, drawing unspoken requisites for what is involved
in recognizing what is good, what is not, what is merely adequate,
what is hopelessly false. No one agrees on the requisites. No one, for
example, believes that contemplative silence of the kind I originally
wanted to practice is much more than an indulgence—self-serving,
unheroic, recusing oneself from the demands of the difficult world,
the world of relationships, and pretending you understand what is
required for an upright existence, a good life, all alone. Asceticism is
solipsism resting on a hard mattress.

In one of the early-morning classes (systematic theology), a few
seminarians have convened around a table to debate questions of the
afterlife and as a possible punishment, under what conditions—if
one imagines, just imagines, the possible manifestations of all we believe to be true—one may be separated from God.

"Separated?" a woman says. "After service and love and working
for social justice, do I deserve to be separated?"

"But isn't that what they believe?" a young man interrupts. "The crazies? The literalists? Like, the very concept of heaven is some reward for piety or right behavior, something you *deserve*?"

Nearing the end of his life, my father found a few notions from a theologian named William Stringfellow fascinating to the point of obsession. When contending with an afterlife, said the theologian, one must see in the manner of the prophets, who quite conspicuously did not excuse themselves from the worst futures or the judgment to come. And that judgment could very well be thus: there is nothing more to existence than the life we have just left. To deny such an option would be to deny the intellect, everything we know, everything we are. It would deny the trial of faith.

"Has anyone here lost someone close?" I ask.

A young man, a Pentecostal, nods. "I have," he says. He waits a moment. "My father died a year ago."

"Where do you think he is, right now?"

The young Pentecostal smiles, a reflex, the smile of panic. "I can't think about that," he says, shaking his head. "I'm not ready to think about that yet."

During my father's funeral, as I listened to a robed priest speak of eternity and earthly reward, I imagined Dad restored to a much younger, more vigorous self and reunited with anyone he'd lost. There was probably a Book of Life at hand, somewhere. And why not? This afterlife was reward for being a good father, a good man. Whether he actually believed he was a good man, if he committed to that level of faith in oneself, was another question. Modesty could have prevented him from answering for his entire life with anything other than a humble conscience—facing the eschaton, poised at the end of existence—and for this he could have been exiled from God as punishment for living as the worst kind of human, one who fails to hope.

Imagine the next world, where a decent, loving, and virtuous life is judged to simply not be enough. Where would he—or I—conceivably go? I want to believe that my father could have accepted whatever conditions arose and upon judgment, standing in the outer darkness in a state of banishment, would still have something of the decency, virtue, and love I knew left in him. In the roomful of strangers, was Dad actually visiting those he had loved, or wronged? Or those who had wronged him? Was he forgiving? Or was I the one paying a visit, trying to express a son's love, assuring him he did fine?

To my mother I describe the unexpected melancholy in the face of the Pentecostal who is not willing to think about death just yet. I have touched a nerve. On the phone I can hear the emptiness of her house, no one calling her name, no one needing her to pause, hold the phone to her heart, and answer. I ask where she thinks Dad is, right now.

She says, Don't be afraid.

IV

From the front doors of the seminary up the street, two streets over, a little ways south to a grassed-in area—the walk is three blocks. The walk is now the hardest part of the day. Each afternoon when we exit the front doors, Bill narrows his eyes and smells the wind. He wants to stay put, standing and smelling the New York wind, something of Harlem, an Indian lunch counter, the Olive Tree Deli, Teachers College, other dogs. He doesn't want to move, but we have to go, I tell him, we can't stay put—I tug at his collar. His nose drags. Twice he falls. Construction workers stare at us. No one asks what's wrong. I hate people. People crowding his path, one complication in a series of complications: torn-up concrete, a steep grade, noise. Something pushes him now—the hind-leg nerves don't communicate to his brain that the legs should stop moving at the curb, so he continues into the street unless I crouch and wrap an arm around his neck, hugging his heavy body in place. One hind leg continues to move up and down, the pedaling cyclist shaking life into his muscles. His nose brushes my ear in what feels like a kiss.

Several years ago, on a drive across Missouri, I pulled off the highway and let Bill out of the car along a dirt road to pee. We had been
stuck in the car for six hours. He climbed out of the backseat and
onto the road, sniffed the air, and sat down. He sighed. I thought his
head was shaking, just a bit. I said, Bill, go pee. He stood and wandered into an overgrown ditch. He rooted around the tall grass, nose
to the earth. Some time passed. I walked in circles and found him
sitting in the ditch. His head still seemed to be shaking. I'd never
seen this. Was he about to seize? He yawned. Apart from the minute
head-shaking, he seemed fine. He clearly hadn't peed. Bill, I said, go
pee. I tried pushing him up. He went from a sitting to a reclining position and then rolled on to his back. Yes, that's very cute. Get up and
pee. He rolled over, then stood and wandered to the opposite ditch. I
followed. Whenever he found a new patch of weeds, I thought, *Here
we go,* then nothing. All of this must have taken half an hour. I
wanted to punch him in the head. I'd been his owner for two years.
If I were a father and he were a recalcitrant child of mine, I'd have
climbed into the car and driven away to make a point. I sat in the sun
and fumed—there were no trees, no shade. Bill stretched out on the
ground, shutting his eyes like a sunbather. I was tempted to leave this
place. He would not see me climb into the car and drive away. Later
he would emerge from the ditch with pieces of weed stuck to his
nose, sniff the air once more, and begin walking in whichever direction. He would walk about half a mile, having no idea where I was.
I could see him stop, turn his ears, wait a beat, continue. I could see
him wait, his dog brain entertaining ambiguities. The sun would set
on Bill sprawled asleep in the middle of a dirt road several miles
away. Later in the evening: headlights, a truck opening its bed, a
young man in a ball cap lifting this slow, oversize dog with strangely
weak legs—or not bothering to lift him at all, discovering him there
on the road with his head shaking and his legs rigid, the man perhaps thinking a stray had gotten into a pond covered with antifreeze
and would die on his own soon enough. Or maybe the man would
take him home and mysteriously discover after a few days that the

dog could not stop seizing, pissing, spitting over a clean kitchen floor. And then what? I walked to the ditch. I tried picking Bill up—he seemed to think this was funny—but I had not lifted him since he was a twenty-pound pup. I manhandled him onto his feet, and he treated it as a game, stepping away from me and looking back, sprinting forward when I ran up behind and shouted. He was a young dog out of doors and in possession of a master who for a minute had considered leaving him on the side of the road.

At last we reach the grassed-in area, and I unhook his leash. After smelling something curious blowing in from the Hudson, Bill falls on his side.

This seizure is weaker than normal and moves through the stages quickly, like a sped-up rehearsal. His muscles constrict until he looks like a statue, mouth agog, eyes shut tight as a fist. The pedaling starts. I'm kneeling beside him and holding his head up, rubbing his fur. The park is suddenly filled with onlookers. A man with dark hair shouts at me, What are you *doing*?

He's sick . . . he's seizing.

The man retreats a step. He wears a suit and holds a cup of coffee. I think he meant to sit on the nearest bench, but he is repulsed by this obscenity in the park. He mutters to another onlooker, a woman, then speeds down the path. The woman's hand is on her mouth—Is he . . . ? she says when our eyes meet. Other figures stand along the periphery as dull shapes. I want to cover his body. I am here to protect him, protect his dignity. I have never considered what he might be saying with the sideways glance, the shamed eyes, begging for a reprieve from indignity. The eyes of a dog. At those times I think I have seen another dog inside him, a perfect one. The one who slipped free and disappeared into spirit at the moment of birth, leaving the dog that needed ten pills a day to survive. Bill stops pedaling. His eyes are dilated, and he is panting his way into the next phase. I don't know if I should let him stand and risk another seizure or get him home so that if this seizure is the first of many more, then he won't have to suffer among strangers. I touch his nose. I think he recog-

nizes the scent. I think the worst filth of New York is crowded along
the ground, and I think leaving him here while I go for help would
make him even sicker. I pick him up.

One arm around his chest and one behind his tail, I am half
bouncing down the road, walking the steep grade, past the workers,
the torn-up concrete. Something rips below my shoulder blade. I am
already running out of breath. Turning a corner, I pray that I don't
trip and drop him onto his soft legs. My arms are going to fail. My
face is contorted. A bus halts to my right. I feel more onlookers appear, gawk, and move in the other direction. Another muscle rips.
I'm talking to Bill. You're fine, I tell him, you're all right. *You're perfect.* His neck is limp. He raises his head once, looking forward. He
is recalling where he is and who has him. It must be like riding in the
back of a van, stretching across the nearest backseat, dreaming. He
lays his head into the fold of my arm. I have never loved him more. If
I dreamed this event—a public seizure, useless strangers, the rush
home—then I failed to imagine Bill's head falling back and finding
a place to rest, his brain somehow overriding the misfires and trusting with a greater instinct that someone is there who promises, and
promises, not to let him suffer alone.

V

Sometime in November he seized what would be the last time, a
grand mal seizure, then only wanted to sleep. He slept for two days.
I brought him his bowl, his water. He didn't move. After three days
he couldn't move. On the fourth day, I phoned a vet on 101st street.

Regarding euthanasia, I had heard that dogs always know.
When death is coming, they *know.* They kindly signal the owner to
make the owner feel it's all right, that the dog understands all about
impossible decisions and options that have been reduced one by one.
I had once heard that dogs dream death, smell it on the wind. What
does it smell like? Of the infirm, or the weakest in the pack? Does it
smell like something is burning? Is the dog afraid? Does he know

he's going someplace new, alone? Bill's attacks always obliterated his senses just long enough for him to seem unsure of what was going to happen next. After he recovered, he kept his eyes on a precious few inches of ground ahead of him, staying upright and walking. A room came into focus. He looked at me until I looked like his master again. Those last moments in a strange city, on his side in the strange vet's office about to die, what he most wanted to do was to go back home. I knew my dog. He didn't know.

All the nightmares I once had of failing him have been replaced with a different dream: Late at night, after a series of seizures, Bill crying in the next room. I am stunned and exhausted and lying on my own bed, waiting for further movement and fearing the familiar sounds of an aura as it begins one more time. But he falls asleep. I fall asleep. Hours pass before I wake to hear his nails click on the wooden floor as he searches our apartment, room after room—at this point I do not know whether I am awake—and I think that he has found me.

I want to call his name. Bill, oh, hello, *Bill.*

Each night an ascetic quiet takes over the seminary like something neatly placed upon it. Early mornings are ghost white, the windows a dense and pretty blue. I am still a light sleeper. Several times I have returned to the room of strangers and shouted instructions at Dad, telling him he did fine, which he does not hear. In a popular psychology of dreams, this means I am talking to myself, pleading, shouting assurances into a mirror. In various soteriological arguments found on the shelves in my seminary apartment, this means that the room could be Dad's heaven, or where he had been banished upon judgment, the place from which he would make the best of things, knowing he could do nothing but be himself, stripped now to the soul. If one honestly believes in a soul, one might consider that the soul itself is good and that this cover of mortal life, with its companions and loves, is hesitant and messy. That is its nature. But the deeper one falls into the bottomless soul, the more one begins to see the potential for goodness, the instinctive motions that hasten our good deeds into being, and the ground of what may assemble the greatest, most selfless and enduring love—*great above all human estimation*—yet reachable only in glimpses, in premonitions and dreams. In dreams there is revelation.

Not long ago one of my brothers called to tell me of a dream where he met up with our father in a large room crowded with strangers. My brother was overwhelmed, clutching at his senses. Dad! he shouted. Dad! How did you get here! He was nearly driven crazy with happiness. But our father said nothing. He smiled, that was it. But a smile! What did this mean? That we shouldn't be afraid? Dad, what was the thing we shouldn't be afraid of?

The Big Kahuna

YANNICK MURPHY

I'd like to write about my Newfoundland, Tom, but I don't have the time. I was going to start writing about him earlier, when I realized I should be grooming him instead. I took out his combs, and my four-year-old daughter, Kit, and I set to work on the porch. Newfoundlands are big dogs. Tom weighs around 150 pounds. The amount of hair he has on him is impressive. Kit and I groomed for a good hour, and we had groomed only one side of him. We had filled up a bucket with his dead hair and would have to empty it if we wanted to keep on grooming, but Tom didn't want us to keep grooming him. He stood up from the porch and looked at me and let out a single, deep baritone "woof." Then he turned to put his mouth on my wrist and let me feel the slightest pressure from his teeth, his way of letting me know there would be no more grooming today. Then the mail came, but the six-foot linebacker-looking mailman did not want to deliver our mail to our mailbox on the porch because the dog was there. Every mailman is afraid of Tom, despite the fact that Tom loves people, and when he meets them, he puts his ears way down and wears a smile and his tail way up, swooping gently back and forth in a friendly wag. So I had to tell little Kit to go take the mail from the six-foot linebacker-looking mailman as he stood out on the sidewalk at a safe distance. When Kit brought the mail back, there was the *Newf Tide* magazine, which I had to leaf through because we want to get a new Newfoundland puppy to keep Tom company and the *Newf Tide* lists breeders.

I went back inside the house with Tom and Kit. I thought I would sit and start writing about Tom, but then Tom went out to the back-yard and stood at his water bowl and let out another "woof," his way of letting me know he was thirsty. After he was watered off, I went back inside the house and sat down at my computer. Kit was quietly working on a floor puzzle in the living room, and I thought now was the time I could start writing about Tom. I had put the mail on my desk, and while my computer was warming up, I decided to leaf through the *Newf Tide* some more. In the back of the *Newf Tide,* there are all these photos of dogs who've recently died, and the own-ers wrote a sentence or so that say things like, "Farewell to our first Newfoundland, our first love," or they say the dog's name and then "Loved and owned by" so-and-so, or "To know him was to love him." And I always get misty-eyed reading them, so by the time my computer was warmed up, my vision was all blurry, and I had to rub my eyes awhile in order to focus on the page.

I was about to begin when Tom started doing this thing that he does before he settles in for a nap. He takes his front paw and scrapes at the floor. He'll scrape the carpet or the tile or the linoleum, de-pending on which room he is in. I don't know why he does this; maybe he thinks that, as he can with dirt, he can scrape up the floor and find a cool place to lie in. Tom was in my office when he decided to do his scraping on the carpet, and I could not think with the terri-ble noise it made.

"Shh, knock it off," I said to Tom, but Tom did not knock it off. The scraping continued. "Enough, Tom!" I said, but still he did not stop. I reached for a rubber eraser on my desk and lobbed it at him. It bounced off his big, square, black head, and he did not even blink. He simply continued to scrape. "Jesus, Tom," I said. There was a hardcover book on my desk, a pretty long, big one. I was considering how much it would hurt him if I threw that at him and that maybe I should opt for a paperback instead, when suddenly he stopped and let his body fall to the carpet with a big *whump* that sent up dust motes, and some of his old shed hairs floated through the air because the vacuum and I have not crossed paths in a good long time. I thought I would vacuum earlier, but I put it off because I have this essay to write about Tom.

Good, I can begin writing now. He's finally asleep, I thought while I sat at my desk. But then Tom started snoring. Tom snores louder than Jeff, who is my husband. Tom snores so loud that when I am talking on the phone and Tom is snoring in the background, the caller sometimes asks me to call back, that there seems to be a bad connection, an awful static on the line.

It is not easy to get Tom up once he's asleep.

"Tom, get up," I said, and walked over to him and shook him. He did not stop his snoring. I pulled up on his collar, but all that did was make him roll over onto his side, and the snoring did not stop.

"Tom, get up," I said again, bending down low and lifting his big flap of an ear the size of a man's toupee. Tom does not have the best hearing, so sometimes speaking directly into his ear helps. Tom opened up his eyes, but then he closed his eyes again, and the snoring went on.

"Tom, squirrel!" I said, because sometimes this works, and he will get up and run to the backyard, looking for a squirrel that is not there. Tom opened up his eyes again, but this time he looked at me. I was crouching low down to him when I was talking into his ear, and he must have thought I was there to play with him. He took his front leg and threw it over my back and pulled me down beside him on the carpet. He can do this because he is so strong and big. Then he stood over me. When he does this and I try to push him off, he just digs in, and I can't move him at all. A feeling of complete helplessness comes over me, and I start to giggle. When I giggle, he begins to lick my face.

Now is the time to talk about Tom's tongue, which is always hanging down outside his mouth. Tom's tongue is so long and huge it verges on obscene, and Jeff, my husband, loves to tell women who comment on the size of Tom's tongue while he's walking Tom that if you think his tongue is big, you should see his member. Jeff has a strange sense of humor, but luckily he mumbles, so half the time no one can understand what he's just said.

When Tom licks me, his slobber gets all over my face. It also gets all over my ears, because Tom likes to lick ears. He likes to nibble at my lobes, ever so gently. You could not believe for a dog that big he could work his front teeth so that they could nibble this gently, but he does.

Also, Tom's slobber really stinks. It is a distinct smell that other Newfoundlands also have. After he was done licking me, he walked off and lumbered to another room. Tom doesn't just lie down on the floor, he collapses onto the floor. If he is in the kitchen, you can hear his bones falling there onto the hard linoleum. It sounds like someone just set down a sack of logs. I could not get up and go back to my computer quite yet; I had to go to the bathroom and load the soap up on my palms and scrub my hands and face. I had to pull some soap through the strands of hair by my ears and rinse that off, too; otherwise I would smell like Newfoundland until I showered the next day.

By this time Kit was tired of doing her puzzle by herself in the living room. I spent a while helping her, and then I began thinking how I'd better get back to the computer and start that essay. This is when Tom came into the room and sat down next to me and started to bark. I don't wear a watch. I don't have to. Tom lets me know that my other children, Hank and Louisa, will be home soon and that Jeff will be home soon, too, and that it's time to start cooking dinner.

Tom barks and barks at me until I get up and go into the kitchen and start pulling out the ingredients from the fridge. He follows me into the kitchen and then crashes down, with his chin resting on the floor and his eyes open, following my moves. In our kitchen, if Tom is lying down, he is so big and long that he blocks my path from the sink to the refrigerator. He also blocks the cupboards where I keep my baking pans and dishes. He also blocks the stove, so that I cannot open the oven door. I usually have to spread my legs wide and step over him in order to go from one part of the kitchen to the next. Sometimes I misjudge, and while he is lying down, I step on his tongue, which as I said before is always hanging out. Cooking is not all that easy to do with Tom around. But at least when I cook, he stops barking, because I am now in the kitchen making the family dinner, which is what I'm supposed to be doing at this hour, because he knows that during our meal he gets fed.

There is some dog-training advice that says you are to feed your dog after the meal so that he knows he is not the big kahuna and that you are the big kahuna instead. Tom and Jeff are not aware of this advice. At dinner Tom is the perfect height for resting his chin on the tabletop, and that is what he does. Jeff always puts some food from his plate in front of Tom on the tabletop, and Tom extends his long, pink tongue out and licks it up. This makes the tabletop all slobbery, and after dinner I have to use extra soap and water so that the table does not still feel slippery from the slobber.

After dinner Jeff and Kit and Hank and Louisa and I sit reading in the living room for a little bit. But this does not last long, because Tom comes into the room and barks. His way of letting us know that it's time for his walk. "You go walk the dog. I've got to work on this essay," I say to Jeff, but Jeff says we should all walk together, since the kids have not had much exercise and we have not had much exercise. Hank and Louisa get on their bikes, and Kit gets on her tricycle, and Jeff and I walk taking turns holding Tom by his leash.

We walk Tom on the streets in our neighborhood and through the city-college campus near our house. When we walk by people talking on their cell phones, Tom thinks they are talking to him, so he pulls toward them wagging his tail. A lot of the time, people are walking over to say hello to him, and at the same time they are saying, "That's the biggest dog I've ever seen." Or they are saying, "Is that a bear?" Or they are saying, "Look at the size of that tongue!" Other times people are not walking toward him but stepping back away from him, afraid, sometimes flattening themselves against the nearest wall and sucking in their breath.

Once, on one of our walks, Tom was invited into the room where the city-college orchestra practices. The conductor was so amazed at how big and beautiful Tom is that the conductor wanted to show the rest of the orchestra. Violinists raised their bows and violins in the air to protect them, and sheet music sailed off metal stands when Tom crashed through the room. The tuba players, who were big guys, seemed to have a particular affection for such a big dog, and they stuck their faces close to Tom and hugged him, and Tom barked at the distorted reflection of himself in the big brass bells of their tubas.

Taking Tom for a quick walk is never an option. Every time we take him, there is at least one person who wants us to stop in order to pet Tom. Often the person who has stopped us had Newfoundlands when he or she was growing up. Lately we have been telling the person that we are also in the process of finding another Newfoundland puppy, and the person replies that they are such great dogs, you can't have just one. Of course we agree.

Some people who stop us do not know that Tom is a Newfoundland, and they insist that he is a black St. Bernard. Jeff tells them, "Yes, you are right, he is indeed a black St. Bernard," because Jeff does not want anyone else who is the type of person who insists he knows something when he's wrong getting a Newfoundland. Jeff thinks he is preventing the breed from being overbred and sold to dumb people by not disclosing the true name of the breed. If the breed is overbred, Jeff is afraid the gentle nature of a Newfoundland might turn.

There are some people who don't assume right away that Tom is a black St. Bernard, and when those people ask what kind of dog he is, Jeff tells them he is a Newfoundland, and then Jeff feels it's his responsibility to tell them a little bit about the breed, like how they were brought over to this continent by the Vikings and how they were once the most popular breed of dog in America one hundred years ago and how they are now trained to jump from boats and low-flying helicopters to save drowning victims' lives, because they love to swim and protect people. Then Jeff will lift up Tom's huge black paw and show them how Tom's paw is webbed between his toes and how this makes him an excellent swimmer. Jeff will also show people how Tom's heavy coat is perfect for swimming in cold waters, and he will have them run their hands through Tom's coat and fan back his topmost hairs.

Most of all, though, Jeff impresses upon these people how Tom is the world's most gentle, low-key dog. He is loyal and loving toward us, and he never asks for much. Newfoundlands, Jeff explains, are not the kind of dogs that constantly come up under your hand for a pet. You do not have to worry about them around other dogs because they are friendly and good-natured, and you do not have to worry about robbers because anyone who comes through the door is always afraid of the huge black dog, because the huge black dog is running up to that person at full speed, because the huge black dog thinks that anyone who has come through the door has come through for the sole purpose of becoming his lifelong friend.

When we return home from our walk, Tom walks straight to the backyard and stands by his water bowl. If one of us takes too long to go back there and give him some more water, then he gives a bark or two.

After the children brush their teeth and get into bed, Tom comes in and lies on their beds, the water he drank dripping down his chin, his chest, and onto their covers. When this happens, the kids begin to yell and scream that their beds are getting soaking wet, and Jeff and I have to go in there and tell the kids that Tom is just saying good night to them and that their beds are not getting too wet. We tell them to say good-night to their dog and give him a kiss and a pet, which they do, and Tom looks up at them gratefully with his big, soft, brown eyes, and then he decides now's his chance to lick them, and so he starts on Kit, the littlest. He starts to lick her all over, since she is not yet wearing any pajamas, and she runs from the room holding her hands slapped to the cheeks of her bottom to keep Tom from licking her there, and she's shrieking, "Ahh, Tom's lickin' me!" as Tom chases after her, and so Jeff has to tell Tom to leave the kids alone and let them get some sleep. Tom then gets up and usually walks into the bathroom and collapses there to sleep on the cool tile floor.

I begin to think how I can sit down at my computer now and finally start that essay about Tom, but then Jeff tells me it is too late for that. He thinks I should just get up at five in the morning and start writing the essay after I've had a good night's sleep. Jeff's idea sounds like a good one, so I go to bed.

I fall asleep quickly, but a few hours later I am awakened by the sound of Tom scraping the floor with his paw in the kitchen. He is scraping so furiously that he knocks over one of the kitchen chairs, and it crashes to the floor. That's all right, though. I know it's just Tom. I fall back to sleep, but only to be awakened an hour later by the creepy sound of someone walking through the house, making the floorboards creak with his weight. I listen long enough to realize that we are not Sharon Tate and her friends and it is not Charles Manson come to slay us in our sleep, but that it is just Tom relocating from his spot in the kitchen and walking past our bedroom door and into the living room.

I shut my eyes, and sleep comes again. But two hours later I am awakened. This time by the bedroom door flying open and banging against the wall. *Oh, my God,* is my first thought, *it really is Charles Manson come to slay us in our sleep!* But then it is just Tom, who comes to the side of the bed and puts his nose into Jeff's face and smells him, checking to make sure he is all right, and then Tom flops down to the floor, sliding his body against the side of the bed as he goes, which makes the bed shake, and then Tom starts snoring so loud that I can hear the loose panes in the windows of our old house start to make a soft *tick-tick-ticking* sound as they vibrate in their rotting frames in response to Tom's body vibrating with his snoring.

So it is 4:00 A.M. now, and I am wide awake. Now is as good a time as any to get started on that essay. If I had woken up at five, it probably wouldn't have been enough time to start in on the essay. I have Tom to thank for getting me up extra early. I sit down at my computer. I think of all the wonderful things I will say about Tom. I think of the stories I will tell how he pined for a day by my daughter and would not leave her side when she had the flu. I think how the essay will put Old Yeller to shame and make Lassie look lazy. I have such high hopes for the essay—it will be a work of art, a tribute to a great dog and my family's love for him. Then my eyes start to well up with tears at just the thought of what I will write, and it is not until I take a tissue and wipe the tears away and blow my nose that I can finally start typing.

Our Little Jack, the Runner

BARRY HANNAH

It was nearing Christmas, ten years ago. Dark, bleak, raining, fog and high mists. We'd had Woody for just a few weeks. He was a corgi and shepherd mix, a blend low to the ground with big ears and a sweet snout whom we'd taken from the brood of a mother owned by a friend of ours, Chico Harris. Woody's little chubby figure was so dear that the college girls who lived next to us on Eagle Spring Road would knock at our door and ask if they could play with him for a while or walk him.

Woody was a born digger and roamer, completely set in a lane that drew him to folks and adventures. We neutered him, but to our grief he still had to run wild. Chico told us his mother was so crazy to get out of his home that despite his putting Tabasco sauce on the windowsill, she chewed a hole in the wooden frame and escaped.

At dusk one night, Woody found a running pal in a loose Labrador and went off with him. We looked all over our suburb and then much of the town, calling for him for three awful days. A friend in the neighborhood who jogged everywhere finally came to us with the news. Woody's corpse lay on a curb on Price Street, where the speed limit was twenty miles per hour. We buried his little body in the backyard near the willow tree.

I was so depressed I couldn't work, eat, or sleep much, and my wife, Susan, couldn't forgive herself for allowing Woody outside at dusk. We shared the emotion of the writer Samuel Beckett, who said that at the death of his Kerry blue terrier he wanted to climb into the grave with him.

Anybody can avoid an animal if they drive thirty in this small city with wide avenues. But I've seen police speeding recklessly, frat boys, coeds talking on their cell phones driving deadly fast in their BMWs around this university town.

A negligent law-school student changing a CD on a hill with a caution light ran over Chico and his faithful companion, the twelve-year-old Wayne, as they walked, just walked across the street right over the hill.

Chico's first words when he awoke in the hospital were "How is Wayne?" He was dead. The awful slaughter almost killed Chico, who has limped around the streets of Oxford in great pain for ten years now.

We held a benefit for Chico called "Wayne's Night." I read a brief eulogy for Wayne, telling the old Indian story of the Great Father splitting the animal and human kingdoms by rending a great chasm in the earth. The dog jumped over to the human side.

So much unbearable sadness led me to the Oxford pound. I was brought to see an Italian greyhound–fox terrier mix cowering at the back of the pen, who then came rushing to me bashfully. His name was Francis, which wouldn't do at all. An old woman incapable of keeping him any longer had dumped him here.

I knew that this was a universal compensation for the unbearable sorrow that attends the loss of a beloved animal. I hardly cared. Grief makes us all a cliché, no?

He was in such distress, so lean and handsome, I had to have him, and he had to have me.

I carried him in my arms after paying the fee for the shots, et cetera. A mere seventy-five bucks, as I recall. The best investment I ever made. Sorrow was leaving me as I took in this trembling animal's sorrow and petted him. Abandoned by some person who had given him the name Francis. Who could have left this exquisite creature in the pound?

He clung to me as I headed over to the university museum where my wife worked to introduce her to our new pal. I wanted to call him Bob, but my wife won out with the name Jack, and she was right, because his beautiful running and jumping, like a jack-in-the-box, made his name perfect.

His whole life this wonderful creature trembled, frightened of something, it seemed. Maybe it was just the mixed breed. His little body was handsome, white fur with black saddle spots, tiny pencil-thin ankles, and feet with needle-sharp toenails that could put serious scratches on you. But the dog meant no harm. He meant to hug you close and get rid of his fear.

We had nine years with this fawnlike dog. He became my writing pal, curled up on the floor under my feet or more often in my lap as I typed. He was feather light, maybe ten pounds. Ten pounds of racing dog wild to run up the hills, around the yard, and down the steep road we live on. His uncanny speed and grace made you glad in the untouched hollows of your heart when you had the vision of Jack running, with our other five dogs.

Gentle readers don't need to be told how much a dog gives you. Jack was a delight. Nine years of spiritual lift through cancer, the medical and financial catastrophe that hit both Susan and me. Our money, even with health insurance, was turning into Monopoly cash. Jack and the other dogs lifted us, despite the trouble of their care, which Susan mainly handled after she quit the museum staff.

Came the leash laws and we built a fence around our large yard. But Jack was slim and could make his way through two loose pickets of the fence.

Jack was not an alpha dog. Unfortunately, we had another terrier mix, the very chubby Jill, who was a car chaser. She was alpha, and Jack began imitating her, snapping at tires and running perilously ahead of them, because he could. But we lived on a dead-end street, and the neighbors, old people mostly, were kind and courteous enough to drive slowly until the dogs gave up the chase.

Jack last ran and jumped down the neighbor's hill on Easter three years ago. My wife was in the front yard when Jack was hit and heard the thud. The little creature fought for his life all night with Harry, our vet, trying to save him. But Jack lost. Harry couldn't bring him back, staying all night with him, bless Harry. I was in Knoxville reading at the university and seeing my son and his wife and their children when Susan called.

In Knoxville, I went instantly into serious decline. An ex-drunk, I began drinking vodka and orange juice as fast as I could, crying. I'd not had a drink in fifteen years.

I don't have to instruct you on sorrow. My health dropped, my work was poor, I was drinking bourbon at home and raving about a lawsuit.

The driver of the death car, a Suburban, sent, get this, an arrangement of hibiscus flowers in condolence. Susan sent them promptly back. In a nanosecond the woman had made road offal of our trembling beauty. Couldn't she have driven slowly, paying attention to the road, where squirrels and deer and loose dogs play? No. She did not even have the honor to offer to pay Jack's vet bill, about six hundred dollars.

I moved my twelve-gauge pump with number-four shot to the front door. I follow Christ and cannot, of course, shoot a person. But I can damn well shoot a car. I've never seen the woman, but I know the car. All four tires and windshield.

———

My sorrow remains raw. I'm better as I remember the sweet times with Jack, who's buried with a stone angel over him in our backyard, where many of our pets have found a home as we wept. But this follower of Christ cannot *be* Christ. My rage is still undiminished.

The shotgun leans, loaded and ready.

You will say I am sick. You betcha.

Schnauzer, Talking

LEE MONTGOMERY

My dog reads lips. It is a Sunday afternoon, and I'm lying in a hot bath watching the dog watch me. He stands on his hind legs, places his front paws on the edge of the bathtub. *Time for dinner?* I mouth. His head cocks to the right. *Is there anyone here who wants to go for a hike?* His head cocks to the left, his ears fold forward at floppy disheveled attention. I give him a whale eye, bare my teeth, flick my tongue—dog talk. He jumps down, runs out the door, down the stairs and back. He climbs up on the edge of the tub again. I hold out a palmful of water that he laps at. I then push my hand forcefully into the water and swish it around at the bottom of the tub. He waits there, looking into the water. He looks at me. At the water. Me. Water.

"Blubblubblub," I say, and go under. He jumps to attention, studying the situation. "Blubblubblub," I say again, spitting a plume of water into the air. He cocks his head and whines.

It's a toss-up who might be stranger, since I am supposed to be a grown-up operating in a "sophisticated" world, but let us put that aside for a moment and consider this dog and his particular doggyness or lack of. His name is Pnut. He is a schnauzer, the miniature variety, now eight years old, a male, black as ink, stocky. He measures two feet long from the tip of his nose to the tip of his tail, one foot high with shortish legs. At two feet around, he is far from svelte, a bit tubby at twenty-four pounds. He has silky ears shaped like valentine hearts, a little bigger than silver dollars. He wears a beard, eyebrows, and has terrifically bad breath due to the teeth rotting out of his head even though we brush them almost daily and take him for biannual cleanings. He is undisputedly a dog, but doesn't always act like one. His overall gestalt is that of an old gentleman with a bit of the jack of hearts thrown in—and, when excited, a Spanish flair, something of a flamenco dancer. My husband, Tom, says if you put your ear up next to Pnut's head, you would hear Ferris wheel music.

"The dog part," Tom instructs Pnut almost daily. "Don't forget the dog part."

We have another schnauzer, a rescue schnauzer named Luna, a four-year-old black-and-silver female, who *is* a dog, *an alpha dog.* She takes her job as lady of the house quite seriously. She patrols the perimeter. She runs errands. She chases squirrels! But not Pnut. He has an active inner life; he's part dog, part something else—a mystic or an empath of a higher order.

He is particular. He does not bark for his bone. He does not jump. He waits until you offer one to him, and then he gently takes it in his mouth, puts it down, and looks up at you as if to say, *Thanks, I am grateful to you and your generosity,* finally trotting off to hide it for later or sitting down for a good long chew. He is picky about where he eats his bones. Like a dog, he buries them in the yard, but not if it's raining, because God knows dogs in Oregon do not like the rain. Often he carries them around the house, hiding them under couch pillows or in the bed.

He cannot deal with loud noises. He runs for cover when he hears planes overhead. He shivers at the sound of the garbage trucks turning the corner, trembles at the sound of thunder, and shudders uncontrollably on the Fourth of July at the sound of fireworks. He does not bark to come in. He sits by the back door and waits. He does not bark when people arrive. He throws his snout in the air, lifts his front two paws off the floor, and hoots like an owl. He only barks—and does so quite seriously—when guests begin to gather their things *to leave*. He follows them around and barks, barks, barks, at least an octave higher than his pal Luna. What he's saying, we can only guess— *Hey! Hey! Where are you going?*—as they head out the door.

He also talks. Incessantly. He talks when you speak to him. He talks when you brush his teeth. He talks when you pat him, give him a bath, pick him up, put him down, open the door, shut the door. He varies notes for different expressions. He can actually keep a tune. "It's so nice to have a man around the house," I sing, and his chat—a low pitched growl-like thing—follows the notes: *Do re mi fa . . . .* "Somewhere over the rainbow . . ." same thing. I pat his bottom, and he *grrrrs* to the rhythm, sounding a bit like a cross between a Muslim prayer call, a bear, and the grinding of a car engine with a carburetor problem.

"Does this hurt?" we ask Pnut, placing a fingertip on his head. He growls a response. "Does this hurt?" We move the finger gently down his back. He growls louder. We continue on this track a few more times, finally sticking our finger in the air. "Does this hurt?" And he growls even louder. We take out our hand, shape it into a mock gun, and make shooting sounds. He collapses, growling. People's reactions are always the same. They laugh and then look very concerned. "Is he okay?" they ask with alarm. "Sure." I point to his tail, a stublike thing, which is wagging rapidly. "Pnut," I say. *Grrrrr,* he says back, and wiggles harder, so hard, in fact, that the stub moves back and forth five wiggles a second and then his whole bottom wiggles, too, hinging at the hip—*right, left*—the tail stub actually acting as the propeller.

He also sings a high-pitched song when he sees anything worth noting at the front door. He stands on his hind legs looking out the French door overlooking the street and starts slowly, a very high-note yodel, swirling into a wild howl reminiscent of coyote calls, into a hysterical sirenlike singing.

"Don't be so gay," Tom says. "Pnut, don't be so gay."

And Pnut chases Tom and hoots shrilly.

Pnut *loves* the ocean but does not like to swim. No, he likes to wade into the water so it covers his back but not his head, often standing in the water with just his head poking out. He loves baths, especially since we put in a huge claw-foot tub with a hand shower. As the warm water cascades down his back, he groans with pleasure issuing instructions: *A little to the left, a little to the right.*

He enjoys pats but adores a good tickle and moans his delight as you lightly graze your fingertips over his head. He also likes to sleep on the chiropractic pillow, enjoying the fancy foam, the give in the pillow, and the support of his back, because he sleeps on his back, head on the pillow, feet in the air. And when we first got our fancy Tempur-Pedic mattress, Tom renamed it the Tempur-Pnut because no one could convince Pnut to get out of bed.

Grrrr, he says. *I would prefer to stay here, thank you.*

In his early years, we called Pnut "Wiggle Bottom" or "Mr. Pnut Wiggle Bottom," so rapidly he shook his ass. And we didn't give him the traditional haircut but shaved only his head, letting the rest of him grow out into this wild Afro so he resembled an English sheepdog, a sort of miniature black English sheep schnauzer. When people asked what kind of dog he was, we told them he was a Welsh Highland Sufi sheep schnauzer.

Later we nicknamed him "Stinky." Luna is "Stinky," too. Together they are "The Stinkies," and our home, a beautiful little Victorian in downtown Portland, is "Stinkytown." And while Stinkies share character qualities, they also approach life differently. Luna conducts her life chaotically, like a dog. Pnut has a different philosophy. He approaches life logically, almost ritualistically. He is a firm believer in routine. There are things he must attend to every day, and he does so each day at the same time, never varying his route unless we are on vacation. First order of business after being pushed out of bed is to go outside to pee. After that he sniffs around the kitchen, checks out the food bowl, has a drink, but only if the water is clean. If not, he stands around the sink and smacks his lips until someone cleans out the water bowl and draws fresh, cold water. Next order of business and big event of the day before following the sun around the house is Stink Patrol. *Sniff, sniff sniff.* He searches for stink with religious devotion. Bathrooms first. Check the toilet, the laundry hamper, the wastebaskets for snot rags and other goodies—for example, used tampons, already-chewed gum, leftover food, apple cores—and then nose around inside the gym bags. On a good day, he finds my husband's gym shorts and pulls them out of the gym bag and sets about chewing the crotch. On a very good day, he'll find my underwear in the hamper, too, and on a three-star banner day, he can raid the suitcase and steal the underwear of some unsuspecting houseguest, chewing the crotch out and then hiding it under the couch for us to find only later, much later, after Pnut has used it for his other daily practice.

Masturbating.

As Tom says, *Twenty-four pounds of pure chocolate love who loves the love*—and who makes love to himself all the time. Or, I should say, makes love with his dog bed, nightly, after his dinner.

He has been doing this for as long as I can remember, disappearing after dinner, finding his dog bed, pushing it around the room with his snout, and then folding it carefully into quarters, jumping on it, and going to town. If he has a bone or has found someone's underwear to throw in the middle of the dog bed before folding, all the better. He does this with Jeffrey Dahmer–like ritualistic devotion, at the same time every night. The vet says he does this because we never had him fixed, but I've never neutered any dog, and he's the first one who seems to be driven to this daily. Tom and I have learned to turn our heads, but it makes no difference to Pnut; he carries on no matter what: dinner party, house full of people. On vacation Pnut seems to think that he deserves two sessions a day, so he rearranges his morning schedule and delays Stink Patrol to throw around his dog bed. I usually find him later in a heap of delighted, ecstatic exhaustion, inside the dog bed or under it, chin on the edge. As the Sufi mystic Jelaluddin Rumi once wrote, *Love has taken away my practice and filled me with poetry.*

Luna sometimes has enough and barks at him to stop, but he doesn't pay much attention to her, or anyone for that matter. We have all learned to work around his schedule. When we have people for dinner, Tom will shut the door to the kitchen, only to peek in a little later to ask, "Is our little friend done?" If so, he will keep the door open and people will trickle back to keep me company while I cook. If not, we wait.

When Tom and I first moved to Portland, Oregon, one of the many marvels of the Pacific Northwest—-besides a Nazi-like recycling company, eternal darkness, the term "hunter moon" (versus "harvest")—was our new hometown newspaper. There was the "Writing in the Rain" column, the Metro section (full of the most phenomenally kinky low-rent small-town news), the hunting-guide special sections, and, completely new to us, a pet column. I love animals, but I had never noticed pet columns in any newspaper in any city we had lived in so far (Los Angeles, Boston, Paris, New York). The column was accompanied by a photograph of the columnist, a cheerful woman with a face shaped like the aforementioned moon, and her dog, a tiny thing with a pointy nose and ears like a fox. Early on, the pet column was buried deep within the lifestyle section, but each year the column has moved forward in prominence and is now frequently trumping other columns about art, fashion, and architecture. Reading it has become a family tradition. Whoever gets up first—usually Tom—makes coffee, lets Luna out, grabs the morning newspaper, and then gets back into bed, where we lounge, read the paper, and catch up on the pet column.

"Uh-oh," Tom announces. "She's stepping out," he says louder. "Above the fold!" We all wait for the performance, the dogs, now firmly ensconced in their proper spots, Pnut sitting between my legs stretched out, draped out over my thigh, and Luna buried under the covers between us. Tom will begin with the headlines—BIG MEN, LITTLE DOGS! Or, as he did a few months ago, PET PSYCHIC ON SATURDAY!

The pet psychic caught my attention. Maybe, I thought, she would have some insight into Pnut's rituals and the masturbation deal.

"Do you tell him where you're going and what time you will return?" is what she comes up with. We are sitting in our living room on a Saturday morning.

"This is what I suggest," she says. "When you leave, let Pnut know where you're going and what time you will return."

Tom and I look at Pnut, who is sleeping on my lap.

"He wants to know where you're going," she insists. "And while you're out but about to head home, give him a little psychic hit, let him know you're on your way. He likes to know what's going on," she said. "He does not like to *not* know what's going on. It gives him anxiety. Do loud noises startle him?"

We nod.

"He shivers when it thunders," Tom says.

"Loud trucks and fireworks," I add. "He has to climb on your lap." I pat him gently, rub his belly; he groans.

"Does this hurt?" I ask him.

"He does not like to be made fun off, you know," the pet psychic says. "He knows you're making fun of him, and he does not like it."

He growls in agreement, but I continue.

"Smile," I say. He lifts his top lip, wags his tail, and growls louder.

"He doesn't," the pet psychic says.

"Oh, pooooor Pnut," I say. "Well . . . what I really wanted to know about is this thing he does. I've never ever seen a dog do this. He does it daily at the same, every night after dinner."

The pet psychic looks at me. "And?" she asks.

"Well, he masturbates. I guess there's no other way to say it."

The pet psychic looks at me blankly but says nothing.

"Daily, same time every day," I continue. "And . . ." I shrug.

"Well," she says. "Anxiety."

"Oh?"

She looks at the dog for another explanation. The dog looks back at her. And they stay transfixed like this for a full minute.

"He wants you to know that he has no plans to stop," she finally says.

"He doesn't?" I ask.

"No," she says. "None."

In 1970, Bob Dylan recorded a song that went, *"If dogs run free, then why not we"* and it became a popular slogan when I was a student at Antioch College. One could find it scrawled everywhere—on dorm walls, bathroom mirrors and stall doors, outside walls of administrative buildings, and on the sidewalks. I was surrounded by the notion, barraged daily, never mind that there were leash laws popping up all over the country, which made it not wholly true. Even so, dogs were free-sort-of: unencumbered by problems in consciousness, problems of overthinking, overanticipating, problems I've long suffered from. But one winter, our first together when Pnut was just a pup, I found great solace in the freedom of Pnut's dogness.

Winters here in Oregon are something to behold. The sky falls. Darkness descends. One lives in a fog, literally. It is short, a few months only, but there is a tunnel—a dark, dark tunnel. At its height the darkness fills sixteen hours of every day. During our second winter, I was struggling with not only the physical darkness but my own inner night. After a year of hell and stomach cancer, my father had died during the previous summer. Two days following his death, while we were in Boston with my family, our beloved schnauser, Dick Diver, whom we had owned for thirteen years, died from kidney failure. The loss of two beloveds was more than I could bear. Even months later, I was still bewildered and miserable; I felt like I lived underwater.

But wherever I went, I was followed by our new puppy, this wiggling ball of fur, who was so very happy about everything. The little bundle embodied light. He whirled! He was only a dog, but he was fucking effervescent.

In an act of desperation, one afternoon I followed him around the house. We wandered. We slept on chairs, couches, hung out, looked out the window, sat in a sun spot or two, or by the heating vent. We had a drink, stared at each other, stared at the floor. I had been reading Rumi: "What I thought before was God, I met today. . . ." I looked at the dog. *In a dog?* I knew I needed to do something different. I needed to simplify my outlook, my expectations. I needed to do something about my life. And even as a goofy, stinky puppy, the dog, the mystic, helped me do that.

Rumi writes:

> *The morning wind spreads its fresh smell.*
> *We must get up and take that in. . . .*

The perverted part came later and though I do believe the world might be a better place if we all made love to ourselves and each other after dinner, I doubt everyone is ready to embrace the ritual as heartily as Pnut does. Meanwhile, we try to do our part; we try to be good dog owners and abide by the psychic's suggestions. So far, though, Pnut is a dog who remains true to his nature, and we to ours. "Pnut," I say, "we are going to lunch and should be back . . . uh, in a few hours . . . hmmm, around three P.M., okay?"

Grrr, okay, he says, then climbs the stairs and looks down on us and hoots once before turning away and disappearing from sight.

Never Just Dogs

JAYNE ANNE PHILLIPS

Dogs are never just dogs. If you get involved with a dog, you reassess your sense of corporeal/incorporeal relations. Let's face it: loving a dog, being loved by a dog, is simply not understandable until one loves a dog—in the domestic, parental, familial, partnering sense. I'm not talking about people who run dog teams or breed dogs or have numerous dogs simultaneously—maybe that's different—but about the usual one person–one dog scenario. The relationship becomes central in the locus of your life and defines the dog's life, which, sadly, is far shorter than a human life. Dogs don't know this, and it doesn't concern them. We know, but we try not to think about it. Human lives are short enough, but a dog's life—metaphors aside—is shorter by seven times, in that every year of a dog's life—if we're to believe the accepted maxim—counts for seven. Seven is every dog's number. If one is the loneliest number, seven is the magical reveal: seven planes of existence, seven deadly sins, seven years for every cell in the human body to make itself anew (supposedly). Seven days in every week of a dog's life with a human, and a human's life with a dog.

———

Families with kids should have dogs, or cats, or both. My mother "didn't like cats," but we had two dogs, whose tenures were separated by several years. Sam the pedigreed dachshund was my mother's choice, miniature, reddish and shiny, chasing a ball on the grass in the old home movies. My mother really liked him; he was "smart as a whip," very clean, didn't shed, bit my brother, and was gone. In the middle of my childhood, there was Polly, whom we all loved. She was a long-haired collie mix, brown and white, with a flag tail, a puppy from the pound, who grew up to chase the cows in the field across the house, nipping at their hooves and dodging nimbly out of reach. Worse, she chased cars up and down our rural road, veering away at just the moment it seemed she'd be swept under the wheels. She had the run of the country and came back with burrs in her fur and fat ticks in her ears. Her collar said POLLY and she wore tags, but one day she didn't come home. We drove here and there, on blacktop routes and dirt roads, looking for her. My father said she'd gone out chasing cows and some farmer had shot her. That's why we'd never find her. He said it sadly, with a shake of his head. Dogs are hard-wired to do what they do, he said, and farmers were entitled to shoot animals on their land. I'd seen desiccated possums and raccoons in the ditches beside our road, diminished to flattened skeins of silvery skin and smashed bone. I thought of Polly in a more private place, a ditch or a field, lying on her side the way she slept, in her collar, until her collar was all there was, like a grave. She stayed in my mind for years, lying in tall grass within a few fields of our house, her collar flat on the ground in snow and rain, like a necklace she'd slipped out of. We never had another family dog. We kids were getting to be teenagers, and my parents had other problems, too.

I got my own place in college, and a cat, a long-haired Persian I named Katya. Katya was supremely independent, but we lived in sync. Her cat box was beside the toilet in the tiny bathroom of my attic apartment. We used to pee simultaneously at the start of every day. Katya wasn't a snuggler, but still, voiding is intimate. I mean to say, I wasn't *looking* for a dog, but Katya and I moved into a rambling, falling-down house with numerous other people and animals.

My circle of friends included the exotic Judy, a brilliant import from Berkeley, California, who found herself in Morgantown, West Virginia, because her geology-professor father took a job at WVU. Not being gainfully employed, she came along and became a student again. We called her "Our Lady of the Clouds" because of her cloud of frizzy hair, her pale complexion, her soft voice. She had played her flute on the streets of San Francisco and Berkeley, and here she was, in her trenchant sadness and wire-frame glasses. She was a hippie in the post-hippie world of the mid-seventies, and she'd been in therapy for many years. She was able to cry for no apparent reason, silently, with no facial expression. I say "able" because to me, who'd learned not to cry, Judy seemed free, "in touch" with herself, able to go about her business in any gathering or revelry, her wide blue eyes pools of tears, tears coursing down her face. She was a Jewish earth mother, tall, bountiful, big-breasted, in her jeans and long-sleeved peasant blouses, her layered clothes that covered every inch of her. Judy reigned in a comfortable, ramshackle house at the top of Pine Street hill. The house was crowded with roommates. A vegan couple even lived under the porch; they'd spread a big rug on the bare, shaded dirt and set up housekeeping.

Judy had a dog named Dervish, a beagle mix so named because she stood up on her hind legs and twirled in circles when she was excited. Dervish had the brown-eyed basset gaze of a dog guru, the look of a thousand sorrows. She lived in glorious freedom even during estrus, and she'd recently had a litter of pups. Most of the pups looked like her, but one had green eyes, a fluffy reddish blond coat, a pointed snout, a nose that was pink instead of black. Dervish was known to consort with Rusty (weirdly, my own father's childhood nickname), a golden retriever–collie mix and dog-about-town. Judy pointed him out to me on the street. Female dogs, of course, can carry the progeny of any number of male partners in the same litter,

depending on how many interested parties gain access during their
heat. At Judy's one night, various friends and strangers clustered
around the pups, who were on their feet now, rousting and tum-
bling. People said the one puppy looked like me, her coloring, her
thinnish face, and I should take her. Judy did need to find homes for
them all, and she (physically) gave me the dog—a roly-poly pup, like
a furry baby. I was reading Russians, and I thought she looked Rus-
sian, like Katya.

I named her Sasha, but I should have called her Nomad. She was
my dog for twelve years, and we lived in probably twenty-four different locations in that time, many of them hundreds of miles apart. We
had a mobile history. I later wondered if it was ethically right that I'd
adopted Sasha at that time in my life; then again, it was unlikely a
settled housewife or a wealthy matron would have stepped forward
to claim her out of our circle of acquaintance. She was certainly no
latchkey kid. She went wherever I went, every day. "Hippie Dog
Goes Everywhere," one boyfriend said of her. The first time Sasha
and I moved to California, I gave Katya and her kitten to a farm
wife, sobbing as she drove them away.

Sasha and I made several (yearly or twice-yearly) cross-country
trips, always by car, sometimes with groups. Roughing it. Camping
if we stopped. She once drank an entire orange-juice can of cooling
bacon grease in the middle of the desert, with no noticeable ill ef-
fects. She definitely ate from the table and leaped into any car with
anticipation. Sasha perfected her own rider's stance, braced on the
front seat, chin on the dashboard. She preferred the wide view. The
cars were secondhand, and there were a few mishaps: the white-ice
episode in Colorado, and the spin-out on a snowy country road at
night in West Virginia. I'd taken the old road home for nostalgia's
sake (always a mistake), because the drifts were so high and beautiful, and in fact the car landed in one after spinning twice very fast.
The car was still running but I opened the door and Sasha streaked
out. This was before cell phones, and the snow was falling heavily.
The road was deserted. I convinced her to get back in and then drove

the car out, rocking and rolling it while she cowered on the floor. We were always alone when we had wrecks. Meaning we were together. I fed her, and she endured with me.

People said she was high-strung. I said she was intelligent. She knew by instinct which boyfriends were good drivers and, all other things being equal, expressed her strong preference for them. She was upset if I brought home strangers, people who did not know her and had not made up to her on other occasions. She thumped her tail in morose greeting but was made very nervous by the sounds behind the bedroom door. She paced in the hallway, nails ticking on the wooden floor. The next time I came home, invariably alone, she'd have peed in my bed, right in the center of the mattress.

Going back, though—her first year was stable. We lived in Morgan-town, and she grew up near her mother, Dervish. No leashes, no tags, no rules other than being house-trained, which she basically taught herself. Now people have cages and complicated systems for house-training dogs that take weeks and months and pounds of equipment. I don't understand this. I had a rolled-up newspaper that I tapped on the floor a couple of times. There was that one morning when Sasha was a small puppy, lazing in bed with my boyfriend and me, and she squatted and peed at our feet in the rumpled bedclothes. She saw the expressions on our faces before she even finished, and she immediately began licking up the urine. She was so perceptive— empathic? sensitive?—that I had only to say no in a particular tone to influence behavior she could learn to control.

Of course, there were the other behaviors. Sasha had detached first digits on her paws. The vet who gave her the requisite shots said she was a throwback; she had the genes of a hunter/tracker. In fact, she was passionate about squirrels, rabbits, even birds; they drove her to insane frenzy. She hunted in fields by popping up above the tall grass at intervals like a kangaroo, then diving in low. Her first action upon hitting the beach in Trinidad, California, after a week's drive

in my yellow Nova, was to down a seagull and break its neck. Everyone on the beach thought this quite unusual, as seagulls are not
known for their kind natures or gullible, trusting personalities. I told
her not to do that again. She was also a ferocious barker. She barked
at intruders until she knew they were invited, then compensated by
smiling and wagging her flag tail in welcoming circles, panting with
happiness and leaning in to be touched. Only the mailman was her
nemesis. She was particularly enraged by mailmen. Mailmen wore
uniforms and were never invited in; they were faceless enemies, approaching and penetrating the perimeter again and again on nefari-
ous, deliberate schedule. We had to put a basket on the front door for
the mail, as she ripped to shreds anything pushed through the mail
slot. The affront and threat of repeated assaults on the mail slot,
things shoved through as she hurled herself bodily against the door
and snarled and bared her teeth! Who could understand this? Why
did it persist in the face of her maniacal defense of home? Even the
look of the mail slot inspired growling and guarded stances. I learned
to nail a large piece of plyboard over the lower halves of my various
apartment doors, or she scratched the doors themselves to splintered
shreds and bit hunks out of the molding.

But for the most part, Sasha was friendly, happy, communicative.
Sit. Lie down. Speak. That stuff was effortless and . . . well, come on.
Everywhere we went, she traveled about a half block ahead, racing
along in her sideways lope, looking back to sight me. She sat at every
street corner and waited, straining, for me to say "Wait" or "Go," at
which point she raced across and continued ahead. She waited for
me outside buildings and restaurants. She was a familiar sight in
Iowa City, back when the Writers' Workshop was housed in the
English Philosophy Building, known as EPB. We'd go in the back
door, which was beside the river; that is, I went in the back door, and
Sasha waited by the bushes on the right side of the walk. I would be
inside for three or four hours, longer, but somehow she was always
there waiting when I came out. She'd been in the river, she'd been

around, but she was back, having had herself a good time and recon-
noitered the territory.

Our first abode in Iowa City was two rooms I rented in the back
of the Means Real Estate (or was it Insurance?) office on Washington Street. Mr. Means weighed over three hundred pounds and was
very generous to rent to a girl with a dog; his agency worked on the
other side of the wall. I could always hear typewriters clacking and
phones ringing. The apartment was actually a big square kitchen, a
tiny bathroom with a metal shower, and a narrow enclosed porch.
The porch/bedroom, slatted windows all around, looked out on the
parking lot of the Means Agency, where I had a free parking space
for my gargantuan Chrysler Torino. The next fall I lived way out of
town on a farm, briefly, and then in the top two rooms, third floor, of
a very funky building whose apartments shared hallway bathrooms.
Why did I have such awful apartments? I think it had to do with
having a dog, and limited financial resources. Sasha was worth my
adaptability. She interfaced with every detail of my personal history
and, in Austin, with history to come. Not my history, thank God.

Again, back. Corporeal relations, history. This was before Iowa, on
the circuitous way back from Oakland and San Francisco and New
Mexico and Boulder. Post-college, pre–graduate school. I'd been
waitressing in Boulder, caught mono, and fainted on the street when
things were far along. I'd wondered why I had that odd, come-and-
go rash, but I didn't go to doctors in those days. Since there was no
treatment, I only had to pay the clinic for the blood tests and the doctor for the examination. He said my spleen was enlarged, I didn't
look well, and he would drive me home. My friends brought food by.
Sasha was no problem. I only had to open the door and let her out,
and she came back on her own. I was too sick to move for a few
weeks, then decided to go home to my divorced mother, save money,
apply to grad schools. My mother had found me a job as an aide in

the school system, and my high-school bedroom was still intact. My mother would live in the downstairs of the house with her toy poodle, Jenny, and I'd live in the upstairs with Sasha. I didn't yet own a car, but I found a ride east with a friend who had a pickup truck. He was driving back anyway, through Austin, and he was willing to take me and my dog. I mailed my books. There wasn't really much else. He was driving, he said, that was the only thing. He didn't like other people driving his truck, but he was glad for the company.

Now we're coming to the history part, the part about dogs and people and what they're hardwired to do. It was the seventh year with Sasha, when Sasha was seven and all the cells of my body were making themselves anew in her company. We were in Austin, staying with friends of the driver of the pickup, in a green residential neighborhood near the UT campus. Austin was nice; Austin was just great. The house was bordered on one side by an ashram and on the other by a gracious bungalow with a For Rent sign in the window. The girl next door was moving out, and she invited me over. The place was four rooms, and beautiful. An ironing board folded out of a little door in the hallway, and big ceiling fans cooled all the rooms. She said I could have the apartment; she was looking for someone to take over her lease. She even had a week's rent left that I could use up, and she was leaving some of the big furniture: the bed, the table, a velvet overstuffed couch. I was sure I could find a job in walking distance; the thriving student ghetto was full of restaurants. As I walked through the rooms, Sasha lay on the rug, nose on paws, watching me. I told the girl I needed an hour to think and to talk to the guy in the pickup. It wouldn't take more than a few minutes to untie the tarp on the bed of the truck and move my duffel bag.

I walked back to the house with Sasha but bypassed the entrance and walked over to the ashram. The green backyard and garden was open to the public; the ashram rented rooms to seekers and taught yoga classes. I envisioned myself living in Austin, writing, working at a job, taking yoga, meditating in this garden. I felt that fate had delivered me here, into this estimable town and beautiful opportunity. Surely I should stay. It would be hard: marooned all winter in my hometown in West Virginia, working in a school system of which I had no fond memories, me and my dog living with my mother and her dog, much as I loved my mother. And I wasn't in a hurry about graduate school. The garden was full of blue and yellow flowers and bordered on one side by a narrow gravel walkway, a pass-through from the street to the neighboring house, a rooming house, as it turned out. A slim blond man on crutches, in jeans, long-sleeved shirt, his hair pulled back in a long blond ponytail, went by, entered the house. I sat on a bench. Sasha was by the flowers. Then I heard the shots, and Sasha yelped and spun around. Kneeling over her, I saw the gun still pointing down from the upstairs window, and the face of the blond man looking down. Then he stepped away and pulled the drapes.

Someone from the ashram heard the shots. Other people gathered around. The guy that lived next door was strange, they said. He'd shot her in the hips with birdshot, six or eight neat little holes, but she could move her legs, and someone gave us a ride to a vet. The vet fished out the pellets, shaved her around the wounds, bandaged her, gave me some antibiotics, and we went back to the ashram. I called the police. Now we were all standing in the garden of the ashram: me, my friend with the pickup, his friends, and the yoga teachers from the ashram. Sasha was under the bench, her hips and hind legs wrapped in gauze.

The cops arrived, a fat cop and a thin cop.

"Whatza problem?" asked the fat cop.

I told him that a blond man on crutches had shot my dog from the second-floor window of the house just next to us. That house, that window.

They listened, looked up at the house, shrugged.

"Shot your dog, did he?" said the fat cop. He cast a glance at Sasha. "Dog live?"

"Doesn't it worry you," I asked, "that someone would shoot a gun out a window?"

The thin cop was chewing a plug of tobacco. He spat. "Weallll," he said, drawling out the word, "*AH*'ve *keeled* dogs in *mah* yard."

That was pretty much the end of the conversation. The cops got back into their car.

I didn't stay in Austin. We got into the pickup and drove away. Later I remembered the shooter, not ten years before, in the tower on the UT campus. I wondered if he'd been blond, and I pictured him on crutches. Now I know the whole story, of course; the tower shooter was blond, an Eagle Scout, an ex-marine, and able-bodied, strong. He'd dragged his footlocker of weapons up the last three flights of stairs to the observation deck of the tower. The ashram shooter was merely a late-seventies alter-ego echo of the real thing, but the thing is always real if it happens to you. I wondered how the blond man on crutches was hardwired, and if he had further aspirations concerning guns and windows. And if the woman moving out of the beautiful apartment was moving out because of him.

Sasha recovered. We went to graduate school, we went to work, we bought a triple-decker and became landlords, we met someone, we blended families, we got married. We had a backyard wedding. Sasha was among the guests and jugglers and mimes and renaissance musicians, wearing a white bow on her collar that had always said SASHA. It was May; the dogwood was in bloom. The baby and the children were there. The baby, six months old, was learning to say "Sasha." By now it was almost twelve years.

The end of the story? My mother attended the wedding, too. She lived with us for the last thirteen months of her life, with her little dog, who was sixteen, and blind and incontinent. Years multiplied by seven, Jenny was a hundred and twelve. We went away for a week, and my older brother came as caretaker; my mother was bedridden, and she asked him to have Jenny put down. He took her to a vet and then buried her in our backyard. I wasn't there, but I have a recurrent memory of seeing her body, smaller than a cat's, wrapped in a towel in the front seat of the car. My mother died two months later, in her hospital bed at our house. I was with her, just after midnight, that November night. The sound of her agonal breathing had filled the room, the hallway, the house. I slept the rest of the night in the bed beside hers, the twin bed fitted out with flannel sheets, her bed until the last weeks. Devastating, devastating, to know what death really is, that kind of death, every inch a struggle, a torture, a reverse labor of life toward death. And then the intense relief, the release and peace and exhaustion, to see her face relax, to know it couldn't hurt her anymore. Sasha stayed out of the room until I lay down; then she came in and slept on the narrow rug between the beds.

By then Sasha was not well. She'd already had surgery, but we didn't do the chemo. We went to the park with the reservoir every day until her back legs failed; then, in spring, we went to sit in the grass and look at the water. At the end of the story, I wouldn't take her to any office. She was in her own bed, moved to the first floor of the house, sedated when the vet came with the shot. Still, she barked softly once or twice. I lay down with her, and then he approached. I've never had another dog. The baby who was learning to say "Sasha" grew up with his brothers, and with cats. I kept Sasha's picture in my office for many years. When my son was nine, he wrote a poem about her. "Quiet, with a woof . . ." As though the sound had penetrated his baby sleep in the room above.

We never stop thinking about our dogs. We're animals too, hard-wired that way, our attachments multiplied by seven. In their heaven, do dogs think of us? No. But when we see them again, in the incorporeal dimension they've taught us, they recognize us: it all comes back. They come forward, running and then loping, out of the field, across the lawn, down the hill, vibrant. There are no more multiples of seven, and dogs are finally dogs.

Damned Spot

MICHELLE LATIOLAIS

For all the last years of my husband's life, we owned an English bull terrier named Damned Spot. He came from a white-and-black brindle line, Fidelis Sebastian of Silmaril, but he was completely white and looked almost exactly like General George Patton's bull terrier. The name Damned Spot started out as a joke—a gag, really, to get my husband's mother to swear—and as years went by, it became funnier and funnier to hear Hilda saying in her sweet Arkansas accent, "Now, Damned Spot—you stop that!" Damned Spot obliged us in this gag, as he would not respond to just the name Spot—though Hilda had tried this shortening many times—and when Damned Spot lived in Michigan and the ladies who worked for the vet there declined to use his full name, he would not budge an inch of his very muscular seventy pounds when it was his time with the doctor. He stood his ground like a marble table, his tongue lolling out, his teeth in a crazed smile. I hesitate to suggest there was cognition or intellection in his eyes—he was one of the dumbest dogs I ever met—but certainly one could read a kind of sentiment that went along the lines of, *Why don't those women stop making noise and pay some attention to me, ME, DAMNED SPOT?*

Paul and I always relished saying to these staunch Michigan ladies, "You need to use his full name; he won't respond to just half of it," and he wouldn't, which was an almost endless source of amusement for us and one of the few arenas in which Damned Spot performed to our specifications. Bull terriers do very little that they do not wish to do, and they do even less of what you want them to, but Damned Spot seemed somehow at the vanguard of comedic excellence when it came to his name and his refusal to respond to just half of it. I realize, as I write this, that he was a bit of an artist, something I've failed to consider until now.

English bull terriers were created a couple of hundred years ago by crossing English bulldogs with an English white terrier now extinct. The breeder, James Hinks of Birmingham, wanted the broad chest of a bulldog but not the dwarfism in the limbs that makes bulldogs' legs bow. Bull terriers have a normal bone structure, perhaps even supernormal, as their legs are exceedingly straight, if not stiff. When Damned Spot barked, his front legs lifted off the ground as though he were a chair leaned back. I have heard some controversy over just what-all else is in the breed—perhaps some dalmatian—but no matter what, they were originally bred for dogfighting, which is the point of their recessed eyes. In other words, it would be hard for an opposing dog to sink its teeth into them. Because of the phrase "dogfighting pit" and the dogs who were consigned there, bull terriers are often confused with pit bulls or the American Staffordshire terrier, but these are distinct breeds from bull terriers, with very different traits and personalities. Bull terriers are hugely affectionate and loyal, and one must read their strength within that context. I have often been thrown halfway across the kitchen by an affectionate nuzzle from Damned Spot, or moved entirely off the bed as he insinuated himself as close as he could possibly be. For years I had to make sure the doors to the bathroom were closed when I drew a bath, because if they weren't, I would come into the bathroom to find Damned Spot, his eyes a bit glazed, luxuriating in a cloud of Kneipp Herbal Bath, juniper or almond blossom or spruce. Damned Spot loved his baths, and asking him nicely to get out of yours was to forget the hedonist you were addressing. Either you agreed to sidle yourself up along one side of the bathtub or you waited your turn.

Paul had originally wanted an English bulldog, but, being bookish people, we consulted—breeders, dog encyclopedias, veterinarians, owners—and what we encountered was information we did not love. Not only were bulldogs very expensive, most of them having to be born cesarean section because their heads had been bred so gigantean, but they were constantly at the vet's with dermatological issues, not the least being rashes that broke out within their neck folds. This chronic malady entailed Vaseline-ing the dog's neck twice a day and years of prednisone, an expensive prescription as prescriptions go. Bulldogs were also known to be magnificent farters, and droolers, and rather stupid, and I looked at my husband with a kind of pleading in my eyes. How exactly English bull terriers came into the negotiations I'm not sure, but we had friends who had relatives who knew breeders, and soon we were in conversation with a couple in Florida, the Cavanaughs. Fidelis Bull Terriers. We waited through one litter, and then a video arrived of a second litter, and puppy after puppy was put atop a short table in a fairly destroyed backyard for my husband to choose from. The Cavanaughs bickered at each other in the background, but all you could see of them were hands and an occasional profile. It was a strange video, an artifact of sorts, the pay dirt of documentarians, and though I did not see this video until well after Damned Spot had arrived in our lives—I was commuting from Los Angeles to Michigan at the time—I relished its weirdness: it took special people to love these canine insurgents enough to *own* them, but it took strangeness of a higher order to actually proliferate them on earth! The video captured much of this.

To lend a fuller sense of the general reception of bull terriers, I must tell you of a passage in a little-known John Fante novel in which a bull terrier is shot dead at point-blank range on a beach in Malibu, California. When I first read this passage, I did not—bull terrier owner that I was—reel back in my chair in surprise and anguish. Rather, I understood the sentiment precisely. That said, I admit that when Target Discount Stores launched their advertising campaign with a white bull terrier whose eye spot was instead a red target, I balked. An early name for bull terriers was White Cavaliers, and indeed much in the behavior of these dogs *is* cavalier—and cavalier in the face of all that Western civilization holds dear—but that is much of their value, too, their irrepressibility, their one-dog insurgency. To keep a bull terrier in your sights, to make one the mascot of your commercial ambitions—or the target of your murderous rage—is understandable. They are indeed spectacular-looking, and spectacularly badly behaved. But if you know bull terriers at all, you know well that they will not submit to our uses—and this is a fine thing. Paul and I amused ourselves by gauging the destruction that one bull terrier loose in a Target store would wreak; we thrilled to the hordes of protective mothers hurrying their children from the too-bright aisles of merchandise, and we debated the time it would take even an experienced bull terrier owner to capture her wildly careening pet and get him back on a leash. It might only be a matter of minutes, but bull terriers—being physicists, too—expand time to allow the utmost mayhem.

Because so few people have actually ever seen a bull terrier, Damned Spot often had celebrity status when he went places—and indeed he loved to be photographed and would stand completely still, all vain attention, while the cameras clicked. What he thought was going on is anyone's guess, but somewhere in the deep reaches of his DNA, he knew about pomp and circumstance; he knew about show. Certainly Elgar had written that music for him!

Sometimes people—and they would almost always be men— would know that General George Patton had a bull terrier named Willie, who was much beloved by Patton, but for the most part people have not seen English bull terriers in the flesh. Even fewer have been around them for any amount of time, as not many are silly enough with their lives to actually attempt to raise a bull terrier—it is virtually impossible to do so anyway. But the Budweiser beer ads with their bull terrier mascot were a constant and almost singular source of identification for people. "Hey," people would exclaim on seeing Damned Spot, "it's a Spuds MacKenzie dog!" And they would often go on to object, "But Spuds MacKenzie has a spot on his eye. Plus, he isn't overweight like your dog." I would—though not always patiently—explain that Spuds MacKenzie was a two-year-old *female,* not completely grown, and that full-grown male bull terriers were like this, and that Damned Spot was not overweight, though obviously he wasn't built for speed on the veld either!

Sometimes they backed slowly away from me.

It's hard to know where to start in relaying the story of an obedience course that taught me more humility than any one human being should have to simper within—and taught my dog absolutely *nothing.* Perhaps a starting place would be to tell about how each of the ten classes ended. The instructor, dressed in jungle fatigues—I kid you not, it was Michigan, and the Michigan Militia met rather too regularly in the Kalamazoo town square—the instructor would visit each owner and his or her pet and have a few words—and of course the retrievers sat there like they were getting fucking manicures—and the dog trainer would come to us, and come to us last—she knew about power—and she would look at me, and then she would look down at Damned Spot, his teeth bared in his characteristic crazed smile, his tongue lolling out, his paws planted foursquare, barking ecstatically, and then she would look up at me again, and she'd shake her head with dismay, and then she'd say with the most practiced derision, "Well, he *is* the happiest dog." "Oh, fuck you," was on my lips every time—she was so smug! But, of course, it's not as if she was wrong. It's just that I hadn't come to obedience school to be reconfirmed in thoughts of my dog's profound idiocy—I knew that full well. This was a Benjy among dogs, a real Lennie if there ever was one, and I needed help, not confirmation of a reality.

For the first two weeks, the instructor watched me be dragged around the large circle the dogs and dog owners formed, and then, at the start of the third class, she moseyed her green-and-brown self over, swinging what looked to be a linked torture device. "This," she stated importantly, "is power steering. I suggest you purchase one immediately." What she held out to me was a choke chain with spikes. I sputtered. "That's vicious," I finally managed to say. "I could never use such a collar."

"Hold your hand out," she commanded, and I did, and she wrapped the spiked collar around my hand and then constricted it, and the spikes were angled in such a way that they threatened but didn't actually impale. It felt horrible, grisly. I purchased one directly following class.

To sum up this obedience course, I'll tell you about the last class, the class wherein one's pet passes an exam—oh, yes!—and one receives a certificate that one can frame should one so wish! This last class was perhaps the most formalized of glimmerings we had that Damned Spot would never-ever-not-on-your-Nelly be a trained dog, but—and this is an interesting "but"—he'd be incorrigible like no other, and in this incorrigibility our love took root.

If you have ever been to doggy obedience school, you know the drill: the Sit; the Walk in a Circle in which the dog heels perfectly, never pulling on the leash; the Down; and then the Three-Minute Down in which the dog rests alertly for three minutes by your side. These simple tasks do not seem to be a problem for most dogs to learn, and the retrievers slide out the birth canal knowing how to execute them, but a three-minute anything is not in bull terrier DNA, believe me, and so we're all there lined up on this last auspicious day. Damned Spot has succeeded passably—I use that term loosely—in walking and sitting, et cetera, but now it's time for the Three-Minute Down. He *is* down, but I'd say at thirty seconds he bounds up laughing his fool head off, barking away. *What are you asses all doing!?* he seems to be shouting to the others. I push on his back to get him down again, and he goes, but it's like trying to deflate a rock, and he's down for perhaps twenty seconds this time and then he's up for the finale and will not be put down, and he barks and barks until all of the nine other dogs—even the golden retrievers, I'm very, very, very proud to say—bound up barking, too. Happiness takes the day. Anarchy reigns.

We loved to tell the story of Damned Spot and the Stetson Chapel wedding, because no matter what, Damned Spot's irrepressibility always amused us, his refusal to do much that didn't strongly feed his most sybaritic impulses. He was a marvel of hedonism, a Falstaff of a dog, though of course it was no matter of conjecture as to whether he had Falstaff's wits—he didn't. Nonetheless, there was something completely marvelous in the hugeness of his spirit, and in Michigan, where we lived rather uncomfortably for three years, he was a singular source of happiness. Not even Michigan could get this dog down!

We had a house on the campus of Kalamazoo College, a beautiful little two-story brick house built in 1928. It was just down a sweet wooded path from the quad, which was a miniature of Monticello, or the University of Virginia, moreover. Stetson Chapel sat primly at the top of the quad and though obviously not Monticello, quite lovely in its Palladian windows and bell tower where students rang changes almost daily. Every weekend, during the spring and summer, elegant weddings took place at Stetson Chapel.

We set out for a walk one day, and before we could lean down to clip on Damned Spot's leash, he shot down the path, looking back once to say, *Watch this you idiot parents of mine!* (We were always so grateful he couldn't actually speak, as his physical articulations were stinging enough.) He was bounding up the hill to Stetson Chapel, to a wedding party being photographed, a regiment of groomsmen and bridal attendants, but more specifically Damned Spot was bounding for the bridal gown fanned out down the long sloping terrace, a cathedral-length train extending on the grass three or four yards, and all Paul and I could see was a deliriously happy Damned Spot rolling himself onto that vastness of peau de soie. We are screaming our heads off at Damned Spot to stop, hurtling our bodies after him as fast as we can, knowing full well that he is not stopping for God nor money, treats nor estrus, and finally, at the last possible instance, the groom steps out of the picture and down the hill the necessary three or four yards and reaches out his hand and grabs Damned Spot's collar and hoists him into the air and away from his gorgeously attired bride. We are full of admiration for this young man. Gallantry is not dead—not as long as there are curs like our boy in the world! Plus, this groom had just saved us thousands of dollars; we had no doubt about this whatsoever. Plenty of tuxedoed moneybags were standing there with not one whit of amusement on their faces. Instead you could see the dollar signs flashing in their eyes, it was so colossally clear their thinking: you will pay for having ruined my daughter's wedding, my niece's wedding, my daughter-in-law's wedding. Conversely, Damned Spot was joyous at the prospect and could not understand why no fun was being had at this far-too-elegant and sedate affair. Once again a sentiment was resident in his eyes. This time it went something along the lines of, *Look, I match the bride. I'm dressed all in white, little mud on my paws, but hey, basically dressed for sanctity!* The smile on his face was as crazed as it ever had been.

Extremity has a way of leading us to language, and Damned Spot— because he was the dog he was—garnered many nicknames: Cowboy, Spot Meister, Piglet, Shark Dog, this last because for a time in his youth, the most prolonged youth imaginable, he ate anything and everything he could snatch up with his beautiful white muzzle. In fact, Paul relished telling the story of Damned Spot's having a movement on the sidewalk that rang with pennies, a sort of zoologic slot machine; our young nieces and nephews knew never to put money in their mouths. One morning in Michigan, after a particularly raucous New Year's party the night before, we heard an odd crashing and then a Morse code of thumps, and then silence for a time, and then another crashing and the *tap, tap, tap*. Struggling up through murky heads, we finally roused ourselves to tread downstairs and see what our boy was up to. We watched from the kitchen doorway as Damned Spot knocked champagne bottles over and then held their necks down, lapping up what few drops he could get. He had already done this with several beer bottles, but it took the heavier topple of champagne bottles to finally wake us. It had been a big party, and Damned Spot had availed himself of enough alcohol to spend the rest of the day significantly subdued. One of the world's more pathetic sights is a hungover bull terrier, but perhaps even more pathetic were his parents missing their darling thug, even for a day.

On Damned Spot's walks, small children would hunker their little diapered selves down and start petting him, and their mothers would ask what the nice doggy's name was, and we'd say it, and of course the children—having such aural fidelity—would repeat his name immediately, before their mothers could suggest an alternative or a shortening to Spot. We would crack up when little tiny children would stand on the sidewalk, waving their even tinier hands, hollering, "Bye, Damned Spot, bye!" And they always got his name right, and they never tried to shorten it or censor it or alter it in any way. God bless them. Paul and I always expected our niece or nephew to be sent home from school for cussing when they had in fact merely been naming their aunt and uncle's dog. The precision of children is to be greatly admired.

Damned Spot's name, children using it, this all seemed like rather innocent corruption to us, but then—of course—there was the quite intentional allusion in Damned Spot's name to Shakespeare, to a guilt-addled Lady Macbeth wringing her hands:

"Yet here's a spot. . . . Out, damn'd spot! out, I say!"

And so thus of course "damn'd spot" being a literary allusion somehow elevated it out of the gutter and onto the sidewalk of civility, if not into the edifices of high culture—kind of like where the pigeons roost. There was no end to the range of this dog's name, and of course the literary allusion was dead on, completely mimetic, as Damned Spot had no spots, just as Lady Macbeth has no actual blood on her hands as she wrings them, and some people got this and found it pretty funny. And some people didn't and were, like, "Uh, but your dog, it like has no spots? Why did you call him Damned Spot?" The best response to this was just to bend down and scoop up the beloved dog's dejectus, because if you stood there and explained, people's faces went into the just-what-you'd-expect-of-a-college-professor look, and working one's way out of that straitjacket of a stereotype was impossible. Or if you said Damned Spot's having no spots was "ironic," you might end up explaining to a fifty-year-old person what "ironic" meant.

There was blood in Damned Spot's life, as there was blood in his name. He had been in the house the day my husband committed suicide, or perhaps he had been in the yard where my husband actually held the gun to his head and pulled the trigger. I did not know, nor did the detectives, as there was no blood on Damned Spot, though one morning about a year after Paul had died, I got an answer—at least I thought it was an answer—to the question of where Damned Spot had been when it happened.

Most nights I could not sleep through the night, and I wandered the house crying, and Damned Spot followed me, and sometimes when I had stood in a room too long without moving, he would bark at me, and I would lean down to him and hold him—he was so great to wrap your arms around, his massive smooth chest—and then we would go back to bed. In order not to hear myself weeping, I covered my head in pillows, and this one night I slept very, very deeply, so deeply that by ten o'clock the next morning I was still asleep. I felt something nudging me frantically in the side. Damned Spot was standing by the bed, and then he leaped up onto the bed and continued to nudge me, over and over, and quite desperately, and I said something to him, but my face was still under pillows, and I was trying to wake up, and then I did finally wake up enough to pull the pillows from my face, and looking into Damned Spot's eyes was like looking into a pure distillation of terror. "Damned Spot, I'm okay," I said to him. "Hey, guy, it's all right. I'm okay. . . ." and I knew that Damned Spot had tried to wake Paul up that day as he lay in our backyard with a bullet through his temple. My husband had been prescribed eighty milligrams a day of Zocor—a cholesterol-lowering drug—by a Kaiser Permanente doctor, and he had dutifully taken it for nine months, the highest dosage on the market. The scientific literature linking low serum cholesterol to decreased brain serotonin activity covered the dining-room table. Damned Spot had lived these last eighteen months in a state of shock akin to my own, and he had sat on my feet as I read this literature about the connection between low cholesterol and suicide.

On August 22, 2005, I stood at the high stainless-steel table in the veterinarian's examining room as Damned Spot died. He was as beautiful as he had ever been, his profile against the white towel, his eyes as dark and impenetrable as Apache tears. Perhaps there had been a kind of brain cancer? There had definitely been fibrotic lung disease—I had X-rays of his chest—but of course he died that day from a lethal injection. He lived for a year and a half after my husband's death, and he had lived with a woman who could not breathe, who was often desperately distraught, a woman who clung to him sometimes as though we both were drowning. The vet said, looking up at the X-rays on the light board, "I've never seen fibrotic lung disease in this breed, and it's pretty rare in dogs at all. Cats get it, but this is quite unusual." But I knew immediately—and I'm not a very woo-woo person—I knew that Damned Spot had taken as much into his own body as he could. I had spent a year and a half gasping, struggling to breathe—it was as though my heart were constricting around my lungs—and I had passed out several times, once my head hitting down on the computer keyboard. I had no doubt whatsoever that this dog had absorbed as much as he could absorb from his mistress's grieving, that he had tried to take it into his own body.

Alive, I called them "my guys," "my white dogs," and now they both were contained in small boxes that when tilted made the sliding, pebbly sound of dirt scattering on a coffin.

A Hundred-Dog Life

RON CARLSON

There was Bouncer, an English boxer, benign and slobbering in the lap of Harry Match, may he rest in peace. Bouncer could have been a gargoyle. Harry was a welder who worked with my father at Chicago Bridge and Iron on the old west side of Salt Lake City. The dog waddled around and let himself be handled in the green grass. *I'm short,* he seemed to say. *Reach down and do whatever you want. I'm beyond this, and my name is Bouncer.* I was four years old and stayed with Harry and Ann for a weekend when my parents were traveling. I sat in their grassy yard with my buddy Bouncer—neither of us could read—and from there we could see the corner of Edison Elementary School one block away, a beautiful red sandstone building named after the inventor, and I wondered what in the world they would do to me there.

And Fenn's dog Buster, a black collie mutt loose in the neighborhood, everyone's dog for a day a week, who mounted a long-haired white mongrel bitch one day down by Linda Putnam's house on Wasatch Avenue. Linda was in our sixth-grade class at Edison and would graduate from West High with the rest of us, a girl I was always friends with. Buster and the white dog copulated vigorously and then got stuck and then, still connected in a confusing display, stood exhausted, embarrassed and in pain, back to back. We didn't know what to do, but finally Linda's dad came out into the yard and hosed them apart. Evidently water could dissolve the evil bond, and a moment later, tail down, shamed, and miserably wet, Buster crossed to us, and we walked back to Sorenson Park. Fenn and I were about to be twelve, young enough for it to become mythology, and later that exhibition certainly kept us virgins an extra year at least. For months that followed while I was idling in the park between ball games or riding bikes, I heard ten explanations of what had occurred, and they were all physically impossible. None of the explanations was comfort. Buster had a white blaze on his throat.

There was Mrs. White's ten-foot wolfmonster with its myriad gene pool and broad forehead who would attack silently, running without barking until he was biting the chain-link fence inches from where we walked to Edison Elementary, and so we crossed the street before we came to her house. We walked on the other side of Wasatch Avenue for two or three years after he died.

My buddy Butch had Tiny, a German shepherd with a hip problem who was happy to lie down anywhere, even in a hole full of water, comfortable in the world as it was presented to him. He was silent and good-natured, another dog who was glad to be petted and glad to be left alone. Fenn and Butch and I played Cup Baseball at Butch's house and Off the Wall and the thrilling Annie-Aye-Over with old tennis balls. These were all balls we had found at the park, old and ruined, some of them rubbed to the rubber, but they served. Tiny loved these things, and for a dog that didn't run or jump very much, he could field a loose ball like a magnet, and if we arrived to begin a game, we learned to look in his mouth first. You'd try to get it out of his molars with two fingers, but two fingers would not suffice. He'd lie there in the weeds, the keeper of the ball, while you delicately plucked at the wet rubber locked behind his teeth. It required both hands, one on the ball and one covering his snout, and even then it took a full minute while Tiny did not move but watched you above him, as if he weren't involved in this negotiation at all. Finally the ball would slip free, covered in dog saliva, which is chemically much more sophisticated and substantial than human saliva and led to some innovative pitches, including a wicked screwball. In the middle of a game of Off the Wall, Fenn used to roll the ball over to the dog to grease it up, and we had to outlaw that. The rule was, if the dog got the ball on his own, well then. But to pander was illegal. Tiny was a big dog. When we slept out in Butch's yard and you left your sleeping bag, you'd come back and find the wet dog in there.

Smokey was a black hound that volunteered as our dog when my parents moved to north Phoenix, Arizona, thin as a cartoon dog and dear, who while standing in the bed of the pickup would duck when we crossed under overpasses and who prowled the desert with us on all those outings. In 1966, Phoenix was just waking before exploding in growth, and there were arroyos and hillsides festooned with cacti where now Barnes & Noble and Office Max anchor malls. Smokey's ears stood up like drawings of a dog's ears. Several mornings in the shadow of Cactus Mountain, which is now in the center of a sprawling subdivision, my father and brothers and I called in coyotes using my father's wooden calls, two pieces of polished walnut twisted together to make the scream of a wounded rabbit. We saw rattlesnakes draped in creosote bushes, lying in wait for whatever creature might huddle beneath them, and once we witnessed a titanic flash flood at dawn, raw and roaring like a living figure from a dream, and later in the sunny day we camped, and Dad cooked us a campstove breakfast while Smokey drifted the perimeter chasing rabbits. That plain and those mesas are now houses, as there are houses everywhere.

Corby was the beagle mix who lived with the Delmars when I was a freshman in college in Houston, Texas. Corby was a cordovan-and-white dog confused by all the traffic in the house, always looking to be out of the way, his backside disappearing into the next room. Everyone was confused by the traffic in that house. Every Sunday, Mrs. Delmar had a breakdown, and everyone but me knew to leave the house. I could hear her in the laundry room, screaming. She was a lovely large woman, but on these Sundays she swore brutally. I sat still in my upstairs room until Mr. Delmar would come home, coo to her, and then take her to dinner. I lived there that spring and had an eclectic group of friends who went to coffeehouses and fished off Galveston in the Gulf of Mexico, and I think I was dating one, but was never sure. It was the year I read *Paradise Lost*.

Then I was at college at the University of Utah. Salt Lake City was the name of the Kranes' dog, named by their sons, a purebred gray sheepdog of some kind with long hair that prevented you from seeing his eyes. He lived to escape and run the neighborhood off Michigan Avenue in Salt Lake. David Kranes was my professor, the first person to encourage my writing, and I was so happy to be invited to his house and then become his friend. I was there sometimes late at night with a fresh story, and David listened to my first stories while Salt Lake City lay at his feet, and he told me what each promised and what I might do to amplify that promise. The dog waited always to see if the door might be opened wide enough for him to slip away or if it might be left ajar, and I know it wasn't my visits that led to his fatal flight, but there came a day.

In all my life I have met only one St. Bernard, and that dog was named Ferdinand. He lived with Pete Adams on the prep-school campus in Connecticut where I taught after I'd graduated from the University of Utah. Ferdinand was a big and healthy beauty, a sort of classic, and I got to know him well the winter that the Marchants' dogs were in heat. He waited outside the dorm apartment door, so close I had to talk him into getting up and backing away so you could pass by. He was reluctant in his large way, and what word would that reluctance be? I've seen it in others. I've seen it in myself. In the spring when the snow melted, there was dog shit everywhere on campus, and Ferdinand, being largest, was overly blamed for the display. Teaching was hard, impenetrable at times, and I was always reading as I walked, these dogs in my peripheral vision.

Geoff Marchant had come from Princeton and he taught English, as did I, and he had two dogs that first year, Ernie and Vicky, and Ernie was a beautiful mutt named after Geoff's hero, Ernie Banks, and Vicky had been kicked by a horse and had a dent in her forehead that never bothered her at all. When you petted that dog, you put your finger there.

Thunder was Grace Becker's dog, a little black dog that could run in great circles. Grace taught French at the Kent School, which was a commute from our campus, and I remember mornings when Thunder would get out and begin those circles, threatening to go absolutely wild, running huge arcs on the lawn so fast that he was at forty-five degrees in a constant turn, and Grace out on the porch worried in her stocking feet calling, "Thunder, Thunder."

The Markses had two large black Labs called Sophie and Sadie, and when Sophie was killed by a car there at Route 112, the other dog went into permanent mourning. When you crossed the campus to the rink, you could see her on the mound by the old tennis courts waiting for her sister's return. Before those two, the Markses had a big red hound named Matt who got hold of one of our cats once and opened him up. The cat was Basil, named after the F. Scott Fitzgerald boy character, and he was an animal without instincts who would nose up to any creature big or small expecting to be well met.

The whippet Missy was Robert Hawkins's dog, and she was a precise and polite beauty who walked with him everywhere and sometimes came to class. In his tweeds with that dog, Mr. Hawkins looked the perfect prep-school master. He knew grammar as well as any human being, and he taught it without compromise.

Blair Torrey had the black-and-white spaniel Bumbles, or Mr. Bumbles, given to him by students who the rumor was had given the dog LSD as a pup. The dog was a good dog mainly, but when you knew the rumor, then he seemed a little off. He was a beautiful dog and looked like all the pictures in the Dick and Jane readers. Blair was a man meant to teach and coach, and he taught the rest of us how. Many winter mornings I arrived early at the English department's office to find him there peeling an apple with this pocketknife and reading Lear or Zorba or the endless student compositions and taking the papers as if they were important messages, and I began to see the way that they *were* important messages. There were also a lot of young teachers who came to school those years and saw what he did and decided that if it was going to take all that, then it wasn't for them. Blair was good with Mr. Bumbles all those seasons, and that dog had as much exercise in the school woods as any domesticated animal in Connecticut.

Rupee was my brother Regan's dog, who resembled a black Lab but was smaller, and perhaps the smartest dog I've known. He had a canny look of appraisal, alert at all times, and he could climb any fence. He was a cool, purposeful dog, who may have assembled steps, used tools, in some of his escapes. But he always came back and was devoted to Regan. My brother was living alone, working at my father's welding shop and drag-racing his old Ford pickup at a track way west of Phoenix. Regan restored a '60 Thunderbird, a beautiful turquoise car with that sill along the door tops. Once, hurtling down the I-17 interstate from Flagstaff to Phoenix with all the windows down, Regan looked and Rupee was standing all four feet outside the car on the narrow ledge, leaning into the seventy-mile-per-hour wind. Without slowing down, Regan reached across and grabbed Rupee's ankle in his fist and hauled him into the car.

Brandy was a retriever who started out as David Posner's dog, and I saw him at David's mother's high-rise apartment near Lincoln Center in New York, where he once broke through a wall, having been left alone during a thunderstorm. That dog feared thunder greatly but was a sweet, benign auburn beauty, who then appeared with Tommy, David's roommate from Brown, the year that Tommy taught at Salisbury School, where Brandy many days went to class in the old library. Lifetimes later, this fall, David and Tommy's oldest kids will meet as freshmen in Providence. If you ask about the good dog Brandy, his ownership is still a question.

A tough night in the mountains of Wyoming was changed by a dog, Scout, who burst into a snow camp I'd made with my fishing buddy, Roger, after three days of snow. Behind him came his owner, John, also stuck here high up in the big woods. The next day we were faced with a ten-mile walk through the snowfields, when Scout circled wide and gathered the range cattle there, leading them down in a file that made our hike out on the packed snow a walk in the park. Scout was an Australian shepherd.

That year I got the Australian shepherd Max, my first dog, my only dog. Of course he was brilliant and handsome, and we were closer than brothers. He was a good dog to me and to my baby sons, whom he herded all his days. He sat closest to me when I wrote those first stories. Once, from the bed of my pickup when we'd come upon a flock of sheep crossing Highway 191 near the summit above Vernal, Utah, Max barked and a thousand animals startled and fled into the sage. I remember him, two legs up on the truck bed, a king.

And now in this dog year my dearest dog is Maggie, the Farmers' beagle, who when I come to their door whines and spins until I get on the floor, such is a dog's love, and she sleeps with me, sliding into the guest room after the house is asleep and creeping from the foot of the bed until we wake nose to nose under the covers, her eyes an entire language of secrecy, companionship, and affection.

And the hundred others and two hundred, some of them pups, you dogs, just over there and over there, lying on the rug or circling home like the theme of love in our lives or hope for the next thing always, hope on four feet, how I still must touch you for luck and look in your eyes for a sign. I love you all, and you were a good dog, Max. Thank you, old souls, for being the dogs for me.

Becky Hungry Coyote

J. C. HALLMAN

In 1989, I was twenty-two years old and a student at the Iowa Writers' Workshop. I lived down the street from Charlie D'Ambrosio when he bought his dog, Kayla. A dog was something I'd thought about for a while, but the little pup peeping out of Charlie's canvas satchel sealed the deal. To help me choose mine, Charlie dropped in my mailbox a manual written by the Monks of New Skete, an unorthodox Eastern Orthodox monastery in upstate New York that made its living raising German shepherd dogs. The monks had written two wildly successful books about their breeding and training programs, *The Art of Raising a Puppy* and *How to Be Your Dog's Best Friend.* I forget which one Charlie loaned me, but both offered practical instruction in dog training and in the quiet, sincere spirituality that came from working closely with animals. With the book's help, I chose my own German shepherd dog, a silver puppy that I named (officially) Becky Hungry Coyote, for Becky Thatcher and the Indian Guide name my father had given me when I was seven years old.

Charlie and I agreed that the monks were interesting for more than just their dog advice, but it wasn't until thirteen years later that I got a chance to explore my curiosity. I had embarked on *The Devil Is a Gentleman,* a book about America's religious fringe and the philosopher, psychologist, and religious thinker William James. In 1902,

James had written *The Varieties of Religious Experience,* a comparative study of the prophets and mystics of the fringe movements of the time. The book was a bestseller, and bits of James are still recognizable in the religions that have come about in its wake. I planned to re-create the effort, setting up journeys to an array of movements that would demonstrate how James's thought continues to inform religion today.

I thought of the monks at once. They were a stretch for a couple of reasons. While their brand of Orthodox Christianity sometimes put them at odds with the larger Eastern Orthodox organization, it wasn't clear that they really amounted to a new religion. Too, the monks had been critical of James, because James was suspicious of religion practiced in groups. But I didn't care: this was a pilgrimage. I arranged a weeklong retreat and told the monks that I wanted to talk to them about how their dogs informed their faith. I hoped that if I could get them to open up, whatever logic they offered might tail back to James's thinking on personal religious experience. But what I wound up discovering was that the best connection between William James and the Monks of New Skete wasn't religion at all—it was the dogs themselves.

The James family (including the prolific but chronically unread Henry Sr., the novelist Henry Jr., and diarist Alice) had kept many dogs when William James was a boy. Dogs figured in family letters and stories throughout James's life. In medical school James participated in laboratory experiments that involved the partial removal of dogs' brains. Ten years later the lab experience, he wrote in a letter to his brother, suggested to him a "parable" that he thought might be useful to theologians: an experiment dog lying on an operating table was in a kind of hell, but if it could be made to understand the larger benefits of the procedure, he suggested, it would willingly submit to the fate. A decade further on, James revisited his apocryphal dog in an essay hauntingly titled "Is Life Worth Living?":

> He lies strapped on a board and shrieking at his execu-
> tioners, and to his own dark consciousness is literally in a

sort of hell. He cannot see a redeeming ray in the whole
business; and yet all these diabolical-seeming events are
often controlled by human intentions with which, if
his poor benighted mind could only be made to catch a
quick glimpse of them, all that is heroic in him would
religiously acquiesce.

That dogs offered religious metaphor was something James inherited from Darwin. Darwin had suggested that the deep love of a
dog for its master revealed something about man's love for God.
James echoed the sentiment in claiming that man stands in igno-
rance of the larger universe in the same way a dog inhabits its master's world without understanding all its devices and furniture. In
letters to his children, James was less academic about it. An accom-
plished artist early in life, he drew quick sketches of the dogs he encountered while traveling. Writing from El Paso, in French, he
described one lazy dog that was afraid of thunder:

Another was from Geneva, and James called him "nice & fat &
warm":

Yet while James was playful in these letters, the idea that dogs could illustrate something about spirituality was still present. To his daughter Peggy, age eight, he wrote of one pup, "His tail keeps wagging all the time, and he makes on me the impression of an angel hid in a cloud. He longs to do good." And to his son Aleck, ten, he wrote of a dog called Dinah, "I care for you & her equally; and you must care for her more than for yourself, for she is your better self . . . and more loving faithful devoted to you than *you* can be to any living thing. You are like a God to her."

In 1909, a year before his death and thirty-five years after his "parable," James appeared to change his mind on vivisection, which was performed by a scientific community he had since become suspicious of. He lent his name to a fervent antivivisectionist movement of the time, and his defense of their tactics had religious rationale:

> So long as the physiologists disclaim corporate responsibility . . . [then] so long must the anti-vivisectionist agitation, with all its expansiveness, idiocy, bad temper, untruth, and vexatiousness continue as the only possible means of bringing home to the . . . experimenter the fact that the sufferings of his animals *are* somebody else's business as well as his own, and that there is "a God in Israel" to whom he owes account.

I packed all these anecdotes away with my clothes when I went for my retreat with the Monks of New Skete. I don't intend to retell the whole story here, but I stayed on long enough to get a sense of the place. I met Brother Christopher, their lead trainer; Brother Peter, a sweet man who had been at New Skete for almost his entire life; and Brother Marc, who had the mien of a philosopher and whose own dog, Oka, was pregnant during my visit. The monks were reluctant to talk about their dogs and their faith for a time. They were eminently practical about their business; there was nothing transcendent about their dogs, they said. Their females were "bitches," their litters were investments, and in general the monks were suspicious of the kind of canine fundamentalism that could result when the master-dog relationship served as a substitute for alienated relationships among people. They were far more interested in what they called their "Orthodox Catholic" faith—a Christian oxymoron. The liturgy in English made for some awkward-sounding translations, but nevertheless I came to think of the monks as attempting to heal the thousand-year-old rift that had separated Christianity, East and West. I got used to the days bookended by prayer, matins and vespers, and I helped out in the puppy kennel, where classical music was played for the dogs on a stereo system. Eventually the monks opened up a bit about the program, agreeing with Darwin and James in that they allowed that the master-dog model could demonstrate how even a hierarchical relationship could prove to be a natural, organic boon for all involved.

"We do have authority, among ourselves, and with animals," said Brother Marc, at a roundtable discussion I arranged with a few of them. "But when you work with animals, you realize that authority does not mean manipulation. Authority means precisely service. This is what the good news of the Gospel was. The experience of authority, helping others, being in charge of and responsible for animals, teaches what we believe God is like."

Oka's temperature dropped at 2:00 A.M. on my final night at New Skete. Marc tapped lightly on the door of the guest quarters, retrieving me so I could watch him whelp his bitch. New Skete was settled in behind a mountain, outside a small town on the New York–Vermont border, and its nights were desolate and thick. We moved through the pure pitch to the puppy kennel. Oka was lying in a plastic tub in a whelping room, a heat lamp pointed down at her. There was an equipment tray ready with a suction bulb to clear the puppy's airway and dental floss to tie off the umbilical cord. Music played in the background, choir boys shrieking prayers, and a litter of puppies in the next room yelped for a while when they heard us come in. Oka looked worried. It was her first litter, Marc said, and she wasn't quite sure what was happening. An X-ray had revealed that she was carrying just one puppy, which was rare and an economic quandary for New Skete. The single dog would take a great deal of effort to raise and would be far less efficient than a multiple litter. Litters generally consisted of six to eight puppies, sometimes as many as thirteen. It wasn't uncommon for two or three to die in the birthing process. The first and the last had the hardest time of it, Marc said. "Sometimes they've gotten an infection two or three days before. They come out decomposed. They fall apart right in your hands."

Oka was shivering even though it was warm in the room, but Marc was reluctant to turn up the heat—it was the temperature drop that kept her from being lazy. The dog began to tear at a pile of newspapers in the tub, ripping with paws and teeth, answering an ancient call to nest. "Boy, you're fierce!" Marc said, petting the dog and sniffing at the air over where she stood. "Yes, you are. You're getting into it now."

We sat groggy through the night, waiting for the contractions to begin, Marc telling stories of litters gone bad, about intubating puppies whose dams did not produce milk properly, about performing a kind of primitive CPR on entire litters that came out not breathing. Marc had read once of an old practice of giving martinis to women who resisted labor, and sometimes he gave his dogs dishes of beer to settle them.

"I feel something," he said, kneading Oka's abdomen. "Maybe it's just your last meal. I don't feel it kicking. I hope it's alive."

He helped Oka tear the newspapers for a while but paused at one sheet that had a picture of John Paul II on it. "Oh, the pope!" he said. He moved to tear it again, to create a schism between himself and the pontiff even more literal than the one the monastery was trying to undo. Then he thought better of it and tossed the page back into Oka's bin.

Brother Peter arrived around 5:00 A.M. with coffee. It was time to artificially inseminate his own bitch, Nikki. He prepared a large syringe, and Werner's *Bridal Chorus* played as he readied her for the injection, lubricating a gloved finger and stimulating Nikki's vaginal canal to trigger the peristalsis that would move the sperm into her. When he was done, the monks began to worry about Oka—contractions had begun, but she seemed reluctant to push through it. They speculated that the puppy, because it had received all the nutrients of the pregnancy, was too large and might suffocate in the birth canal if it didn't come out quickly. There was concern because matins was not far off and Peter would soon have to leave.

Oka looked between the two men as they talked, baffled but faithful, for some reason confident that they would help her regulate the painful season. They gave her a shot of oxytocin to accelerate the labor, then tried positioning her in various stances to move the puppy along. Peter reached inside but couldn't get a grip.

"Grease won't help," he said. "You don't want to make it slippery. I keep feeling the back of the skull."

"No," Marc said, feeling for himself.

"No? There's no feet there, it's not the tail."

"Oh, God. I've got the jaw, I think. It's big, Peter. I don't know if it's going to get through."

"You think I should get Stavros? He's got narrower fingers."

"It's really small. The opening."

"I know. I'm afraid to put my finger in there. I keep pushing it back in."

"Come on, girl."

"Jesus, Mary and Joseph," Peter said.

The strings of some violent concerto climbed rapidly along scales in the background, and I swore I heard a voice from somewhere back in the kennel.

"What's that?"

"Oh, that's just a puppy."

Peter and Marc rested on their haunches for a time, and then Peter decided to cut her. He tore open a sterile scalpel head, pinched it, and leaned in behind Oka to begin the work of widening her vulva. Marc held her head and grunted echoes of the noises that Oka made, her face taking on an indescribable dog emotion built of pain and instinct, and if she wasn't transcendent, I wanted to argue, then why would she let these men hold her and tear at her, why did she know they meant her no harm?

"I felt the snout coming out," Peter said, taking a break with his hands bloodied. "I went into the canal. I think it's alive, thank God. But I don't know how far I can go with this surgical stuff."

Several more attempts failed, and they considered calling in a veterinarian. Then Peter had an idea. We all climbed into the tub with Oka to hold her upright, enlisting gravity in the effort. I held her up by her paws until my back strained, and Oka groaned deep and jammed her muzzle in under my jaw. Peter cut her until her vulva was wide enough for a fist, and she yelped as he pressed her sex even wider. The puppy finally fell out of her, and Oka collapsed in the tub, and we were all jubilant for a time, and Peter quickly tied the cord and snipped it and held up the puppy and said, "Here you are! Little girl!" The puppy was a slimy mound of black, a huge tongue sticking out of a tiny crease of a mouth, its eyes still closed and its body limp as a sock. Oka delivered the afterbirth on her own, a purplish jellyfish. "Now she can eat that," Marc said, and Oka went for it as the monks tended the puppy, gobbling it up but getting its fat balloon caught on the lower part of her jaw. I unhooked it with a finger, and down it went, and Oka pressed her ears back to look up at the men, for her puppy.

And now the monks realized that the puppy was not alive. It wasn't breathing. They worked to resuscitate it, holding it before them in two hands, performing compressions with their thumbs and pumping air into its lungs by putting their mouths over the whole of its wet face. Oka watched as they passed the limp shape back and forth.

"I don't think it's going to make it," Peter said.

"Keep massaging it."

They tried for ten minutes or so, the music in the background wandering now, someone's odd twistings, a maze like a mathematical search over the possibility of arpeggios, until finally resolving on a chord.

"It looked alive but . . . Come back," Pete said.

"Well, I think that's it."

"Okay. Oh, dear. Well, little girl. I'm sorry."

Peter looked up and seemed to hear the music for the first time and recognize it.

"Whelping to Bach," he said.

Up at matins a little later I felt an acute need for God, perhaps the first time I could earnestly say I'd felt such a thing during my entire time studying William James and religion. But even that was a little silly. The monks were neither farmers of dogs nor pet owners, and I was reacting like the latter, a fanatic on the verge of tears for a death that had an upside: the puppy would have strained New Skete's resources, and now Oka would know what to expect with her next litter. I felt the music of the awkward New Skete liturgy in my bones: *God is risen from the dead, conquering death by death, and on those in the grave restoring life.* "And here religion comes to our rescue," James had written,

> and takes our fate into her hands. There is a state of mind, known to religious men, but to no others, in which the will to assert ourselves and hold our own has been displaced by a willingness to close our mouths and be as nothing in the floods and waterspouts of God.

Now, okay. James isn't talking about any of his dogs *there,* and, truth be told, dog spirituality is part of a low, common wisdom evidenced by bumper-sticker axioms: DOG IS MY COPILOT; LORD, PLEASE HELP ME TO BE THE PERSON MY DOG THINKS I AM. I'd indicted this sentiment myself, railing against a Vermont Dog Chapel that was open "to all dogs and to people of any faith" and fretting over a "Blessing of the Animals" ceremony in my hometown. There was a silly side to this, too. The night of whelping to Bach rounded out my time at New Skete, but it seemed that my cynical side wasn't quite finished learning how dogs and the religious spirit interact. At home I had Becky, my own dog, now more than thirteen years old.

The monks had been surprised that Becky had lasted that long. Thirteen was the magic number for German shepherds. Hit thirteen, they said, and you're in the "Thirteen Club." Becky died shortly after her sixteenth birthday.

I'm skipping past a whole life here—the life, actually, I want to celebrate. Obviously, there are many anecdotes that make up that life, and the worry with dog stories, I think, is that many, even as they seem to capture something about the spirit of a particular animal, are actually pretty interchangeable. We think dogs are expressing their personality exactly at those moments they're doing what all dogs do. Better, I think, to leave the terms abstract. When Becky died, one thing that surprised me was that I found out that I had thought of her all along as a kind of audience. I read aloud when I write, and Becky must have heard everything I'd ever done twenty-five times or more, and because she didn't know the meaning of the words, she was better prepared than anyone to tap into Eliot's "aural imagination." I used Becky to imagine how my own work sounded, and she was there at the moment when my work began to mature. This implies something about how dogs can inform the literary life, and as I look back on Becky's life, I find that she was something of a literary nexus.

In her first year, we spent a lot of time with Charlie and Kayla. Charlie moved to a small house on a farm outside of Iowa City, and the four of us sometimes went for walks across the downed corn, the swaying fields littered with machine-stripped ears that made perfect dog toys. On those walks Charlie and I put our heads together to work out the business of storytelling (I received much more than I offered), and the dogs worked together to extract the largest branches they could find from twisting irrigation creeks. Becky's link to the literary world would eventually be much more literal, and makes for a comic genealogy. One night she was in the car when Writers' Workshop director Frank Conroy needed a lift from the postwork-shop watering hole, the Mill, to the more hard-core writers' bar, the Foxhead. Becky painted Frank's face with her tongue on the drive; he seemed to like it. That same year Lan Samantha Chang, who would succeed Frank as director of the workshop a decade later, spontaneously offered the nickname "Becky the Sea Dog," an exclamation that inspired a few children's stories with Becky as heroine, which I wrote, illustrated, and distributed myself. (I've since heard of them popping up as far away as Germany.) Becky had her share of literary references, too. She made a cameo in Tom Grimes's *WILL@ epicqwest.com,* and while she was no Dark Lady, she has appeared in a poem or two. For most of her life, Becky was more famous than I was.

Sam Chang's comment was prescient in that I eventually lived near a beach and spent hours throwing clamshells instead of sticks, whizzing the ovals just above the sand so Becky could chase them like game. Becky followed me on the writerly road trip I arranged for myself: I read *On the Road* on the road, and Becky the Sea Dog swam in the Atlantic and Pacific oceans, the Gulf of Mexico, and Lake Michigan all within a few months of each other. She adapted easily—better than I did—to the many moves that are part and par-cel of the literary life. These included several stints back in Iowa City. During the last I lived above a bar on the downtown mall. This made for some odd nights, and on one of these—and this, I assure you, was the result of a misunderstanding for which I carry no blame—I blacked out and came to in an orange jumpsuit in the local drunk tank. Several months later I moved about a mile out of town, as Charlie and Kayla had done. I was at work on William James by then, and the time came for my retreat to the Monks of New Skete. While I was gone, Becky, now a member of the "Thirteen Club," creaky as you'd expect her to be but sneaky in her ability to slip away, fooled her dog-sitter and set out to look for me, limping the mile through traffic back to my old bar apartment. The Humane Society found her and took her to the pound.

Punch line: both my dog and I were arrested on the pedestrian mall in Iowa City and spent a night in jail.

But that's the kind of dog story I tend to be suspicious of. All dogs follow their masters home, and besides, it says nothing of what I'm driving at about dogs and faith. Becky stuck around for another several years, enduring two more moves, one to a city whose asphalt left her claws bloody because she could no longer lift her feet all the way off the ground, and then, finally, to a kind of paradise, a home at the end of a long grassy boulevard, an arboretum that got no traffic at all except for occasional convoys of deer. I was living on campus at a small college, as writer-in-residence. Early on in my tenure, I arranged for Charlie to visit, to read and teach a class. One of my students was named Becky, and she had a young daughter: Kayla. We all smiled at the coincidence, and the memories came rushing in.

Becky faded over the next four or five months. She kept up her morning routine of a trip out and around the front yard—working dogs love their jobs—but she was slowing down, her eyes and ears going, sphincter control failing. It seems a universal rule that if we don't die fast, we all die very slowly.

On the morning of her final day, I remember very distinctly that Becky stood at the bottom of the porch and sniffed the morning breeze. A dog's nose is ageless, and I liked thinking of the way that just the scent offered her a portrait of what was afoot in the world. It didn't matter that she was old—she could still take the measurements, and it was a pleasure for her. The world tasted good, is probably the only way we can understand it. It had been a long time since Becky could run—an MRI in a "people hospital" had once revealed inoperable damage to the disks between her vertebrae—but sometimes she would forget and attempt a trot. She gave it one last shot that morning, following a friendly cat.

That afternoon she turned for the worse, as they say—it became clear she would die very soon. I carried her into the yard to pee, but she couldn't stand, and I picked her up in my arms and paced the lawn, sobbing into the scruff of her neck, which was still as loose and soft as it had been when she was a puppy. Becky had always been small for a German shepherd, tipping the scales at sixty-five pounds in her prime, but now she was just thirty-six pounds. Back inside, I laid her on the spot in the bedroom she favored for sleeping through the night. Her heart was racing as though she had just come in from a run. She seemed uncertain, but not fearful. That night I lay down on the carpet beside her and stayed where she could see me for an hour or so, until her eyes closed and she fell asleep.

I woke at 4:00 A.M. for no good reason. I got up to check on her. She was awake again, her eyes moving and open wide, and she seemed to be seeing not just the bedroom but something more as well.

Had I not awakened, I would surely have gone on to guess that Becky had died peacefully in her sleep, but what I saw as the night proceeded leads me to conclude that no one dies peacefully, that such a thing isn't even possible. Her heart now felt like some insane boy pounding on a drum inside her chest. Twenty minutes later her bladder and bowels voided in a sudden gush. The relaxation of involuntary muscle is sometimes used as an indicator of death all by itself, but Becky kept moving for a while after that, and I was struck by how hard it was to decide that she was finally gone. I realize that I'm not establishing anything new about this kind of moment. As deaths go, this was a pretty good one, and in fact I think it's the ordinariness of it that is important. Even now I linger over the details that are generally subsumed into obituary idioms. For some time after the shit and piss came spilling out of her, I had the strong sense that Becky was still fighting to stay alive for me, that there was a loyalty that had been bred into her and was her job, and that she was striving to do her job. Our relationship was a hierarchy, surely, but while I was supposed to be the more transcendent member of that relationship, I had absolutely no power over how it would end. There is something to this that is so fundamental and ordinary that it would be unremarkable, except for the fact that we generally do not address it. We buy the myth of the peaceful death. Becky's eyes kept moving, and her claws curled. Her head pointed in toward her chest, and her mouth opened wide in a long spasm that looked like a scream. Her chest stayed warm, her nose was still cold. I knelt over her for a long while. Eventually I shone a light in her eyes and saw the fixed black disks through the clouds of her cataracts. But it was not until I felt the chill of her flews and turned away from her that I learned what I still needed to know.

I thought, *It will be nice to see her again.* Later, telling this story to others, I changed the grammar: *It would be . . .* But most honestly it was *will,* and that I think is what I learned about dogs and faith. Don't get me wrong: I didn't have any special insight into the architecture of the universe at that moment—I didn't peek into some dog Valhalla where Becky was already back to chasing clamshells—but nevertheless there is something to how that thought arrived, organic and fully formed, before I'd had a chance to intellectualize the experience at all. It was a moment in which I was permitted a glimpse into my own nature, and what looked back out at me was an expression of human loneliness and of a painful longing that was the sure result when people first became curious about their mortality. The Monks of New Skete had taught me that dogs can take us outside ourselves; William James had taught me that consciousness was just as likely to interfere with the self as comprise it. Later in the morning, I bought five bags of ice and laid Becky in the back of my car. I drove two hours to a facility that permitted individual cremations, and I set her in the oven and closed the door myself. Dogs heal a schism, too, I think. It's not the chasm between us and heaven, but there is a glory on the other side, hidden in ourselves, and we're more inclined to reject it than embrace it. My dog let me touch that glory briefly, and that is what I carry.

Dog on Two Legs

LYDIA MILLET

I remember the way things died. First there were the caterpillars
we put in jars, collected from a row of trees near the schoolyard,
where they festooned every low-hanging branch for a couple of weeks
in spring: they may have starved or they may have suffocated. We
took them home in droves, punched holes in the lids of jam jars and
stuck twigs and leaves into the jars with them; but rather than spin
cocoons most of them perished there, airless and immobile, their
dried-up bodies curling into forlorn little loops. Now and then one
survived to emerge as a butterfly, and in anticipation of this we took
the tops off the jars once the cocoons were spun.

We were careless with the lives of hermit crabs gathered at the
ocean in summertime, too. We picked them up by their shells and
put them in homemade terrariums. I don't remember what we did to
feed them; probably nothing. They smelled more than the caterpillars when they went. The caterpillars gave off only a faint, moldy
emanation if you put your nose to the mouth of the jar, but the hermit crabs speedily imparted a powerful odor of putrefaction.

Insects, in general, died well, more neatly than beasts of bone and
flesh. In the yard we found lovely cicadas, with their bright colors
and gossamer wings, and beetles and potato bugs; on windowsills it
was houseflies most often, houseflies and dull-colored moths. All of

these looked, in death, much as they had in life. There was no new vulnerability or repugnance to being dead, with them. They lay still and gathered dust, but tended to retain their forms.

We also witnessed the many deaths of our pets, a pageant of species that moved through the various rooms of our house like gunshot ambassadors. There were too many to count: a fish named Sauve Qui Peut—Soaky Poo in the household vernacular—dozens of finches, mice, hamsters, guinea pigs, rabbits, and through it all two venerable cats. We never had dogs. The animals died in various ways: the birds by being eggbound, a hamster by choking, some by wasting, some by kidney infection or old age, but most by no means visible, since there were no autopsies. (Or necropsies, more properly, the distinct term for postmortem animal dissection.) The deaths were often sudden and unexplained, and met painfully with my fondness for the individuals involved, which was always deeply felt and sometimes histrionically displayed. Was it our fault? Was it nature? Was it something the animals themselves had done?

Also our family was captivated by stories of talking beasts and the magic lands whence they hailed, so I spent much of my youth waiting for the private moment when an animal might finally consent to let down its guard, open its mouth, and speak to me in the King's English. In stories, magic revealed what I had always suspected: that animals were people in disguise. But in real life, the animals' common distinguishing trait was this: they were the things that died. I saw hundreds of them depart, if you include the caterpillars, long before I encountered a dying person.

And yet I wouldn't say these animal deaths taught me a lesson. That's the conventional way of looking at children and animal death: these less important, mini-deaths serve a didactic purpose as proxies for human death, showing innocent children what the reaper looks like. The animals are an introductory course in life's finitude. But in fact—beyond the fact that animals' true role is far less utilitarian than this, far richer and more complex—I don't think I understood death at all by seeing them die. I couldn't have, because even now, at the tail end of my thirties, I don't understand death. Rather what I saw was the diversity and mystery of dying and my own powerlessness in its face; what I felt was a loss that could never be fathomed—the animals' presence had been ineffable in the first place, and so now was their absence—and the confusion of my own possible complicity.

But as children grow up they seem to lose the grip they once had on the agony of this separation, this permanent severing of live self from dead other. Defensively we teach our young to cease to identify with the pain of others past a certain "appropriate" point whose threshold is quite low—to assimilate and dismiss such nonrelevant pain in order to attain the well-adjustment of selfishness. Our denial of the importance of animal death is a logical part of the distancing act implied by maturity, of the creation of a hierarchy of meaning that allows us to function smoothly and without constant crises of anxiety. And the suppression of the bond we instinctively feel with animals, which we deny more and more as we age to avoid facing up to the puzzlement of our similarities, allows us to ignore any possible responsibilities to them as well. Hence the acquired skill of dismissing the importance of animal death often brings with it the habit of also dismissing their life.

As they become adults children learn to objectify "lower" animals more and more—animals that are safely, visibly different from people—and to dismiss the deaths of these animals also, as less; they learn that animals do not feel as we do, are not intelligent as we are, have no consciousness of death, and thus suffer less. *We* are the sole owners of suffering, is what many children are trained to believe by the time they become adults. *We alone* live in awareness. Because animals do not see death the way we do, their suffering is inferior in quality—machinelike, neurons firing, without emotional or narrative context.

And yet animals are the ones who die.

This, more than any other thing, we know about them—not only children but all of us, who see their corpses everywhere every day,

whether as roadkill or shoes or coats or on the dinner plate. Because
animals die all around us and are seen by us after death, it becomes
the case that by conceptually and emotionally affirming our separation from the animal kingdom we try to push our own death away.

We may die too, at some point, we may be forced to acknowledge,
but our death will not be the same as their death. Our death, for instance, will often give onto a glorious afterlife, because we partake of
a soul. Animals, who unfortunately lack the benefit of a soul, become more dead than we do. Their deadness is meat. Ours is holy.

And even if not holy, from the secular-humanist perspective, our
death is enlightened. It is not an animal death, a blunt-force trauma,
but a sensitive and tormented parting that leaves behind a sheaf of
memories, a legacy of influence and affection.

With insects, which we most often see dead—indeed see dead all
over the place, littering our landscape with the minor specks of their
bodies—the victims are so far removed from us as to be unthreaten-
ing, so different from us in their essence that they provoke no auto-
matic identification or anxiety. Fish, perhaps a slightly greater twinge;
birds, maybe still greater; and mammals are closest of all, since
we identify with them most strongly. Their deaths clearly cause us
greater distress.

Among familiar mammals the two kinds closest to us, in our
daily lives, are of course cats and dogs. You'd think, with all our
elaborate conceptual, linguistic, and even legal efforts, as a species, to
establish separation between other animals and ourselves—to elevate
ourselves through this distinction to ensure we don't "act like animals" or "die like dogs"—that we would strive to keep animals at
arm's length. But instead, while in myriad ways seeking still to af-
firm our inner differences from the beasts, we surround ourselves
with them. They adorn our lives everywhere, with dogs and cats
alone numbering in the billions and their images proliferating across
all media. We do not live without them.

Though my own family had been cat people I grew more interested in dogs as I aged; cats began to seem all the same, echoing a

lovely and remote archetype, while dogs, and particularly purebreds, were like intriguing character actors. Each physiognomy evokes a type—less an archetype, maybe, than a stereotype, which is what renders purebreds inherently comic or tragic and also makes them approachable. But mutts also broadcast specific personhood in a way cats do not. Cats offer many distant aesthetic amenities, while dogs offer a kind of amplified sociability, with the foibles of all social creatures.

The dogs with noble aspects were the ones I admired most—tall, proud, intelligent dogs with solemn faces, dogs that enjoyed the liberation of running and jumping, swam eagerly in the surf and were adept at hiking up mountain trails.

But when push came to shove what I got was a pug.

My pug fetish started with an ancient, overweight, wheezing individual named Hombre, whom I met in a living room in Albuquerque; he was a wreck, a disaster. He waddled around emitting labored snorts. After that meeting I launched an obsessive pug-research project that soon revealed the worst distortions of the breed—most notably the way they struggle to breathe through nostrils the size of pins in their nonexistent, almost concave noses. (Some pugs undergo surgery in which their nostrils are excavated with a scalpel, enlarged for easier air passage.) Still I was captivated. When I first announced to my husband that I wanted a pug—this was before we were married—and showed him a picture online, he said only, "It's an abomination."

It couldn't be denied. The fact that purposeful inbreeding has not only shaped an animal in the subtle particulars of its ears or tail but subjected it to constant respiratory torment can only be denounced.

And yet, at my insistence, we got a pug.

Much has been said by scholars of the dog, cartoonists, and devisers of witty greeting cards about the resemblance of owners to their dogs or dogs to their owners. Physically the possibilities are limited and the humor broad, but in less material terms the resemblance is genuine. Because we tend to identify so strongly with our dogs, and our dogs, at least to my eye, come in their own enigmatic way also to identify with us, it's not a stretch to say that most people see in their dogs qualities they admire, and may decide to bring a particular dog into their home for its apparent embodiment of these qualities. Nor is it a stretch to assume that people try to take on those qualities themselves, so that what they attempt in themselves and what they project onto their dogs are often one and the same. So where exactly in my pug do I see myself?

My pug, name of Bug, is not the sharpest dog in the drawer. She likes food; chiefly, in life, her pleasure comes from food. She dances around in circles, bobbing up and down with a certain lack of balletic grace at feeding times. She breathes loudly and sneezes volubly on people, provoking exclamations of dismay, even horror. She wants to play more than she's played with, giving her an abject aspect; when people come to the door she falls upon them in hyperactive and frenzied abandon, whether or not they return her affection. I can't bring myself to say she is the opposite of dignified—there have been moments when it seemed clear to me that even Bug's minimal dignity exceeds my own—but many others tend to view her with a mixture of sympathy, alarm, and forbearance.

I may perceive certain similarities between Bug and myself—I, too, fixate overly on my food, metaphorically dancing around it when it comes; I, too, can have an eager-to-please, abject aspect, particularly under the influence of behavior-altering substances—but I definitely don't see her as a vanity pet. She's not the gorgeous Weimaraner being walked on the Upper East Side by a well-groomed woman in heels; the glossy retriever or hound trotted out by the upscale, macho hunter; the teacup Chihuahua owned by the perky college girl; or the high-maintenance bichon frisé on the lap of the society matron. She's something else.

And clearly, that something is only part dog.

We all have our concept of "dog"; even though dog types vary almost infinitely, there remains an essential dogness we can identify. Bug seems to chronically fail the test. People unaccustomed or unsympathetic to the breed constantly say things like, "But that's not a real dog!" or "Is she even a *dog*?"

Because Bug openly undermines the notion of a natural animal, mocking the nobility of her wolf ancestors. She couldn't survive a day in the outdoors, much less a life in the wild. She has no protruding jaw or sharp teeth to bite with, no large ears to hear with, no long legs to run with. Her tail's no good for swatting flies, curled into a little corkscrew as it is. When she tries to swim, she can't even float: she sinks immediately. Her whole being contradicts the notion of virility, of the predator, of savagery and muscle. In fact, more than most dogs—already domesticated, highly inbred forms of a wild ancestor—Bug the Pug is a hybrid.

On the face of it, the pug choosers among us value the presence of comic relief in our lives above some other presences—possibly, you could say, above morality, even, or kindness. For who would suffer a dog to snuffle the way mine does whose guiding light, in life, was charity or justice? (Plainly, the most virtuous among dog owners must and do choose mutts.) It should be noted that legions of my fellow pug owners deck out their dogs in elaborate fancy dress and parade them at massive pug costume parties, thousands of dressed-up animals strong.

Yet the pug's defining characteristic is not humor but poignancy. Her face is permanently fixed in one expression: plaintive and bulgy-eyed longing. It's a look so powerful I have to remind myself constantly that my dog is not heartbroken. And she likes to stare at you, just sit near you and stare up at your face for a long period of time. If you respond even slightly—a twitch is sufficient—she begs and prances excitedly. She's a physical embodiment of need, with an expectant demeanor that asks a perennial question. What the question is from her point of view is unknowable and possibly food-related, but to me it feels most like, *Will you love me, love me, love me?* And in fact it can be oddly stressful, exerting a constant pull on the conscience, to be near a half-dog, half-human face that poses that question unceasingly.

That which is poignant is at once "profoundly moving" and "keenly distressing" to the mind or feelings, according to the dictionary. It combines the tragic and the comic such that the apprehender of poignancy is conflicted, caught eternally between ridicule and melancholy, identification and objectification.

What makes Bug so poignant is the fact that the half of her that's not dog is pretty much, well . . . human. Her frontward-facing eyes and flat face, with features configured as our own are, give her a humanoid aspect it's impossible to refute. What makes the sight of a pug so aesthetically and emotionally excruciating is its juxtaposition of a human face with a dog form and a dog consciousness.

We try to separate ourselves from animals, yet we do not wish to live without them, and they infiltrate all corners of our lives. We push them away and pull them near. Throughout all this cohabitation we desperately emphasize the elemental differences between ourselves and them. With dogs in particular, we love them as we condescend, discipline as we display, mix up disgust and pride. In general, we work hard to keep the hierarchy, and the distinction, clear. What makes the pug unique is its transgression of this separation, which confuses the viewer. The pug openly violates the human-animal boundary.

People have chosen to fashion the pug deliberately down through the centuries—according to the American Kennel Club, from as early as 400 B.C. pugs have been the favored companions of Tibetan monks and Chinese and Japanese emperors, who bred them all the time to be more and more flat-faced and humanoid as the millennia passed. The pug is not alone as a humanoid dog but is arguably the most extreme example, beating out the likes of French and English bulldogs and even Boston terriers with its supremely humanoid countenance.

Yet what pugs resemble most of all, even more than people, is the bulgy-eyed demon figures of old Chinese scroll paintings. Is this a coincidence? The round, protruding eyes, the square face shapes of the demons, bear such a close similarity to the geometry of the pug that the first time I saw the scrolls, in a museum, I thought of pug dogs rather than men. And Bug begins to seem, to me—and this, like her, is both a laughable and a serious proposition—like a caricature of a god, the kind of god that comes in the shape of a composite monster.

There are Hindu deities that are part man and part animal, all the mythological creatures that combine us with other mammals, or birds, or fish, or even plants—the fauns, the mermaids, the dryads and naiads. The images of composite gods and the composite monsters are manifold throughout history. Even Plato was at a loss to describe or understand their multitudes, complaining in *Phaedrus* of the difficulty of explaining "the forms of the Centaurs, and then that of the Chimaera . . . a whole crowd of such creatures, Gorgons and Pegas, and multitudes of strange, inconceivable, portentous natures" (Frans Ilkka Mäyrä). In fact, so confusing are the half-man, half-animal gods that he has to give up thinking about them and focus instead, in a famous line, on himself: "I dismiss these matters and . . . investigate not these things, but myself, to know whether I am a monster more complicated and more furious than Typhon or a gentler and simpler creature, to whom a divine and quiet lot is given by nature."

Maybe one such confounding and holy monster is the pug.

After all, dogs have become almost our own creation. With no other animals have we had such a long history of manipulation and design, of making varieties. Dogs are a kind of animal art form, neither the "other" of wild animals nor the "us" of people but suspended in between. And the oddness of the pug in particular—even the extremes of feeling provoked by its appearance—is typical of art, which does not explain but merely offers, which is itself a thought-provoking object that cannot be fully parsed and is often met with confusion or distaste. We make art to approach the sublime, creeping up to the altar—but we can never touch its essence, only circulate vaguely and hopefully around it.

Still our desire to be close to communion with the universe of sentience we don't know, to be on the verge of touching it, is always with us. And the existence of pugs points to one more way we're drawn, despite ourselves, to a union with animals that supersedes our separation from them—be it ever so absurd, at times, ever so befuddling and tormented. With pugs it's as if the mysterious and personal affinity we feel for animals, and for dogs in particular, wished to express itself in a living being.

With her hybrid, homuncular appearance, in her exaggerated fusion of *Homo sapiens* and *Canis familiaris,* my dog rejects the separation of man from animal that we're taught from youth to assume as, arguably, she rejects the separation of art from nature. She disallows an easy dismissal of animals for their otherness, and with it the easy dismissal of both their lives and their deaths. Sure, she's still an animal, and animals are still the ones that die, predeceasing us endlessly: but her face will always be with me. She simply cannot be assimilated.

Of course the humorous, arresting, extreme configuration of her face doesn't require an interpretation—some may register it as freakish and choose to move on—but unlike Plato, I find myself compelled. I don't hold with the idea that enlightenment will come to me from looking inward alone. After all, it didn't work for Socrates; he died, in the end, without perfect self-knowledge. Instead I keep looking out. I don't want to turn away from my monster.

Bridgette

VICTORIA REDEL

I said, "No dog."

For weeks then months I said, "No dog."

I said, "Period. No discussion. I'm not budging."

My younger son said, "I'll never ask for another thing. No more presents, ever, not even birthday presents. I'll never want anything else."

I said, "No dog."

My other son said, "It's not fair. You had a dog growing up."

It was true; we had two dogs. First there was Lucky, a rough collie puppy left in a basket at the front door of our house. I grew up taking rides on Lucky's strong, agreeable back. She loved us; she loved us loyally, territorially, fiercely, and, unfortunately, violently, ready to tear into anyone who walked up our slate front walk. When we were forced to get Lucky out of our suburb and onto a farm, my father announced, "No dog. Period. No discussion." We girls did then what daughters do with resistant fathers—picketed through the house with Magic Markered signs saying UNFAIR DAD and CRUELTY TO KIDS, and we cajoled, and then, when all else failed, we threw our arms around him, kissing, cuddling him and saying *please please please please please* until he relented and JoJo, the Maltese, became the most pampered member of our family for the next twelve years.

I said, "No dog," though memory had softened my resolve.

My younger son, quick to hear the emotional crack, said, "Come on, Mom. A boy and his dog. Hours romping together, exploring the forest. Isn't it a part of a healthy childhood?"

"Not so fast, smartypants," I said, "We live in the city." I toughened right back up thinking about the morning, noon, and night walks with a dog. Thinking about the rain-or-shine or sleet-or-hail walks with the dog. Thinking about the dreadful poop bags.

My son said, "But, Mom, you read to me about Maxi the Taxi Dog every night of my long childhood. He doesn't need flowers and fields. He loves the city."

Then I made the big mistake: I looked at my boys, the keen, open faces of childhood. Didn't I really believe, city or country, that a home was better with a dog in it? Didn't I believe that the more love in a home, the stronger the home? I allowed myself the image of these boys happy to return home after the long school day, greeted by a wagging tail, a dog that wrestled or retrieved balls, a dog that snuggled on the floor with them while they watched Sunday television.

My sly younger cuddled close. "Let's save a dog, Mom. A stray."

My unbudgeable heart collapsed.

"You'll have to feed the dog," I feebly insisted, and watched them nod though I knew, of course, that they would have nodded their heads to the most draconian stipulations—no candy on Halloween, in bed by 6:00 P.M. until you graduate from high school—because they knew—just as my sisters and I had known—a parent could always be worn down, and now it was just a matter of time and a couple more flimsy promises until a dog was living in our home.

The day we went to have our first look—our it's-only-a-look, our don't-expect-anything, especially-that-we'll-find-the-right-dog look—was the first Saturday after 9/11. Friends were talking about moving out of New York. We'd spent the week helping sort donated clothes

at the Chelsea Piers skating rink. There were sandwiches made outside St. Vincent's Hospital to be brought down to the World Trade
Center site. I'd put together a go-bag with flashlights, sleeping bags,
water, and cash. Looking to enlarge our family, looking for more responsibilities, seemed a little crazy. But that uneasy morning walking up to the pet store where the rescue and adoption group had set
up their crates, the happiness and comfort and security that a dog
would surely bring my sons seemed like good thing, a healthy thing
in an unhealthy world. Suddenly, adopting a stray seemed like part
of making a better world. If I wanted a world where people showed
responsibility and compassion—a dog seemed a way to encourage
this in my sons.

But even in a better world, I wanted a beautiful dog, and at first
Bridgette was not my idea of a beautiful dog. A mutt—New York
City style—clearly part boxer, and from there the guessing began—
ridgeback? pit? shepherd? Wasn't there something beagle about the
angles of her face? Even the name she'd been given, Bridgette, hardly
seemed what I would have chosen for a dog. But my younger son,
Gabriel, and my partner of seven years, Bill, thought Bridgette was a
winner. Gentle, unruffled by the city traffic when we walked her
around the block, she seemed steady and sweet. Bill said the dog had
the focus and ease we wanted in a dog. Gabriel said Bridgette was
perfect. I saw my son's happiness. And then the thing about loving
kicked in, and suddenly I noticed that she had arresting eyes—dark
mascara and a soulful, serious look. She was lean, muscular, and a
perfect combination for a city dog: big but not too big.

Before I knew really what was what, we had agreed to take
Bridgette home for an overnight, and the adoption folks were giving
us a crate and food. We'd talk in the morning to make sure we were
the right fit. By the time we were at our building we were laughing—of course the fit was right. Our stray walked into the apartment as if she were home.

———

Gabriel was right. Bridgette was the perfect dog. At a year old, she
was already house-trained. She listened. She was easy about the dog
crate. She wasn't a barker. She made herself quickly a part of our
family. Gabriel fed her. Jonah, my older son, was teaching her tricks.
Bill was the night walker. I learned that the city is actually an easy
place to have a dog. There are lots of dog runs, and the parks have an
off-leash law between 9:00 P.M. and 9:00 A.M. I'd roll out of bed and
across the street to Riverside Park. Even in the 7:00 A.M. winter dark,
there was a neighborhood scene of other dog owners. We talked, the
dogs played and chased squirrels. Above us a resident hawk hunted,
flying between the limbs of the linden tree.

We all seemed the better for it.

On January 1 I was out early, Bridgette off leash roaming Riverside Park. I was tired, a little hungover, and grateful to be in 2002. It
wasn't that there was any evidence that the world would be any better this year, but getting out of the old year and into the new one
seemed somehow a good thing for my city. Friends hadn't moved.
Friends, whose children had been in the school next to the towers,
where there was so much dust that teachers had trouble seeing the
children as they evacuated the building, were working in close and
effective community with their school even as it was housed in temporary quarters.

Then suddenly dogs were fighting, that terrible fierce snarl of
dogs in a knot of fighting. Though she'd never been in a scrabble before, I immediately recognized the sound of my dog and ran to where
she and another dog were in the thick of it. We got them apart. The
other dog was yelping. The owner was screaming. I leashed Bridgette.
She was calm and heeled at my side like the poster dog of good
behavior.

The owner screamed, "Who are you? Who the fuck is your
dog?"

"Is your dog okay?" I asked after she'd checked; it had stopped
whimpering, but she kept saying, "Who the fuck are you? What's

wrong with your dog?" She scowled at me with suspicion. Bridgette had never gotten into a fight. This felt like the playground—where with a single push or tantrum your kid becomes a problem child, a hoodlum. And you the delinquent parent.

When I knew that everything was okay, I said, "Have a peaceful year," and I left the park trying to hold on to some moral superiority or at least good manners.

But I was shaken. What had happened? Was Bridgette the aggressor or was she just protecting herself? There was no chance for a post-playground conversation. I chalked it up as a dog moment. But over the next few weeks, Bridgette got into more fights and began snapping at dogs, while on the leash.

One night at home, while we were all in our evening routine—I was cooking dinner, Jonah was plowing though homework, and Gabriel was on the kitchen floor giving Bridgette smoochy kisses along her belly and on her face—then, with me right there in the room, Bridgette nipped at Gabe.

There were clear red marks around Gabriel's nose and mouth that lasted for a few days.

I was told to call an aggressive-dog trainer.

A dog, I learned, comes into its full temperament at a year and a half. So my Bridgette's easy nature, her I-want-to-love-everyone behavior, could, it seemed, be permanently shifting. I learned there were ways to manage this. Maybe my youngest couldn't cuddle with Bridgette because the dog would interpret the behavior as too submissive on my son's part. Dogs are pack animals, and we all had to put Bridgette in her place as lowest pup in this pack. Suddenly all the talk in our home was about restriction.

In trying to learn about dog aggression, I found every bit of contradictory information. "There are no bad dogs, just bad owners," claimed one expert. Others claimed that the dog was just trying to convey some information or that some dogs found kids annoying. We were instructed not to be strict with the dog. We were instructed to be demanding and tough. We were instructed to be attentive but not overly attentive. Others blamed it on careless breeding of aggressive dogs. There was talk of encroachment on space, that we hadn't been reading signs properly. But what were the proper signs? I had been right there. Bridgette and my son had been playing for a considerable time when, without a warning growl, she nipped.

I told the boys that our dog was on probation. I could sadly accept a dog that wouldn't be able to play in the dog runs or run off leash in the park. But I would not accept any attacking behavior of humans.

We settled into the new life. Stricter, watchful, but we still loved our dog. I worked with trainers. I harbored hopes that with real discipline she'd shift back to the 100 percent sweetheart we'd first brought home. She never managed to play again with other dogs. I found places for her to run, off leash, alone. But she seemed content at home, and we all adjusted, as a family does to make room for the unexpected problems and limitations of those we love.

Then, a year later, without warning, she nipped again. Again the younger. Her biggest fan. Her advocate.

And a week later she bit him full on in the face.

I was in the room and when Gabriel came up from the bite, crying, his face already masked in blood, he said, "Mom, I'm fine. You can't give her away."

His brother stepped in to calm him while I called the doctor, who made arrangements to have a plastic surgeon meet us in the emergency room.

Seventeen stitches later we were home.

In the next weeks, I was given every kind of advice. One friend who had a farm full of animals and dogs said to put the dog down, that a dog that bites will invariably bite again. Our vet said that there wasn't a question—I would need to find another home for the dog. The dog-adoption group said I should crate Bridgette whenever kids were in the house. And that my son and Bridgette should work intensively with a special aggressiveness trainer.

I tried to explain that there were only five hours per day when children weren't in the house. That I wasn't concerned only with the beautiful bodies of my sons, but that they each had beautiful friends, that their friends had beautiful brothers and beautiful sisters who often arrived with them, and that there were frequently the babies of any number of my friends crawling around my house.

The dog-adoption folks looked at me with disgust, as if I'd confessed to a chaotic, shabbily run, probably unlicensed child-care center. Apparently they were all single and childless.

Word went out to help find Bridgette a new home. People were helpful, contacting friends who wanted a dog and other friends who were inclined to take on difficult situations. But big surprise, it's hard to find anyone who will want a dog that has bitten. People would come over; they'd fall in love with those dark, sweet eyes. They'd be impressed with her good house manners. Maybe they'd even ask if they could have her for an overnight. But the next morning I'd receive a call. They told me they'd fallen in love with her in about two seconds but they weren't ready to take on all the unpredictability. They found it freaky, her sudden lunges at other dogs. A couple said they hoped for babies. I understood.

Even with the stitches still in his face, my younger son was pleading for another chance.

He said, "It really was my fault, Mom."

Maybe he was partly at fault—clearly, over the year he'd been given unmistakable clues by the dog that a certain kind of nuzzling was too intense. He should have known what kind of play would irritate her. Certainly, he'd come to understand what would irk his brother, what would provoke a punch or a flat-out brother-to-brother takedown. But wasn't I right there, in the room, for each nip and for the final bite? And what did I know? That he was kissing his pup just as he did every day. I couldn't believe that lying on the floor with his dog was wrong.

But Bridgette was a stray, our stray, our dog we'd rescued, and now, suddenly, I was contemplating a give-back. Could that be right? Despite her being "the boys'" dog, she and I spent hours together, walking outdoors; she settled under my desk as I wrote. As tough as I'd been about getting a dog, I was now entirely in the rhythm of dog owning. But the obvious truth was, I loved my sons more, and I also loved having a home that was safe, child-friendly. I seesawed, thinking about it. A safe home seemed a given. Yet didn't I believe that it was an obligation of love to hang in there and try to make things work? Wasn't she part of our family action on behalf of a better world? A world where I believed that conflict resolution was essential, that you didn't give up. What was I teaching the boys if I gave Bridgette back to the adoption group?

The woman in the park's question, "Who the fuck are you?," echoed in my head.

When I spoke to friends, they didn't get it. "Come on, we're talking seventeen stitches!" friends reminded me. "Next time it's some neighbor kid's ear." Or "This isn't about world peace." I wasn't sleeping well. Bridgette slept at my bedside, following me from room to room as I worried in the night. But in the early daylight, as I walked Bridgette on a tight leash or let her off leash illegally on the fenced-in empty basketball courts, she seemed a suspicious, unpredictable creature.

Finally one Sunday, a year and a half after we'd rescued Bridgette, I brought her down to the Lower East Side where the adoption group had agreed to board her with the hopes of finding her a new home. I wouldn't let my sons come along. Bill and I cried the whole way downtown. We circled the block two times. When I brought her up the narrow stairs and they buzzed me in, Bridgette was shaking uncontrollably. I comforted her, saying, "It's okay baby," though it wasn't okay, and she was a keen dog with a clear attention to my moods. Despite my warning, they tried to let her in among the other dogs, and she quickly went at one. Then they put her in alone in a small room.

I lied when I went home, telling the boys that it was like doggy sleepaway camp and that Bridgette would probably get more attention there than we could ever give her.

My younger one started in that first night with, "So we'll get another dog."

I said, "No dog."

"Mom, you loved having a dog," he said.

I did. Wasn't that the point? I didn't want another heartbreak.

"I don't want a dog," my older boy chimed in. "Look what happened. It's too much responsibility. It will turn out badly again."

But of course I didn't want that, teaching my boys to shy away from loving because grief might be involved.

So we grieved and talked about Bridgette. What a great dog she was. How she was the 98 percent perfect dog. "But that 2 percent was pretty bad," my elder son said with all his straight-out call-it-as-it-is wisdom. I made weekly calls to where Bridgette was boarding. I did not tell the boys she was still there, unclaimed. Bridgette's story eventually turned out all right. I learned that a person who volunteered at the center fell in love with Bridgette and after months of walking her decided to adopt her. A single woman. No roommates. A perfect situation for Bridgette.

A year later Gabriel declared the period of mourning officially over, and he went into a marathon of pleading, begging, reasoning, insisting, bargaining. Again, he'd give up all future presents. He'd walk her even in the middle of his school day.

Jonah weighed in, repeating that we had no business getting a dog. It would come to no good; it was too much responsibility. And if we were foolish enough to get a dog, he wanted no part of the business.

I agreed with Jonah about the responsibility. Despite my pleasure in those early dawn walks, wasn't it a lot easier to stay warm in bed? But then there was the boy who, despite the trauma of a dog bite, was encouraging the rest of us to keep taking risks that could bring joy.

What if this dog didn't work out either, if, as Jonah said, it would come to no good? I was scared in exactly the ways I knew people to close down, make their lives safer but smaller. Still, I said, "No dog."

I said "no dog" halfheartedly a few pathetic times and then made the mistake of agreeing to visit a litter of golden retriever puppies. I am surprised that an entrepreneur hasn't created a retreat where clients lie down in the soft bedding of puppy boxes and let litters of fluffy four-week-old puppies nuzzle and lick and frisk over soul-weary bodies, creating instant happiness and delight. Or perhaps, at least, I should include in my own living will that my departing body be given the final ecstasy of a litter of puppies. The remarkable thing is only that then and there I didn't agree to two puppies—"Come on, Mom. Brother and sister, they'll never be lonely."

Gabriel wanted to name her Ophelia. The breeder insisted that Gabriel find a name no more than two syllables.

And once again we all fell in love. Even Jonah, who rigorously worked to maintain his moral distance from the whole dog experi-ence for a little while, until he realized that every time he fought with me teenage style or was brought in for a you're-in-some-trouble, son conversation, Brook was like glue to his side. Whenever he got angry, she stayed close, waiting for when, despite his fury, he'd start to pet her and it would begin to quiet him.

Interestingly, our dog, Brook—as in "river," not "Shields"—is a remarkably submissive dog. She'll often come to a statue stop until an approaching dog passes. In play she's always on her back. Often I am having to tell concerned onlookers that indeed she's really fine—rather thrilled, actually—to have two, even three dogs chewing and tugging on various ears and paws. The Riverside dog gang joke when she staggers to her feet, always the muddiest dog, that she's the park's love whore. Call it lucky temperament? Or, is this ever-eager-to-please dog tuning in to our family's need for mildness? We were the ragtag strays this time. The ones who needed a second chance. Sometimes I consider that this time the dog rescued us. But mostly I'm happy for our home to be a place for everyday run-of-the-mill love. Which is exceptional, after all.

About the Authors

Chris Adrian is a pediatrician and divinity student in Boston and is the author of two novels, *Gob's Grief* and *The Children's Hospital*. He owns no dogs.

Rick Bass is the author of twenty-three books of fiction and nonfiction, including most recently a story collection, *The Lives of Rocks*. In June 2008, Houghton Mifflin will publish a memoir, *Why I Came West*. He lives in Montana's Yaak Valley, where he works with the Yaak Valley Forest Council to designate the Yaak's last roadless areas as protected wilderness.

Ron Carlson is the author of nine books of fiction, most recently the novel *Five Skies* from Viking. He teaches writing at the University of California at Irvine.

Tom Grimes is the author of the novels *WILL@epicqwest.com*, *A Stone of the Heart*, *Season's End*, *Redemption Song*, and *City of God*. His fiction has twice been finalist for the PEN/Nelson Algren Award. It has also been selected as a *New York Times* Notable Book of the Year, an Editor's Choice, and a New & Noteworthy Paperback. He received a James Michener Fellowship from the Iowa Writers' Workshop. He later edited a fiction anthology entitled *The Workshop: Seven Decades of Fiction from the Iowa Writers' Workshop*. His recent essays have appeared in *Tin House*, one of which, "Bring Out Your Dead" was cited as a Notable Essay of 2007 by *Best American Essays*.

Barry Hannah is the author of fourteen books. He has received the William Faulkner Prize and the Bellamann Foundation Award, among other honors. He lives in Oxford, Mississippi.

J. C. Hallman is the author of *The Chess Artist* and *The Devil Is a Gentleman*. He lives in St. Paul, Minnesota.

Denis Johnson is the author of several novels, plays, and books of verse. His novel *Tree of Smoke* was published by Farrar, Straus and Giroux in 2007 and won the National Book Award.

Anna Keesey's work has appeared in *Tin House*, *Grand Street*, *Witness*, *Zyzzyva*, and *Double Take*, among other journals, and has been anthologized in *Best American Short Stories*. She has been awarded fellowships or residencies by the Fine Arts Work Center in Provincetown, the Yaddo Foundation, the MacDowell Colony, and the National Endowment for the Arts. She currently teaches writing at Linfield College in McMinnville, Oregon.

Michelle Latiolais is professor of English at the University of California at Irvine. She is the author of the novel *Even Now*, which received the Gold Medal for Fiction from the Commonwealth Club of California. Her second novel, *A Proper Knowledge*, was published by Bellevue Literary Press in spring 2008. She has published stories and essays in several literary journals.

Lydia Millet is the author of six novels, most recently *How the Dead Dream* (Counterpoint 2008). Her 2002 novel, *My Happy Life*, won the PEN-USA Award for Fiction, and 2005's *Oh Pure and Radiant Heart*, about the physicists who developed the atomic bomb, was shortlisted for Britain's Arthur C. Clarke Prize. She works for the nonprofit Center for Biological Diversity in Tucson, Arizona.

Lee Montgomery is the author of *The Things Between Us: A Memoir* (Free Press, 2006), *Whose World Is This?* (University of Iowa Press, 2007), and *Searching for Emily: Illustrated* (Nothing Moments Press). *The Things Between Us* received the 2007 Oregon Book Award and *Whose World Is This?* the 2007 John Simmons Iowa Short Fiction Award. She has been an editor at the *Iowa Review*, the *Santa Monica Review*, and has edited numerous anthologies. She is the editorial director of Tin House Books and the executive editor for *Tin House* magazine.

Yannick Murphy is the author of the novels *Signed, Mata Hari, Here They Come*, and *The Sea of Trees*; the short-story collections *In a Bear's Eye* and *Stories in Another Language;* and two children's picture books, *Ahwoooooooo!* and the forthcoming *Baby Polar*. She is a recipient of the Whiting Writer's Award, a grant from the National Endowment for the Arts, a MacDowell Artists' Colony fellowship, and a Chesterfield Film Project Fellow, awarded in conjunction with Steven Spielberg's Amblin Entertainment. Her short fiction has been published in the *Quarterly, Epoch*, the *Antioch Review, AGNI, Conjunctions, McSweeney's* and the *Malahat Review*, among others, and her nonfiction has appeared in the *New York Times Magazine*. She lives with her husband and three children in Vermont.

Antonya Nelson's most recent book is *Some Fun*, a collection of stories. She teaches creative writing at the University of Houston and divides her time among Texas, New Mexico, and Colorado.

Mary Otis's short-story collection *Yes, Yes, Cherries* was published in May 2007 by Tin House Books. She has also had stories published in *Best New American Voices*, the *Los Angeles Times, Tin House, Cincinnati Review, Santa Monica Review*, and *Alaska Quarterly Review*. Her story "Pilgrim Girl" received an honorable mention for a Pushcart Prize, and her story "Unstruck" was cited in the list of 100 Distinguished Stories in *The Best American Short Stories 2006*. A 2007 Walter Dakin Fellow, Mary lives in Los Angeles.

Jayne Anne Phillips is the author of *Black Tickets, Fast Lanes, Machine Dreams, Shelter, MotherKind*, and *Termite* (forthcoming from Knopf). Her works are published in nine languages, and she is the recipient of NEA, Guggenheim, and Bunting Institute fellowships. She is professor of English and director of the Rutgers Newark M.F.A. program in creative writing.

Writer and poet **Victoria Redel** is the author of three books of fiction and two books of poetry. Her most recent book is *The Border of Truth* (2007). Her novel *Loverboy* was awarded the S. Mariela Gable Novel Award and was a 2001 *L.A. Times* Best Book. *Swoon* (2003) was a finalist for the Laughlin Poetry Prize. She teaches at Sarah Lawrence College and the graduate writing program at Columbia University.

Robin Romm is the author of the critically acclaimed short-story collection *The Mother Garden*. She lives in New Mexico.

Jim Shepard is the author of six novels, including, most recently, *Project X* (Knopf, 2004), and three story collections, most recently *Love and Hydrogen* (Vintage, 2004) and *Like You'd Understand, Anyway*, published by Knopf in September 2007 and nominated for the National Book Award.

Abigail Thomas has written two collections of stories, *Getting Over Tom* and *Herb's Pajamas*; the novel *An Actual Life*; and two memoirs, *Safekeeping* and *A Three Dog Life*. *A Three Dog Life* was named one of the best books of 2006 by the *Los Angeles Times* and *The Washington Post*. Her most recent book is *Thinking About Memoir*. She lives in Woodstock, New York, with her three dogs.

Among her other works, **Elizabeth Marshall Thomas** is the author of *The Hidden Life of Dogs* and *The Social Lives of Dogs: The Grace of Canine Company*. She lives in New Hampshire.

Paul Winner is a 2007 graduate of Union Theological Seminary in New York. Previous work has appeared in *Tin House* and the *Seneca Review*. He currently teaches Shakespeare in East Harlem.

Acknowledgments

I am grateful to the authors whose work appears in these pages and, of course, the dogs we all have loved that inspire these stories: Rosie, Carolina, Harry, Simon, Point, Moose, Shefton, Dino, Lady, Snoopy, Moe, George, Flannery, Odette, Elmo, Lulu, Roscoe, Oscar, The Colonel, Mercy, Charlie, Odin, Ringo, Bill, Tom, Woody, Jack, Dick Diver, Pnut, Luna, Sasha, Damned Spot, Becky, Bouncer, Buster, Tiny, Smokey, Corby, Salt Lake City, Ferdinand, Ernie, Vicky, Thunder Sophie, Sadie, Missy Bumbles, Rupee, Brandy, Scout, Max, Maggie, Bug, Bridgette, and Brook.

My life would be less thrilling without the guidance of my friend and agent Judy Heiblum. I am thankful to her and Sally Wofford-Girand for suggesting the idea of this anthology. I am grateful to all the kind folks at Viking Penguin who have helped assemble such a special tribute to our friends. First and foremost, Kendra Harpster, my editor and fellow dog lover, for her keen eye, enthusiasm, and patience for all things dog. I'd also like to thank Kendra's assistant, Jennifer Dwoskin, production editor Kate Griggs, Nancy Resnick for the interior design, and Maggie Payette for the perfect cover. Special thanks to Fabiana Van Arsdell for putting up with us and keeping the trains running on time.